BEYOND 1989

Modern German Studies

A Series of the German Studies Association

This series offers books on modern and contemporary Germany, concentrating on themes in history, political science, literature and German culture. Publications will include original works in English and English translations of significant works in other languages.

Volume 1:

Germany's New Politics

Parties and Issues in the 1990s

Edited by David Conradt, Gerald R. Kleinfeld, George K. Romoser and Christian Søe

Volume 2:

After Unity

Reconfiguring German Identities

Edited by Konrad Jarausch

Volume 3:

Beyond 1989

Re-reading German Literary History since 1945

Edited by Keith Bullivant

BEYOND 1989

Re-reading German Literary History since 1945

Edited by
Keith Bullivant

Berghahn Books
Providence • Oxford

First published in 1997 by

Berghahn Books

Editorial offices:
165 Taber Avenue, Providence, RI 02906, USA
3, NewTec Place, Magdalen Road, Oxford OX4 1RE

© Keith Bullivant 1997

Library of Congress Cataloging-in-Publication Data

```
Beyond 1989 : re-reading German literary history since 1945 / Keith
  Bullivant, ed.
      p.   cm. -- (Modern German studies ; vol. 3)
  Includes bibliographical references and index.
  ISBN 1-57181-037-4 (alk. paper). -- ISBN 1-57181-038-2 (pbk. :
alk. paper)
  1. German literature--20th century--History and criticism.
2. Authors, German--20th century--Political and social views.
3. Germany--In literature.  4. Criticism--Germany--History--20th
century.  5. Germany--History--Unification, 1990-   I. Bullivant,
Keith.   II. Series: Modern German studies (Providence, R.I.) ; vol.
3.
PT405.B475  1997
830.9'00914--dc21
                                                    96-53154
                                                    CIP
```

British Library Cataloguing in Publication Data

A catalogue record for this book is available from the
British Library.

Printed in the United States on acid-free paper.

CONTENTS

Introduction

BEYOND 1989

Keith Bullivant

When I was asked by Gerald Kleinfeld to edit this, the first volume by Germanists in the new GSA series, it immediately struck me that the only possible subject for such a volume published by the *German Studies* Association was that which is now contained in its title. I also had to face the fact that, having had my own initial say on this matter in my *The Future of German Literature* (1994), I would have to play an essentially background role in the project, letting others individually and collectively now have their say. More by happenstance than design, the contributors to this volume make up a representative cross-section of the Germanists within the GSA in terms of age range, gender, and geography (one is from Europe), with only the West Coast not represented *(mea culpa)*. I would also like to think that the range of the essays in the volume reflects the way in which German Studies has emerged in the last two decades from a traditionally more narrowly focused *Germanistik*.

The re-reading of the history of German culture since 1945 is necessary, in that the collapse of the Eastern Bloc and the unification of Germany so fundamentally challenged the way in which the modern and contemporary areas of our discipline had focused on German culture since 1945. We had divided more or less neatly into FRG and GDR Germanists, and our emphases on major writers, works and themes reflected the prevalent socio-political climate of West or East Germany during the four decades of German division. It has been argued since 1989 that Germany remained unified during that time through literature, an idea very similar to the notion of the *Kulturnation* (cultural nation) promulgated by Grass after 1980 and taken up by others after 1989. And while the idea of the convergence of the two literatures during the 1980s (examined here by Stephen Brockmann) was put forward by Frank Trommler and others at that time, cultural trends since 1989 have demonstrated clearly how very different the two German cultures were. More and more revelations make it clear that Western perceptions of the *Stasi* vastly underestimated the way in which the secret police had penetrated the cultural scene, with even the so-called alternative scene in the former GDR under its close control

The collapse of the socialist states and, more importantly as far as literature is concerned, the discrediting of the ideational substance and the rhetoric of socialism has had its impact on the reading of a whole range of texts, and not merely the crudely conformist ones. Even a major work like Christa Wolf's *Nachdenken über Christa T.* (The Quest for Christa T.), looked at after 1989 minus the *frisson* of reading it as her so-called rueful parting of the ways with the "real and existing" socialist state, is not only inaccessible to younger readers in a country (the USA)where the word socialism has long been equated with an enemy and evil system, but does not stand up in comparison with other substantial treatments of the theme of female identity in West German literature, such as Ingeborg Drewitz's outstanding *Gestern war heute* (Yesterday Was Today).

A further important aspect of that separateness, at least as far as German Studies is concerned, is the way in which, in the context of the Cold War, it for a long time was maintained that, in contradistinction to the instrumentalization of culture and the artist in the GDR, culture in the West – including literature from the East received there – was evaluated according to aesthetic rather than ideological criteria. The change in the reception of dissident GDR writers in the West after they had moved to the FRG, examined here by Carol Anne Costabile-Heming, is perhaps the clearest example of this not being so. Such a view also ignores the standing of an older generation of conservative writers, now essentially forgotten, until well into the 1950s, such as Gottfried Benn, Hermann Hesse, Ernst Jünger, and Gerd Gaiser, of other older writers such as Ernst Kreuder, Martin Kessel, Marie Luise Kaschnitz, Kasimir Edschmid, and Rudolf Alexander Schröder, as well as of critics like Hans Egon Holthusen, Friedrich Sieburg and Rudolf Krämer-Badoni. That particular conventional wisdom also takes no account of the problems of incorporating so much lyric poetry or linguistically and stylistically innovative literature, such as that of Arno Schmidt and the Vienna Group of writers, into the post-1945 canon.

Another more thoroughgoing rebuttal of this notion is provided by most literary histories of the old Federal Republic, which all attest to an amazing congruence with its socio-political history. Even those of us who reject the thrust of Frank Schirrmacher's "Abschied von der Literatur der Bundesrepublik" (Leave-taking from the Literature of the Federal Republic) have to agree that the bulk of literature in the West up to 1989, or at least that which had established itself as part of the normative view, is indeed characterized by a distinctive *Gesinnungsästhetik* (ideological aesthetics) not to be found in the literature of other Western countries during the same period; Walter Pape's analysis of the work of Erich Fried is testimony to this. Important studies such as H. L. Müller, *Die literarische Republik. Westdeutsche Schriftsteller und die Politik* (1982), R.A. Burns & W. van der Will, *Protest and Democracy in West Germany. Extra-Parliamentary Opposition and the Democratic Agenda* (1988) and Cora Stephan, *Wir Kollaborateure* (1992), as well as Klaus Wagenbach, *Vaterland, Muttersprache* (1980/1994), give extensive evidence of the political concerns of West German writers until well into the 1980s, and of their effort, in both their writing and in their public role as intellectuals, to shape the course of the Federal Republic.

Schirrmacher is wrong, however, as Siegfried Mews also argues in his essay examining the ramifications of that article, in seeing literature as carrying out some sort of societal mandate. Nothing could be further from the truth: West German literature from 1945 to 1989 constitutes, in the main (and certainly as far as the authors Schirrmacher names are concerned), a counter-discourse to that of the political sphere. Through writing and their intellectual activities, writers asserted values and articulated concerns that were felt to be under threat in political and other circles of influence: world peace, global internationalism, the caring society, the rights of women and other minorities, and tolerance in general. In the 1970s in particular writers and other artists clearly felt it part of their calling to defend the democratic state as such. The work and life of Heinrich Böll until his death in 1985 illustrates most clearly just what a thorn West German literature could be in the side of the Establishment, particularly in the 1970s and early 1980s.

The work of so many West German writers provided a sort of alternative public sphere, in which matters repressed or in some other way excluded from socio-political debate could be articulated. One negative aspect of this was that for many educated Germans literature offered a morally cosy virtual reality that, in the manner of TV soap operas, could easily distract from the actual reality around them. Looking back, there is little doubt that, stirring and comforting as the Peace Movement of the first half of the 1980s was, and despite the number of people it activated, it was irrelevant to the negotiations between Reagan and Gorbachev. The same was true of the earlier literary protests against rearmament, atomic weaponry, civil rights, and environmental damage. Such topics form an important part of the literary agenda after 1945, as Klaus Wagenbach's *Vaterland, Muttersprache* makes clear, but it is equally obvious that the impact of such writing and any concomitant demonstrations was negligible.

Nevertheless, it would have to be conceded that certain types of literature did in time change the parameters of West German public discourse. One striking example of this is women's writing, examined in this volume by Barbara Kosta and Helga Kraft. Another is literature's ability to mourn, at a time when the "business as usual" attitude of the Establishment led to a failure of the state to address the legacy of the Third Reich and, in particular the Holocaust, in the 1950s and 1960s. Not only did the government of the day indicate in many ways its insensitivity to the issue through the appointments of Globke, Kiesinger, Lübke, Filbinger and others; this was accompanied by the swift and easy rehabilitation of many civil servants and other administrators and judges, not to mention the monetary rewards and state awards heaped on other severely compromised former Nazis (including Hanns-Martin Schleyer), as revealed so incisively in Bernd Engelmann's novel *Das Große Bundesverdienstkreuz* (The Federal Cross of Service, First Class), and Michael Schneider's drama *Die Wiedergutmachung* (Restitution).

The essays of Jennifer Michaels and, in part, Frank Trommler address this issue here in different ways, but are agreed on the central importance of this aspect of German writing after 1945. The role of the documentary drama in the 1960s, and of the later examination of German fascism by the generation of 1968 in changing West German awareness of the legacy of the Nazi past, cannot be over-emphasized. Without that sea change, the sympathetic reception that Daniel J. Goldhagen received – from his audiences, not from his professional critics during his visit to the Federal Republic in the later summer of 1996 cannot adequately be explained. There is also no doubt that Goldhagen's awareness of the coming to terms with anti-Semistism in West Germany, which he addresses in an inadequate footnote, would have benefitted from the historian's awareness of the literary scene of the country. Particularly interesting in the context of this volume is that, while Jennifer Michaels does identify some small degree of relatively late individual convergence in the confrontation of the Nazi past, the main thrust of her essay essentially reinforces the differences between the two German literatures, differences which, in turn, sadly give some explanation for the emergence of ethnic hatred in the former GDR.

The essays by Stephen Brockmann and Carol Anne Costabile-Heming, in looking at the interaction between GDR (or ex-GDR) writers in the 1970s and 1980s, also provide us to some extent with an answer to that particularly thorny question as to which of the former GDR writers are likely to continue to be regarded as important in the future. One aspect of this is that many of the writers who figure in these two essays have long since lived in the West and their work is fully integrated into the literary scene of the Federal Republic, which essentially continues to dominate the media, with the former GDR maintaining, as a matter of necessity, it might be argued, a separate literary world; the exception, such as Jens Sparschuh, still proves the rule. After seven years or so of so-called unification, there are strong signals that that cultural divisions between the two former German states have increased rather than diminished.[1] Another aspect of this question is provided by the essay of Barbara Kosta and Helga Kraft, who admittedly do come up with some of the same names as Brockmann and Costabile-Heming, but whose thematic approach brings together writers from West and East Germany (and Austria) in a way that would not have been possible before 1989. They also strongly reinforce my own view that, while a number of previously key GDR texts may struggle to survive as such, it is much more likely that the feminist texts from the East will continue to play a prominent part in feminist discourses.

The main title of this volume also invites exploration of cultural trends since the collapse of the GDR, of course, and two contributions to this volume do just that. One of the most alarming tendencies since unification has been the upsurge of a right-wing, even neo-fascist movement. The most obvious manifestations of this have been the attacks on foreigners, especially Turks, that have resulted in several deaths, the desecration of synagogues and Jewish cemetaries, and a general xenophobia, especially among the youth of the former GDR, that has been encouraged by neo-fascist organizations from the USA and Canada, and also by a virulent right-wing rock scene. Thes disturbing developments have been accompanied by an intellectual discourse having a number of similarities to the Conservative Revolution of the 1920s. A German review of my *The Future of German Literature* in 1994 argued that I attributed too much importance to this trend, but Jay Rosellini's contribution to this volume concurs with my analysis of the situation. Rosellini explores one of the more disturbing debates since unification, one sparked off initially by Botho Strauss' essay "Anschwellender Bocksgesang" (Impending Tragedy), which then gathered disturbing critical mass with its publica-

---

1. *Cf.* in this connection: Anke Westphal, "Ost-Plünnen: Lieber Sammler, bitte melde dich!, *Die Zeit* (US edition), 14 June 1996, and Anon., "Rückfall in die Barbarei", *Der Spiegel* 26 (1996): 168-71.

tion in the right-wing anthology *Die selbstbewußte Nation* (The Self-confident Nation). Rosellini's essay raises points that are then taken up in a very different way by Nora M. Alter, who in her examination of Helke Misselwitz's post-"Wende" film *Herzsprung* addresses many of the major social and cultural problems facing an increasingly multicultural Federal Republic in the 1990s and beyond, in which ethnic intolerance again takes centre stage.

A fuller examination of the literature that has emerged since 1989 would require another book, and also more time, however. After an initial outpouring of texts on the dramatic changes in Germany by writers from the West, the cultural scene in the West has slipped back into its old ways, by and large, and it is now clear that no immediate changes can be expected. There has been no attempt at all by critics or literary historians to re-examine West German literature from the perspective of the late 1990s. There were some initial indications that there might be an examination of the role played by the generation of 1968 and its somewhat older sympathizers, such as Martin Walser and Hans Magnus Enzensberger, that barely scratched the surface before fading from sight. This much needed examination has still to be undertaken, as has a serious scrutiny of the sweep of the careers of Walser and Enzensberger, whose work reaches from the years of the "Economic Miracle" into the late 1990s. As for Günter Grass, whose writing career spans a similar period, there is a consistency in his position on the question of German identity that is not to be found in his contemporaries.

The effective separation of the two literary scenes has led to the emergence of a highly self-conscious, highly n/ostalgic trend in the East, especially in East Berlin, as can be seen in the pages of the magazine *Sklaven* (Slaves). The cultural division of the country was brought out very sharply by the reception of Günter Grass' novel *Ein weites Feld* (A Broad Subject, 1995), his idiosyncratically critical work on post-unification Germany. In the West the novel was widely criticized, with Marcel Reich-Ranicki being particularly harsh in his judgement, whereas in the East it was well received as a novel that did justice to "their" GDR.

Another key issue has been the involvment with the *Stasi* of former GDR writers, which continuing revelations expose as being far greater than was ever suspected, and which has prevented a fusion of the *two* German Writers' Unions, as former GDR writers have led a vigorous campaign against prominent writers of the Eastern section with a highly compromised past. It is therefore hardly surprising that there have been few signs of literary or other work existing comfortably in the unified country. There are a few exceptions, such as Jens Sparschuh's *Der Zimmerspringbrunnen* (The Sitting Room Fountain, 1995) and Uwe Timm's

Johannisnacht (Midsummer's Night, 1996). 1997 apparently promises us Jens Sparschuh's *Ich dachte, sie finden uns nicht,* Irina Liebmann's *Letzten Sommer in Deutschland. Eine romantische Reise,* and Hertert Rosendorfer's *Die große Umwendung,* all of which are said to explore life in the unified country. All the signs in 1996, however, indicate that, with the continuing economic and concomittant social problems in the East further disappointing hopes of a painless convergence, the lengthy separation of the two halves of the country continues to make itself felt in the cultural life of the Federal Republic. The prognostications about the speed of post-1989 general reintegration of the two halves of the country have been continuously revised, and the same is undoubtedly true in the cultural sphere: until the dominance of those who grew up in the old cosy world of West Germany is eroded by the passage of the generations, German literature is likely to remain as divided as the country itself.

CONFRONTING THE NAZI PAST

Jennifer E. Michaels

In "Schreiben nach Auschwitz" (Writing after Auschwitz), a speech Stefan Heym gave in October 1988 in the Paulskirche in Frankfurt, he observed that the smoke from the furnaces of Auschwitz has darkened the blue of the sky forever and its stench will hang over us into the third and fourth generations (227). His comments, voiced over fifty years after Hitler's rise to power and on the fiftieth anniversary of the *Kristallnacht*, suggest that Auschwitz continues to embody a guilt that has not been overcome (Dinter, 93). In both East and West Germany writers have often been in the forefront in bringing questions about the responsibility for the Nazi past into public awareness. Many have been voices of conscience and have prodded their fellow citizens into remembering what they would have preferred to forget.

The reunification of the two Germanys offers a vantage point for examining how writers in the former Federal Republic and German Democratic Republic approached their countries' Nazi past, how their treatments differed, and how they converged. In both East and West German literature writers used all genres to explore this past. Dramatists and poets made important contributions to the discussion of this topic – Rolf Hochhuth's *Der Stellvertreter* (The Deputy, 1963), Peter Weiss's *Die Ermittlung* (The Investigation, 1965), Heinar Kipphardt's *Joel Brand* (1965), and the poetry of Nelly Sachs, Paul Celan, and Sarah Kirsch are just some of the most well-known examples. Because of limitations of space, however, I decided to focus on the novel and short story, which were more widely used than drama and poetry to confront the Nazi past. Even within these limits, the large amount of works on this topic makes it impossible to be comprehensive. To try to give a sense of the changing nature of the response to Germany's past in the two countries, I chose to highlight works that were either widely read or written by influential authors, but I also include works that signaled a shift in how writers have addressed this topic.

In the immediate postwar years writers in both countries began struggling to come to terms with the Nazi past. In West Germany, the "Stunde Null" (zero hour) or "tabula rasa" – just two of several similar terms used in the aftermath of the war – suggested that the defeat of Nazi Germany would lead to a new beginning, but many soon thought that this new beginning was a myth. Although there was a brief period of denazification right after the war, this was not carried out thoroughly because of the intensifying Cold War (Bullivant 1989, 139), and many former Nazis held important offices in the Federal Republic. In 1952 Konrad Adenauer admitted that two-thirds of the senior officials in his government were former Nazi Party members (Reed, 36). In the 1940s and 1950s West Germany turned its attention to rebuilding its economy and did not encourage its citizens to confront their Nazi past. Many blinded themselves to the continuities with the Third Reich and thought that their country's past could now be comfortably forgotten.

Some of the earliest attempts to confront the Hitler period in West Germany emerged from the Group 47, a loose association of new and relatively unknown writers who hoped through their literary works to promote a democratic Germany, a renewal of German literature, and an existential change in their fellow citizens. Confronting the past was an important part of their writing. Alfred Andersch and Hans Werner Richter, for example, had worked on the prisoner-of-war newspaper *Der Ruf* (The Call), which had published political analyses of the Third Reich as well as photographs of Buchenwald taken by the American army (Demetz, 7). Most of the members of this group were suspicious of political involvement, but they believed strongly that literature should speak out against "fascism, war, nationalism, and all repressive ideologies" (Demetz, 14).

In the early postwar years in West Germany writers such as Heinrich Böll, a member of the Group 47, and Wolfgang Borchert gave voice to the suffering of ordinary Germans. Böll's early short novels, such as *Der Zug war pünktlich* (The Train was on Time), and stories which are characteristic of the "Trümmerliteratur" (literature of the ruins) of the time, are peopled with innocent victims who are trapped in the misery and senselessness of the war and who are wounded or killed at the front, or who struggle to survive amidst the ruins of their defeated country. Like Böll, Borchert writes about ordinary people whose lives the war disrupted and destroyed. In his play *Draußen vor der Tür* (The Man Outside), written in 1946, and in his short prose pieces, Borchert struggles to express the horrors of the Nazi years. Like many writers Borchert is torn between a sense of the powerlessness of language to evoke the agony (Langer, 34). In "Im Mai, im Mai schrie der Kuckuck" (In May, In May Cried the Cuckoo), written in 1946 or 1947, he observes that we lack the words to describe even a second of the war, and stresses the need to break the silence and bear witness. Borchert and Böll are among the earliest postwar writers in West Germany to ask whether the defeat of nazism has changed people's attitudes and whether they have learned anything from the war, questions that later writers pose with increasing urgency, and both are pessimistic that any existential change has occurred. In Böll's story "Der Mann mit den Messern" (The Man with the Knives, 1948), for example, which is set amidst the postwar ruins, the audience watching the knife-thrower's act clearly hopes to see blood flow. Even after the death and destruction of the Hitler years, people are still bloodthirsty.

Instead of examining the political and social roots of nazism, many writers in West Germany in the 1940s and early 1950s depicted it in metaphorical or mythic terms (Ryan, 23). Nazism was seen as a sickness or a madness that had overwhelmed the German people (Trommler, 10), and notions of a Germany possessed by the devil were widely held (Ryan, 14). The Germans were treated as the victims of an inescapable fate instead of as morally responsible individuals, and this view tended to absolve them of guilt since it suggested that they were helpless to resist "the eternal forces of evil" (Ryan, 25). In *Der Totenwald* (The Forest of the Dead), for example, Ernst Wiechert depicts the Nazi years as a struggle between good and evil, which led the East German critic Therese Hörnigk to accuse him of obscuring the social causes of Hitlerian fascism by portraying it as satanic (82). Like many authors of this time, Wiechert, who spent the war years in inner emigration, drew on his own experiences of persecution during his four-month imprisonment in Buchenwald, but by calling his protagonist Johannes he stresses that his was a common fate. Wiechert poses questions about individual responsibility and the possibility of resistance. Although Johannes takes a courageous moral stand for which he is imprisoned, Wiechert suggests that in a society, which Johannes terms the kingdom of the Antichrist, any moral stance can only purify the individual, not effect political change. The text reflects the widespread belief at this time in the "two Germanys" or "other" Germany theory. There is the sadistic Nazi Germany of the Antichrist and the good Germany of the culture of Goethe, inhabited by those who suffer behind the barbed wire and who, despite attempts to brutalize them, retain their concern for others and their dignity as human beings. In contrast to the East German Bruno Apitz's *Nackt unter Wölfen* (Naked Among Wolves, 1958), to be discussed later, Wiechert's depiction of Buchenwald is decidedly nonpolitical. Johannes, who considers all ideology a misfortune, stresses that those who helped him in the camp did so, not because they were communists, but because they were decent human beings.

In the early postwar years in West Germany the most influential text to express this mythic view of nazism as the demonic was Thomas Mann's *Doktor Faustus* (1947), which set the tone for later treatments of this topic (Ryan, 43). Mann traces nazism's roots back through the German cultural tradition to Dürer and thereby suggests that nazism is an inherent and thus inescapable part of German culture rather than the result of political, social, and economic factors. The composer Leverkühn's pact with the devil comes to signify Germany's involvement in an inevitable and fated evil (Ryan, 46). Zeitblom represents those who, in their attempt to distance themselves from the Nazis and retain their decency as human beings, withdrew passively into inner emigration. Although Mann portrays Zeitblom sympathetically, he shows that his inner emigration has not made him immune to Nazi ideology. Despite Mann's mythologization of nazism here, his novel was one of the first attempts by a German author to "unmask fascist attitudes in himself" (Mahlendorf, 554), since he knows that he was also shaped by the same cultural tradition as Leverkühn, and was thus susceptible to the same alliance with evil to which Leverkühn succumbed.

In contrast to the new beginning implied in the term "zero hour" in West Germany, the government in the Soviet Zone and later in the GDR stressed continuity. The new socialist state, it asserted, was the heir to the "good" German cultural heritage and to the resistance against Hitler. Because it defined itself as an antifascist state, whose citizens were the "victors of history" (Reid, 130) it refused to accept responsibility for Nazi crimes. It considered West Germany the heir to the Third Reich and "a haven for former Nazis and a breeding ground for future ones" (Fox, 18). Denazification was carried out more thoroughly in East Germany than in the West. The government in the East made a serious effort to reeducate its citizens and actively promoted antifascist literature as a means to reaching this goal. Between 1945 and 1949, for example, most of the texts published in the Soviet zone confronted the fascist past (Emmerich, 52). This confrontation was, however, shaped by myth. In contrast to the mythologization of nazism as the demonic in West Germany, the East created the heroic myth of a country filled with brave communist resistance fighters. Although writers in the East deserve credit for recognizing the contributions of those in the communist resistance, who were generally ignored in the West, their emphasis on heroic resistance fighters as models and their focus on the antifascist roots of the new socialist state helped to legitimize the government in East Germany. As in West Germany, this myth, coupled with the Comintern definition of fascism as rooted in monopoly capitalism, a view that the East German government continued to hold, discouraged citizens in the East from coming to terms with questions of individual responsibility and complicity since they felt absolved from guilt. As Stephan Hermlin observes, it was too easy to regard the case as closed, "the crimes of the Nazis as something which had been purged by the mere act of inaugurating a socialist state" (cited in Reid, 130).

Antifascist works written by returning exiled writers who carried on the socialist literary tradition of the Weimar Republic shaped the early stages of literature in East Germany. *Das siebte Kreuz* (The Seventh Cross, 1942) by Anna Seghers became a model for later writers in East Germany who explored the Nazi past and the communist resistance to Hitler. Although Seghers first published the novel when she was in exile, it was republished in the Soviet zone in 1946 and became one of the most widely read books in the GDR. Christa Wolf admired the novel and wrote approvingly that it makes clear that fascism was first directed against its own people and that its own people were the first to resist (*Dimension*, 268). Through the escape of the communist Georg Heisler, the only one of seven concentration camp inmates to elude capture or death, Seghers shows a cross-section of life in Germany under the Nazis. A variety of people, some of whom are communists but most of whom are not political, help Georg. The novel is essentially optimistic because Seghers depicts a society in which people are ready to resist the Nazis. Through Heisler's escape she shows that fascism was not invincible. The heroic communist resistance is also central to Stephan Hermlin's works. *Die erste Reihe* (The First Row, 1951) contains portraits of communist resistance fighters who were killed for their opposition to the Nazis, although he also includes a sympathetic discussion of the non-communist White Rose. In the story "Der Leutnant Yorck von Wartenburg" (Lieutenant Yorck von Wartenburg, 1945), Hermlin gives a communist slant to the failed plot by army officers to assassinate Hitler on 20 July 1944, and in "Der Weg der Bolschewiki" (The Way of the Bolsheviks, 1950) he describes the escape by Soviet officers from the Austrian concentration camp of Mauthausen and their subsequent murder by the local population. Another short piece "Die Zeit der Gemeinsamkeit"

(The Time Together), written in 1949, deals with the uprising in the Warsaw Ghetto in 1943. Hermlin emphasizes the courage of such Jewish leaders as Mlotek (who also happens to be a communist), but he portrays the majority of the Jews in the ghetto as apathetic. Despite this rather negative depiction, he at least reminds his readers about the ghettos and the death camps in contrast to most East German writers at the time who, in their emphasis on resistance fighters, tended to ignore other victims of nazism.

Bruno Apitz, who was imprisoned in Buchenwald from 1937 to 1945 for his activities in the communist resistance, draws on his experiences in the camp in his best-selling novel *Nackt unter Wölfen*. The afterword by Max Walter Schulz, another writer who confronts the Nazi past in his works, shapes how the East German reader should understand this and other works on this topic. Schulz argues that it is essential to remember such places as Buchenwald because they keep alive hatred for the murderers, remind people of the victims, and encourage them to admire surviving anti-fascists. Like Wiechert's *Der Totenwald*, Apitz's novel is a powerful account of the brutal world of the camp, but it differs in its focus on the resolute members of the communist resistance in the camp who plan to liberate Buchenwald at the end of the war. With the arrival of a three-year-old orphaned child in the camp, they are faced with a decision: to hide the child means to endanger their plans, but to send the child away would mean his death. Although some of the communist leaders order the child sent away, others disobey and keep him, refusing to betray his hiding place even when the Nazis torture and kill some of them. They successfully hide the boy until they can liberate the camp and join the advancing American units. Apitz's depiction of the Jews in the novel is troubling. The prisoners refer most of the time to this Jewish child from the Warsaw ghetto as the Polish child (Demetz, 27), and the Polish Jew, who had hidden the child in Auschwitz and, at great danger to himself, smuggled the boy in his suitcase to Buchenwald, is treated condescendingly, and his courageous protection of the child is barely, if at all, acknowledged. In contrast to the strong resistance fighters, Apitz portrays the Jews as helpless, fearful, and weak.

By the mid-1950s some of the most prominent antifascist writers began to see that the model of heroic communist resistance did not reflect the experience of most citizens in the GDR who had not been resistance fighters, but had attempted only to survive and had experienced the end of the war as a defeat (Silberman, 531). In the following decade a new generation of writers such as Franz Fühmann, Dieter Noll, and Max Walter Schulz moved anti-fascist literature in East Germany away from the resistance model to depict the conversion of former soldiers and Nazis to socialism, a conversion that frequently takes place in Soviet imprisonment. These texts, which were often patterned on the nineteenth century *Bildungsroman*, replaced, however, the myth of a GDR peopled with resistance fighters and antifascists with that of a GDR whose citizens had quickly seen the error of their ways and converted to socialism. Because GDR leaders considered that the past had been overcome in their country, any discussion of the continuities in thinking and behavior between the Third Reich and the GDR was stifled.

Of the many texts dealing with conversion, which include Noll's *Die Abenteuer des Werner Holt* (Werner Holt's Adventures, 1960/63) and Schulz's *Wir sind nicht Staub im Wind* (We are not Dust in the Wind, 1962), two by Franz Fühmann stand out. His novella *Kameraden* (Comrades, 1955) tells the story of three German soldiers who accidentally shoot the daughter of their battalion commander. Out of a perverted sense of comradeship, they promise to keep quiet, and the Russians are then blamed for her death. Two of the comrades remain silent even when two young Lithuanian women are to be executed in reprisal, but the third, Thomas, tells the truth. Nobody believes him because the version that the Russians were responsible suits propaganda purposes better. The novella, which is "a masterly demolition of the military ideology of comradeship which helps to cloak the most evil of deeds" (Reid, 131), demonstrates Thomas's ability to change and break with the Nazis, but it does not fit in entirely with the new model since it does not show his conversion to socialism. More typical is the autobiographical *Das Judenauto* (The Car with the Yellow Star, 1962), in which Fühmann details his conversion in Soviet imprisonment from a fanatical Nazi to a convinced communist. Even though Fühmann shows that he had begun tentatively to question National Socialism before his capture, the conversion happens too quickly to be convincing, a common problem in many of these texts. Fühmann also addresses German anti-Semitism in this work. Although he follows GDR thinking that anti-Semitism is economically motivated – he and his father hold the Jews responsible for ruining the family business, for example – he shows that its roots are not only economic but also irrational when he draws attention to the widespread belief among the children that Jews commit ritual murder.

The rapidly developing prosperity in the Federal Republic in the 1950s and 1960s encouraged little interest in confronting the past. In their influential study, *Die Unfähigkeit zu trauern* (The Inability to Mourn, 1967) Alexander and Margarete Mitscherlich sharply criticize their fellow citizens for repressing the past. Instead of feeling guilt and remorse, the Mitscherlichs argue, they were content to let bygones be bygones, and thought that if they denied the events of the Third Reich they need not acknowledge their consequences. According to the Mitscherlichs, working through the past is an urgent concern since without the process of mourning, brought about by acceptance of guilt, the past has not been mastered and understood and could therefore return. They criticize the lack of interest in West Germany in teaching the younger generation the lessons of the past, and they address the problem of individual responsibility when they observe that Hitler demanded nothing in which millions were not prepared to follow him. Authors such as Heinrich Böll, Günter Grass, Alfred Andersch, and Siegfried Lenz voiced similar concerns. In Böll's *Billard um halbzehn* (Billiards at Half-Past Nine, 1959), for example, Johanna Fähmel criticizes her fellow citizens for lacking even a trace of grief about their country's past, and she asks what a human being is without grief. These writers began to ask insistently about individual responsibility for the Nazi period. They were concerned not only because many former Nazis continued in leadership positions in the Federal Republic but also because they saw evidence that the ideology and values instilled in the generation that grew up under Hitler had not changed. They discarded the metaphorical and mythical approach used by earlier postwar writers in favor of exploring the sociological roots of nazism.

Alfred Andersch, one of the founders of the Group 47, rejects the notion that people are passive victims of the historical determinism and mass conditioning that dominated thinking about nazism in earlier fiction, and instead, from an existentialist perspective, he stresses moral responsibility and the possibility of individual choice (Ryan, 70). Such thinking, already evident in his autobiographical *Die Kirschen der Freiheit* (The Cherries of Freedom, 1952), becomes more pronounced in *Sansibar oder Der letzte Grund* (Flight to Afar, 1957), in which he expresses his belief that people are not helpless victims of fate but can exert their existential freedom. *Sansibar*, one of the earliest works to challenge the individual to confront his or her past, is "the first literary portrayal of inner freedom that leads to concrete action, thus going beyond the preservation of personal integrity practiced by the inner emigrants" (Ryan, 73). In *Efraim* (Efraim's Book, 1967) Andersch addresses the Nazi persecution of the Jews and the alienation of those who survived. Efraim, a German Jew who escaped the Nazis by living with an uncle in England, returns to Berlin for the first time in over twenty years. Most of the people he meets there are decent, but he feels uneasy and cannot forget the past. By murdering his family, the Nazis have wiped out all traces of his own past. Although the authorities are giving him back his father's house, they cannot show him his father's grave. In *Winterspelt* (1974), the fictional story of a German major's unsuccessful plan to turn his battalion over to the Americans during the Ardennes offensive, Andersch continues his exploration of moral resistance and individual choice.

1959, an important year in the confrontation with the past in West Germany, marked the publication of Grass's *Die Blechtrommel* (The Tin Drum) and Böll's *Billard um halbzehn*. In this novel and in his other important novels in the 1960s and early 1970s, Böll continues to raise questions about individual responsibility and the continuity between the unconfronted past and the present. *Billard* shows the struggle of the three generations of the Fähmel family to come to terms with their country's "spiritual rubble" (Langer, 266). Böll divides people into two groups. The smaller group consists of the lambs, people like the Fähmels who retain their decency and are appalled and saddened by the hypocrisy and opportunism they see in their society. The younger generation, the Fähmel children, represent those "who have inherited a dark legacy for which they do not feel guilty, but from whose implications and consequences they are unable, if they are sensitive, to dissociate themselves" (Langer, 277-78). The larger group consists of the buffaloes, of people like Nettlinger who were Nazis and now are prominent public officials, having once again seized power. This division of society suggests, however, a recurring and inevitable pattern with little hope for change. In *Ansichten eines Clowns* (The Clown, 1963), Hans Schnier refuses to forget the past and protests against his society's collective amnesia. He is surrounded, however, by such people as his formerly racist mother, who by sending her daughter to volunteer for anti-aircraft duty to protect the "sacred German soil" from the "Jewish Yankees" was indirectly responsible for her death. She is now president of the Executive Committee of the Societies for the Reconciliation of Racial Differences. Unlike such East German authors as Führmann, Böll is skeptical of such rapid conversions since he is convinced that people have merely opportunistically changed one set of beliefs for another but have not essentially changed. In *Gruppenbild mit Dame* (Group Portrait with Lady, 1971) Böll continues to stress that the unconfronted past throws a shadow over the present. Some of Leni's neighbors, for example, say she should be gassed because she has a Turkish lover.

In *Die Blechtrommel* Grass moves discussion of the Nazi past away from the German cultural tradition to sociology (Ryan, 58) by situating his novel within the *petite bourgeoisie*, the class that was a fertile breeding ground for National Socialism. Grass focuses on everyday fascism, on daily life under Nazi rule among small shopkeepers, and he shows that nazism would not have been possible without the support of such people as Matzerath, who accommodated themselves easily to Nazi rule.

Through Oskar, Grass unmasks the grotesqueness of nazism and its per-version of values. Grass's demythologization of nazism, which is far removed from the demonic aspects that earlier writers stressed, contin-ues in such other works as *Katz und Maus* (*Cat and Mouse*, 1961), *Hun-dejahre* (Dog Years, 1963) – the other two volumes of the Danzig Trilogy – and *Aus dem Tagebuch einer Schnecke* (From the Diary of a Snail, 1972), which takes up anti-Semitism in Danzig as well as present-day intolerance. In all these works, Grass shows the widespread complicity and collaboration among the Germans and thus challenges those earlier writers like Wiechert, who held a small group of criminals responsible for the atrocities and saw the rest of the Germans as innocent victims. Grass protests against the postwar tendency in West Germany to repress and forget the past. Like Böll, he fears that ways of thinking formed under National Socialism continue to shape the present.

The Eichmann trial in Jerusalem in 1961 and the Frankfurt Ausch-witz trials from 1963 to 1965 spurred a younger generation of writers in West Germany to confront the Nazi past. These trials opened their eyes to the mass murder in Nazi concentration camps, a subject that had rarely been discussed during the Adenauer years. Because they were con-cerned with authenticity, these writers made extensive use of court documents and historical materials. Such plays as Hochhuth's *Der Stellvertreter* and Weiss's *Die Ermittlung* are the most well-known the-atrical examples of this documentary approach to the past. Alexander Kluge's *Schlachtbeschreibung* (The Battle, 1964) is one of the most important examples in prose since it was influential in shaping the doc-umentary novels of the seventies. Kluge uses documents from a variety of sources, including daily Wehrmacht communiqués of the time, to shed light on the battle of Stalingrad from different perspectives and to underscore how official Nazi reports distorted what was actually hap-pening at the front (Bullivant 1987, 44).

In *Deutschstunde* (The German Lesson, 1968), which was a bestseller in the Federal Republic and internationally, Siegfried Lenz continues in the tradition of Grass and Böll by depicting how nazism thrived in everyday life in the Third Reich. Through his protagonist, Siggi Jepsen, Lenz asks questions about individual responsibility and the role of duty. Siggi, who is in a reform school for stealing paintings, reflects on his childhood during the Hitler years when he has to write an essay on "The Joys of Duty." During the war the authorities ordered Siggi's father, a policeman in a small village in Northwest Germany, to prevent his friend Max Ludwig Nansen, whose art the Nazis declared degenerate, from painting and to confiscate his paintings. Jepsen follows this order blindly. It is his duty, and duty for him is more important than everything, including friendship. Lenz stresses that Jepsen's perverted sense of duty, inculcated in him since childhood, helped nazism flourish. Through Siggi, who stole Nansen's paintings to rescue them, Lenz shows how nazism blighted the childhood of those growing up at that time, and continues to exert a paralyzing influence in the present.

As in West Germany, the political climate in the GDR in the 1960s did not encourage a confrontation with the past. Although some novels of conversion continued to appear, beginning in 1959 the new cultural policy of the Bitterfeld Way focused writers' attentions on the rebuilding of the GDR and on socialist achievement rather than on the trauma of the past (Silberman, 532). The questions about individual guilt and complicity that Andersch, Böll, Grass, and Lenz were insistently asking in the West remained unaddressed in the East. Two novels published in the 1960s in the GDR are, however, important for directing the discussion of the past in new directions. In *Levins Mühle* (Levin's Mill, 1964) Johannes Bobrowski tells the story of the Russian Jew Leo Levin, who moves to a former Polish village, now part of the German Reich, and builds a mill that takes business away from the narrator's grandfather, who destroys it. The grandfather's motive for the destruction is economic, but Bobrowski shows that he is xenophobic and anti-Semitic, feelings he shares with the other Germans in the village who dislike Poles, Gypsies and Jews. Although the novel takes place in 1874, Bobrowski implies connections to the Third Reich and the present. By showing that the families of those now living in the GDR were shaped by the anti-Semitism and nineteenth century nationalism that provided fertile soil for the later growth of fascism, Bobrowski questions the contention that the GDR is the direct heir of the resistance against Hitler and the "good" German cultural tradition (Ryan, 131).

Jakob der Lügner (Jacob the Liar, 1969), an immediate bestseller in both parts of Germany, is the other work published in the 1960s in the GDR that contributed in an important way to the broadening of the confrontation with the past in East Germany. Jurek Becker, a survivor of the concentration camps, gives a voice to the Jewish victims of nazism who were either invisible in East German literature or were seen negatively as apathetic, helpless victims. Jakob, who is confined in an East European ghetto in 1943, and who invents a radio and fictional news reports about the advancing Red Army, musters resources such as storytelling to bring hope and courage to his fellow Jews. Through him Becker stresses the indomitable spirit of the Jewish prisoners who despite persecution refuse to lose their humanity. Becker depicts the brutality of everyday life in the ghetto, where people starve to death, disappear, and are arbitrarily murdered, and where the extermination camps are an ever-present threat as Jews are rounded up street by street for deportation to Auschwitz and other camps.

In the 1970s in East and West Germany confrontation with the Nazi past was intense. In West Germany Willy Brandt provided important leadership for this confrontation when he knelt in front of the memorial to those who died in the Warsaw ghetto. In demanding an examination of National Socialism, which was absent from the history curriculum in the schools in the 1950s and 1960s, the student movement of the late sixties also encouraged this development. Members of the student generation saw that their fathers preferred to forget this period. If they talked about it at all, they portrayed themselves as helpless victims (Schneider, 6). Although members of the student generation were not involved in the Nazi period, they still felt psychologically damaged by the past, and they began to ask questions about nazism's connection to the present and its impact on their own lives. In the "Väterromane" (the father novels) of the 1970s and 1980s they scrutinized the involvement of their fathers, and sometimes their mothers, in the Nazi years. These texts reveal the pain of this confrontation because the new generation "observes its former Nazi parents in the late 1970s with feelings of embarrassed pity, distaste and total alienation" (Mahlendorf, 558). In the posthumously published *Die Reise* (The Trip, 1977), Bernward Vesper, whose father was a well-known nationalist author who collaborated with the Nazis, was one of the first in the Federal Republic to explore the damaging impact of the parents' past on the younger generation. In *Der Mann auf der Kanzel* (The Man in the Pulpit, 1979), Ruth Rehmann, who like many German women writers in the 1970s began at this time to examine the Nazi past, explores how her father, a conservative Protestant pastor, could have blindly gone along, and she shows that he did not see anything because he did not look (Schneider, 18). Rehmann believes that the concept of authority and discipline, instilled in him in his childhood during Wilhelminian Germany, made her father into an obedient conformist, unable "to perceive the criminal nature of the Nazi state" (Gättens, 50). In *Hubert oder Die Rückkehr nach Casablanca* (Hubert or the Return to Casablanca, 1978) Peter Härtling investigates the impact of the father generation on its sons through the fictional story of Hubert Windisch, whose SS father had murdered Jews in Holland and later committed suicide. After the war, Hubert tries to hide his father's crimes, but they continue to poison his life. At the end of the novel, he meets a young hitchhiker whom he tells about his father's past. She says that these crimes happened long ago and should not concern him. Her reaction, which gives Hubert hope that he can finally free himself from this past, suggests, however, that some members of the generation growing up in Germany after the war consign the past to the past.

Manfred Franke and Peter O. Chotjewitz are typical of those in the 1970s who drew on the documentary literature of the 1960s, such as Kluge's *Schlachtbeschreibung*, to depict everyday fascism, ask questions about guilt and complicity, and examine how extensively life in West Germany in the 1970s was still shaped by the Nazi period. In *Mordverläufe* (The Courses of Murder, 1973) Franke uses a variety of sources to investigate responsibility for the murder of Jews during the *Kristallnacht* in a small town in the Rhineland. He shows the difficulty of finding out the truth since official records are incomplete, people lie, and memory is unreliable (Bullivant 1989, 144). Those involved in the murders are brought to trial after the war but, with one exception, are either acquitted or given mild sentences. Ortsgruppenleiter Nohl, for example, who led the attack on the Jews and became rich from acquiring Jewish property, is now a respected and well-connected businessman, and he is declared innocent. Franke shows that most of the town's citizens, who now want to forget the past, did not try to protect their Jewish neighbors. He stresses that those who did nothing are nevertheless responsible since not acting is the same as acting. Chotjewitz's *Saumlos* (1979, Hemless) explores the fate of a small Jewish community in a fictional small town. Using documents, Chotjewitz depicts the destruction of what had been a thriving community that had lived mostly peacefully with its Christian neighbors for hundreds of years. During the *Kristallnacht*, however, the village youth, incited by the teacher and pastor, burned the synagogue and destroyed Jewish property. Jewish men were sent to Buchenwald and the remaining Jews were driven out. After the war there is no sign that Jews had ever lived in the town. Their long presence there has been obliterated. The townspeople's silence and the disappearance of official records underscore their reluctance to confront the past and probe individual guilt (Bullivant 1987, 162). Chotjewitz makes clear that the repressed past is still part of the present. Many of the townspeople are enjoying the wealth gained from cheaply acquired Jewish property, and they exhibit the same intolerance toward outsiders that they had exhibited toward the Jews in the Nazi period.

Unlike the GDR, West Germany virtually ignored the communist resistance to Hitler – a result of the Cold War. Although people in the Federal Republic were familiar with the officers' plot of 20 July 1944 and the White Rose, they knew little, if anything, about the communist resistance. Peter Weiss, whose play *Die Ermittlung* helped make people aware of Nazi atrocities in the extermination camps, addresses this gap in his monumental work *Die Ästhetik des Widerstands* (The Aesthetics of

Resistance, 1975-81), one of the most thorough accounts of the communist resistance to appear in West Germany. Weiss's novel, which he originally intended to call *Der Widerstand* (Resistance) presents a panorama of German history in the twentieth century and highlights the resistance to the Nazis in the communist Schulze-Boysen-Harnack group. In the last volume of this work Weiss gives a detailed and horrifying description of the execution in Plötzensee of the men and women of this group.

In 1979 the TV series *Holocaust* was broadcast in West Germany. The GDR government refused to broadcast it, arguing that, because the GDR had a long antifascist tradition its citizens, unlike those in West Germany, were already familiar with the Nazi past (Herminghouse, 259), but many in the East were able to see the series on West German television. In West Germany twenty million people viewed it and their overwhelming response revealed that the new generation knew little about this period and that people felt an urgent need to know more. As Demetz points out, since 1945 "the best and most thoughtful German writers have confronted the recent past," but it was a telecast that shocked viewers into thinking about this time: "My astonished respect for the impact of the *Holocaust* series on German public opinion is not entirely free of a certain melancholy about the rather limited power of good writing" (Demetz, 29). The success of this series encouraged the production of Edgar Reitz's *Heimat* (Homeland), which was broadcast in 1984.

In the 1970s in the GDR the confrontation with the Nazi past in literature began to converge with West German literature in its treatment of individual responsibility and complicity, an issue that Bobrowski had already begun to explore in *Levins Mühle*. Writers in the GDR questioned with increasing frequency the focus on the heroic communist resistance and the conversion of Nazis to socialism since both models, in their opinion, said little about the experiences of most GDR citizens during the Nazi years. This more probing antifascist literature in the 1970s was facilitated by the change in cultural policy in the GDR when Erich Honecker replaced Walter Ulbricht in 1971 and, as in the West, by the increasing urgency with which younger people raised questions about their parents' complicity during the Nazi years (Jarausch, 89). This younger generation had learned about fascism in school and had made obligatory visits to the camps at Buchenwald and Sachsenhausen, where they were told that a communist organization had liberated Buchenwald in the final days of the war. The museum in Sachsenhausen, documented the leading role of communists in resisting the Nazis, and they saw pictures of German monopoly capitalists and displays that informed them about the economic uses of the camps (Fox, 17-18).

Like their counterparts in West Germany, however, they wanted a more comprehensive picture of the fascist experience. Their questioning led to a broadening of the discussion of fascism as writers began to explore the collaboration of their parents' generation. In Klaus Schlesinger's *Michael* (1971), Michael, who mistakenly believes that his father was guilty of shooting Polish hostages, is led to confront his father's past. Although his father was not a criminal, he also did nothing to oppose the Nazis. The novel suggests that "the older generation in the GDR has little more moral authority than its counterparts in the West" (Reid, 134). This confrontation with his father's past leads Michael to question what he himself would have done during this time.

During the 1970s some of the leading GDR writers, like Franz Füh-mann, Hermann Kant and Christa Wolf, confronted their own involve-ment in the Nazi years. This acceptance of personal responsibility for Nazi crimes is central to two works by Fühmann and Kant. In *Zweiundzwanzig Tage oder Die Hälfte des Lebens* (Twenty-Two Days or Half of a Lifetime, 1973) Fühmann declares that like thousands of his generation he came to socialism not via the proletarian class struggle, but via Auschwitz. On a visit to Hungary Fühmann has time to reflect and reexamine his involvement in the Nazi period. He has become skeptical of the quick conversion to socialism he had depicted in *Das Judenauto* because he realizes that change is a process that lasts an entire life. Füh-mann confesses that only chance saved him from guilt because, if as a soldier he had been ordered to go to Auschwitz, he would have obeyed and would have participated in the atrocities. He also recognizes that he must accept personal responsibility for Auschwitz since, although he was not directly involved, by serving in the army he provided the support that made the system possible. Mark Niebuhr in Kant's *Der Aufenthalt* (The Stay, 1977) comes to a similar conclusion. While he is imprisoned in Warsaw because a Polish woman mistakenly identified him as a war criminal who massacred Polish civilians he protests his innocence, but he begins to examine his role in the Nazi years, spurred by seeing the destroyed Warsaw ghetto and by his talks with the Polish lieutenant. Mark comes to realize that although he has not personally committed a crime, the fact that he was in reserve made it possible for others, like his cellmates in the prison for war criminals, to create the mountains of ash in camps like Treblinka.

Christa Wolf's *Kindheitsmuster* (A Model Childhood, 1976) had the greatest impact of all the works dealing with the past in the 1970s in East Germany and was one of the first in the GDR to expose Nazi collabora-tion (Jarausch, 85). Like Fühmann, Wolf confronts the fascist within herself. In this depiction of daily life under Hitler, through Nelly, her younger self, Wolf explores the patterns of behavior she had learned as a child that made her receptive to Nazi indoctrination. Wolf insistently asks how people of her generation became what they are today, and by so doing she broadens her discussion of her own fictionalized childhood to include all of her generation in GDR society. Like Grass and others before her in the Federal Republic, Wolf sets her novel in the *petit bourgeois* environment "where fascism found its strongest mass appeal" (Silberman, 535). In contrast to the resistance myth of early GDR literature, Wolf shows that although there were few fanatical Nazis in her hometown, most people went along and made no attempt to resist. By confronting the complicity of the majority of ordinary GDR citizens and stressing that the conditioning and indoctrination her generation experienced as it was growing up in the Nazi years continue to shape the present, Wolf contradicts the official view that the GDR had made a clean break with the Nazi past. Like the Mitscherlichs, Wolf stresses that only by working through the past can people open themselves to change since memory, in her opinion, instigates moral awareness.

In *Kindheitsmuster*, the narrator's daughter Lenka knows virtually nothing about the persecution of the Jews and the final solution: Eichmann is not mentioned in the hundred pages in her school history book devoted to the Hitler years. This silence about the Jews began to change in the 1970s, inspired in part by Becker's portrayal of Jewish victims in *Jakob der Lügner*. In 1971 Fred Wander published *Der Siebente Brunnen* (The Seventh Well, 1971), a powerful account of Jewish suffering in the death camps for which he was awarded the Heinrich Mann prize in 1972. The book is a collection of stories of people Wander met during the years he spent in Nazi concentration camps. Wander is not interested here in politics or ideology but in people, and he rescues the victims of nazism from becoming anonymous statistics. He highlights those resources, one of which, as in *Jakob der Lügner*, is storytelling, that enabled these Jews to retain their humanity amidst the atrocities. Despite his own experiences in the death camps, Wander expresses his belief in the human spirit. One of many people in the work to give him faith in the greatness and dignity of people is the ten-year-old Joschko, who despite the brutalizing conditions he has experienced tenaciously looks after his younger brothers, determined that they will survive. In *Der Boxer* (1976) Becker turns his attention to the problems of Jewish survivors and their children. Aron Blank, who changes his name to Arno to hide his Jewish identity, is a survivor of the camps whose wife has been shot and who has seen two of his children die. After the war he settles in East Germany and is reunited with his remaining child, Mark, although he is never completely certain that Mark is indeed his son. Aron cannot forget the years in the camps. Despite the financial help he receives in East Germany as a victim of fascism, he remains a complete outsider who mistrusts his society. Because his spirit is broken he is unable to begin life again. In *Bronsteins Kinder* (Bronstein's Children), written while Becker was living in West Berlin and published in 1986 in the Federal Republic and in 1987 in the GDR, Becker depicts how the children of Jewish survivors struggle to come to terms with the past and their fathers' experiences. As in the earlier father novels, the past here continues to poison the present. The older generation, whose members suffered in the camps, continue to be tormented by the past while their children, like the teen-aged narrator Hans Bronstein, struggle not only with this past but also with their Jewish identity in German society.

Although some works, such as Stephan Hermlin's autobiographical *Abendlicht* (Evening Light, 1979), in which he details his experiences in the communist resistance during the Hitler years, continue in the heroic tradition of the literature of the 1950s, other works in East Germany in the 1980s develop the radical questioning of Fühmann, Kant, and Wolf. In "Schreiben nach Auschwitz," for example, Stefan Heym asks his listeners to consider what they would have done during the Nazi years. Would they have protested and tried to help when the victims were rounded up to be sent to the camps, or would they have turned away, not wanting to see, or even have mocked the victims? He also expresses his concern about continuing anti-Semitism. He still hears, for example, that not enough Jews were gassed, words spoken not only by people of the generation shaped under nazism but also by young people. In Helga Königsdorf's short novel *Respektloser Umgang* (Irreverent Discourse, 1986), in which she discusses the Jewish physicist Lisa Meitner, who was forced into exile in 1938, and also how her own family accommodated itself to the Nazi period, she points out the limitations of earlier GDR models of confronting the past. Like many in her generation, she writes, she was born too late to be guilty of crimes but she feels a lack of identification with the past. She was brought up reading reports of people who resisted and, although she admired and honored these victors of history, she did not see herself as one of them.

The way in which writers confronted the Nazi past in the Federal Republic and in the GDR slowly converged. In the immediate postwar years, this confrontation was shaped in both countries by myths that tended to absolve people of guilt and enable them to repress the past. Gradually, writers in both countries began to ask about individual responsibility and complicity and about how thinking instilled in the Nazi years continued to shape the present. This radical questioning began earlier in the Federal Republic with writers such as Böll, Grass,

Lenz, Andersch, and Weiss, than in the GDR where it became insistent only in the 1970s. Although writers in the East were encouraged to confront the Nazi past, they could do so only within certain limits. Such topics as the Hitler-Stalin pact, the role of the German Communist Party in the Weimar Republic, and the vestiges of the Third Reich in the GDR were taboo. With the collapse of the GDR, East German writers have themselves been accused of various forms of collaboration with their former government. By stressing the communist resistance and antifascism in their works, for example, they helped give the GDR government legitimacy. GDR writers found it difficult, however, to distance themselves "from a state that defined itself as antifascist, since to do so would have entailed resisting the resisters"(Fox, 14). But by bringing into public awareness questions of continuities between the Third Reich and the GDR writers such as Wolf challenged the official GDR view of the Nazi years, and warned that "the proud antifascist legacy helped legitimize a new kind of unfreedom in the GDR" (Jarausch, 85). As Helga Königsdorf observed, the government's imposed antifascism threatened to bring about a new fascism (cited in Jarausch, 85). Whether writers in the new Germany will continue to confront the Nazi past, mindful of the words of William Faulkner that Christa Wolf uses to open *Kindheitsmuster* – "The past is not dead, it is not even past" – remains to be seen.

Select Bibliography

Bosmajian, Hamida. *Metaphors of Evil: Contemporary German Literature and the Shadow of Nazism.* Iowa City: University of Iowa Press, 1979.

Bullivant, Keith. "The Spectre of the Third Reich: The West German Novel of the 1970s and National Socialism." *After the 'Death of Literature': West German Writing of the 1970s.* Ed. Keith Bullivant. Oxford, New York, Munich: Berg, 1989. 139-54.

Bullivant, Keith. *Realism Today: Aspects of the Contemporary West German Novel.* Leamington Spa, Hamburg, New York: Berg, 1987.

Demetz, Peter. *After the Fires: Recent Writing in the Germanies, Austria, and Switzerland.* San Diego, New York, London: Harcourt Brace Jovanovich, 1986.

Dinter, Ingrid. *Unvollendete Trauerarbeit in der DDR-Literatur.* New York: Peter Lang, 1994.

Emmerich, Wolfgang. *Kleine Literaturgeschichte der DDR.* Darmstadt and Neuwied: Luchterhand, 1981.

Fox, Thomas C. *Border Crossings: An Introduction to East German Prose.* Ann Arbor: University of Michigan Press, 1993.

Gättens, Marie-Luise. "Language, Gender, and Fascism: Reconstructing Histories in *Three Guineas, Der Mann auf der Kanzel* and *Kindheitsmuster.*" *Gender, Patriarchy and Fascism in the Third Reich: The Response of Women Writers.* Ed. Elaine Martin. Detroit: Wayne State, 1993. 32-64.

Herminghouse, Patricia. "Vergangenheit als Problem der Gegenwart: Zur Darstellung des Faschismus in der neueren DDR-Literatur." *Literatur der DDR in den siebziger Jahren.* Eds. P. U. Hohendahl and P. Herminghouse. Frankfurt: Suhrkamp, 1983. 259-94.

Heukenkamp, Ursula, ed. *Unerwünschte Erfahrung: Kriegsliteratur und Zensur in der DDR.* Berlin and Weimar: Aufbau, 1990.

Heym, Stefan. "Schreiben nach Auschwitz." *Stalin verläßt den Raum.* Leipzig: Reclam, 1990. 227-35.

Hörnigk, Therese. "Das Thema Krieg und Faschismus in der Geschichte der DDR-Literatur." *Weimarer Beiträge* 24 (1978): 73-105.

Jarausch, Konrad H. "The Failure of East German Antifascism: Some Ironies of History as Politics." *German Studies Review* 14. 1 (February 1991): 85-102.

Langer, Lawrence L. *The Holocaust and the Literary Imagination.* New Haven and London: Yale University Press, 1975.

Mahlendorf, Ursula. "Confronting the Fascist Past and Coming to Terms with It." *World Literature Today* 55. 4 (Autumn 1981): 553-60.

Reed, Donna K. *The Novel and the Nazi Past.* Berne: Peter Lang, 1984.

Reid, J. H. *Writing Without Taboos: The New East German Literature.* New York, Oxford, Munich: Berg, 1990.

Ryan, Judith. *The Uncompleted Past: Postwar German Novels and the Third Reich.* Detroit: Wayne State, 1983.

Schneider, Michael. "Fathers and Sons, Retrospectively: The Damaged Relationship Between Two Generations." *New German Critique* 31 (Winter 1984): 3-51.

Silberman, Marc. "Writing What—for Whom? 'Vergangenheitsbewältigung' in GDR Literature." *German Studies Review* 10. 3 (October 1987): 527-37.

Trommler, Frank. "Der zögernde Nachwuchs: Entwicklungsprobleme der Nachkriegsliteratur in Ost und West." *Tendenzen der deutschen Literatur seit 1945.* Ed. Thomas Koebner. Stuttgart: Kröner, 1971. 1-116.

Wagener, Hans, ed. *Gegenwartsliteratur und Drittes Reich.* Stuttgart: Reclam, 1977.

Wolf, Christa. "Das siebte Kreuz." *Die Dimension des Autors: Essays und Aufsätze, Reden und Gespräche 1959-1985.* Darmstadt and Neuwied: Luchterhand, 1987. 263-78.

A FAREWELL TO THE LETTERS OF THE FEDERAL REPUBLIC?

F. Schirrmacher's Postwall Assessment of Postwar German Literature

Siegfried Mews

In the intense, multi-faceted debate that followed the fall of the Berlin Wall one may distinguish three partially overlapping, closely interrelated phases of a literary debate or *Literaturstreit* that evolved in response to the rapid disintegration of the GDR and the forcefully emerging issue of unification. The first of these phases, a close scrutiny of the role and function of GDR literature, was in part triggered by public professions by major GDR writers of their continuing belief in socialism, a project that, after the crumbling of the Wall, had lost both its credibility and attractiveness to the populace at large. Paradoxically, the literary endeavors of Christa Wolf, Stefan Heym, and others to "reform" the GDR variant of the incantatorily invoked *real existierender Sozialismus,* or actually existing socialism, had been interpreted during the existence of the Wall by liberal, and particularly by leftist Western critics, as expressions of necessarily veiled political-critical intent; these critics had found solace in the fact that GDR writers upheld the idea of socialism in the face of an insufficient socialist reality.[1]

1. The literature on these developments is considerable. For a brief survey, see, e.g., Mews, "Fall."

This so-called bonus of assumed oppositional tendencies in GDR literature rested on the privileging of surmised political content over aesthetic construct; with the disappearance of the object of criticism, the GDR, that took place without any overt assistance from GDR writers, the function of these writers came under close scrutiny. In fact, GDR literature was disingenuously and retroactively criticized for not having assumed a strong oppositional role in hastening the demise of the GDR. The compensatory desire on the part of Western critics, who were determined to revise their previously positive evaluations of GDR letters, may be gathered from the vociferous debate that followed upon the publication of Wolf's slim prose volume "What Remains" in June 1990. Wolf's prose narrative gained a degree of notoriety that constituted the culmination of the probing of GDR literature and may be said to constitute the beginning of the second phase of the *Literaturstreit*. The uproar that was caused by the publication of the work can only be explained by the fact that both friend and foe perceived Christa Wolf as the foremost representative of GDR literature, and that her case exemplified the problematic relationship of GDR writers to their state.

To be sure, the soul-searching expected of GDR writers failed to materialize; similarly, a corresponding self-examination of Western writers and intellectuals, particularly concerning their attitudes towards the former GDR and towards unification, was lacking. Apart from a few notable exceptions such as that of Peter Schneider, who in April 1990 criticized some of his fellow writers for failing to take into account the monumental changes that were taking place by reexamining their dearly held beliefs ("Earthquake"), intellectuals in both East and West preferred to succumb, as Rolf Schneider put it, to "leftist melancholia." This melancholia was tinged with nostalgia or, as punsters would have it, *Ostalgie* (i.e., nostalgia about the loss of the *Osten* or East) about the absence of the GDR's presumed material and moral values. Moreover, these writers lamented the disappearance of the GDR's utopian potential – a potential that was not discernable in the pre-unification Federal Republic. After all, notably the writers of *Gruppe 47* (Group 47), such as Heinrich Böll, Günter Grass, and Martin Walser had professed, to varying degrees, their commitment to social and political causes. Hence they were perceived as oppositional voices in the face of a conservative establishment and a powerful political class that – in obvious contrast to the practice of the GDR – tended to treat writers and intellectuals with benign neglect or scornful indifference. By virtue of their oppositional role that they abandoned only temporarily during the period of the Social/Liberal coalition under Chancellor Willy Brandt, writers such as Böll, Grass, and Walser were mindful of the strict separation of the spheres of *Macht* and *Geist* (power and intellect) as well as the comparative powerlessness of the interpreting class. At the same time, unlike some or most of their colleagues in the GDR, they established their impeccable anti-authoritarian, democratic credentials by seeking to subvert the dominant official political discourse.

Although, in part motivated by the lessening of tensions between East and West and the beginning of *Ostpolitik*, in the late 1960s and early 1970s the thesis of two independent German literatures gained currency, the "partial transfer of GDR literature to the FRG" (Schmidt, qtd. in Peitsch, 474), that commenced after the much publicized expatriation of singer/poet Wolf Biermann from the GDR in 1976 contributed considerably to the revision and disavowal of the notion of two German literatures. For example, in the 1980s Grass assiduously promoted the concept of the *Kulturnation* (a nation defined primarily on the basis of the culture shared by its members) as a substitute for both the missing and – in his view undesirable – national unity.[2] Precisely because, as he wrote in *Headbirths, or the Germans Are Dying Out* (1980), "politically, ideologically, economically, and militarily the two Germanys live more against than alongside each other" (6), the notion of an indivisible German literature had to be kept alive. In Grass's view it is literature's inherent oppositional tendency that provided the common bond for writers in both German states. In *Headbirths* this oppositional tendency is largely directed against the attempts in both East and West to abolish and suppress the last vestiges of German unity; Grass's report on the semi-clandestine meetings of East and West German writers in East Berlin, which came to an end after Biermann's expatriation, clearly establishes the antagonistic role of both German states in their suppressing or ignoring of literature – albeit by ignoring those writers who fully supported the GDR.[3]

Although Grass's views were by no means universally shared, they may be considered indicative of a prevailing mode of thought that emphasized the significance of language, literature, and culture as the elements that counteracted the separatist tendencies of the two German states. Peter Schneider, for example, who had participated in the East Berlin meetings reported by Grass in *Headbirths*, articulated the anomaly of Berlin's and Germany's division in his narrative *The Wall Jumper* (1983). The narra-

2. For details, see Mews, "Problem," and Peitzsch.
3. Grass's emphasis on the convergence of the two German states in their comparable treatment of literature is evident from a short passage in *Kopfgeburten* (81) that has been omitted in the English translation: "Danach [after Biermann's expatriation] hatte der Staat das Sagen, der eine, der andere. (Dem einen fällt zur Literatur das immer passende Reimwort [Diktatur], dem anderen nichts ein.)" See also Mews, "*Kopfgeburten.*"

tor's identity crisis results from this division; his "national identity" is grounded in "[German] history and in the [German] language" rather than in his depending "on either of the German states" (126-27).

Yet in the postwall intellectual climate, this comfortable but restrictive dichotomy, which pitted writers against their respective states, was challenged in a major article that, significantly, appeared on the eve of German unification on 2 October 1990. Frank Schirrmacher, successor of star critic and *Feuilletonchef* Marcel Reich-Ranicki at the influential *Frankfurter Allgemeine Zeitung* (*FAZ*), both implicitly and explicitly took issue with Grass's arguments that posited one national literature primarily on the basis of its critical potential. In contrast to Grass, Schirrmacher ignored oppositional tendencies and stressed the propensity for accommodation that he perceived in both the literature of the GDR and of the Federal Republic.

Schirrmacher's article, which may be said to have initiated the third phase of the *Literaturstreit*, shifted the focus from the examination of GDR literature to that of letters in the (old) Federal Republic. Even if Schirrmacher's "Abschied von der Literatur der Bundesrepublik" (A Farewell to the Letters of the Federal Republic) did not generate the volume, intensity, or passion generated by the publication of "What Remains," it offered a challenging hypothesis. Intent on destroying "some myths of West German consciousness," Schirrmacher posited polemically the essentially similar legitimating function of both GDR authors and those in the Federal Republic: "Not only the literature of the GDR was supposed to legitimize its society and to establish new traditions; the literature of the Federal Republic also was aware of this task and carried it out conscientiously."

If one disregards Grass's dissenting voice with regard to the critical potential of East German writers, Schirrmacher's claim about the function of GDR literature is unexceptional; however, the alleged "mandate" of letters in the Federal Republic contradicts all notions about the mechanisms governing the production and distribution of cultural products in a market-oriented society – unless one wishes to invoke the arcane and subtle influence of the collective unconscious or of the dominant *Zeitgeist* as originators of such a mandate. Hence Ulrich Greiner's supporting opinion, which was published in the reputable weekly *Die Zeit*, denounced the basically similar orientations of GDR literature and its Western counterpart as *Gesinnungsästhetik* (German ideological aesthetics.)[4] According to Greiner, the practitioners of such ideological aesthet-

---

4. For the difficulties of translating *Gesinnungsästhetik*, see Bullivant (5, n. 12) whose translation I adopt.

ics dealt with "extra-literary topics," stipulated by their "conscience, the party, politics, morality, the past." But Greiner's assertion is of dubious validity in that the dictates of an individual conscience and the directives of the party apparatus are hardly compatible entities. Yet, whatever the source of the writers' mandate, Schirrmacher argues that the main task postwar authors in the (old) Federal Republic were engaged in was the creation of a new consciousness *(Bewußtsein)* and progressive identity that were eagerly embraced by at least part of the West German public.

In Schirrmacher's view the texts produced by Böll, Grass, Walser, and others merely served to exonerate society and to provide a substitute for its lack of involvement with the past in order to demonstrate to the world the essentially democratic character of the postwar West German society and politics. Such a claim tends to collapse two successive stages of the postwar development in the cultural-intellectual realm, that is, the "literary opposition to the Adenauer restoration" and "its later ossification into palliative dogma" (Huyssen, 137). In a scathing rebuttal of Schirrmacher's thesis about the unproblematic reception of postwar literature Wolfram Schütte pointed out in the local rival of the conservative *FAZ*, the liberal *Frankfurter Rundschau*, such incidents as the repeated diatribes of prominent politicians against leading literary representatives, the various boycotts of Brecht's plays in the Federal Republic and West Berlin, and the rejection of fiction with political themes by conservative critic Friedrich Sieburg, erstwhile *Feuilletonchef* of the *FAZ*. Needless to say, such conditions hardly facilitated the reception of postwar letters.

Among the major postwar writers and founding fathers of the "bundesdeutsches Literaturwunder" (literary miracle) of the Federal Republic that began in the late 1950s and early 1960s Grass serves Schirrmacher as a frequently invoked witness for the presumed legends and myths of postwar letters that the writers themselves supposedly fostered and perpetuated by claiming that they had prevailed in the face of a reactionary and nationalistic *Öffentlichkeit* (public sphere). Even if one takes into account that *Öffentlichkeit* is not a homogeneous entity, an entity that allows varied and contradictory modes of reception, the tenor of the responses to Grass's literary work, which like that of Böll and Walser tended to subvert the *Wirtschaftswunder* (economic miracle) that had preceded the literary miracle, hardly supports Schirrmacher's claim. Although *The Tin Drum* is today acknowledged as perhaps *the* major work of postwar literature, its present-day canonical status tends to obscure the decidedly mixed reactions it received initially . To be sure, on the one hand Grass was awarded the prepublication prize for reading from the manuscript of the novel at the 1958 meeting of *Gruppe 47*; on the other, the Senate of the City of Bremen rescinded the decision of its panel to award a prize to Grass (Arnold/Görtz, 263-81). Such a contrasting pattern of awarding and withholding prizes seems to suggest an antagonistic relationship between literati eager to promote young, provocatively innovative representatives of postwar letters on the one hand and conservative politicians intent on preserving the status quo and rejecting literary experiments on the other. The contradictory nature of the critical assessments is aptly summarized in the subtitle of Franz Josef Görtz's anthology of reviews of *The Tin Drum, Attraktion und Ärgernis* (Attraction and Scandal).

True, to return to Schirrmacher's argument, the negative comments about the novel and its author, which may be subsumed under the headings of "pornographer, blasphemer, nihilist" (Vormweg 55), are not overtly inspired by politics. But the very fact that those critics who perceived in the novel an indication of the loss of traditional values in an entire generation failed to take into account the Nazi past and the end of World War II as crucial contributing factors to such loss constitutes an evasion, and a denial of the political dimension of the novel to which some perceptive critics alluded.

The reception of Grass's works has been amply documented; the evidence clearly suggests that Grass's claim of having to succeed in the face of "a reactionary and nationalististic *Öffentlichkeit*" is essentially justified. But, it is important to note, this *Öffentlichkeit* was not exclusively dominated by reactionaries and nationalists; hence it was unable to prevent Grass's rise to fame and to becoming very much a public figure himself, particularly after the beginning of his active involvement in politics on behalf of the SPD that dates from 1961 and intensified, in terms of grass root campaigning, in 1965. Grass himself drew attention to the fact that he deliberately used his renown as a writer to enhance his stature and efficacy as a campaigner, especially in *From the Diary of a Snail* (Neuhaus, 122) The media attention he attracted as both a writer of fiction and a citizen actively engaged in politics secured him a role of public consequence whose limitations Grass satirized in his 1966 Princeton address, "Vom mangelhaften Selbstvertrauen der schreibenden Hofnarren ..." (About the lack of self-confidence of the writing court jesters). No doubt Grass's deliberate break with the tradition that pitted, in the fashion of Thomas Mann, *Bürger* (bourgeois) against *Künstler* (artist), contributed to his attractiveness as an intellectual media star. As early as 1969 critic Horst Krüger called him "The heraldic animal of the [Federal] Republic" and attested to his status as a national representative in the manner of a well-known trademark, the Mercedes emblem (56, 57). Yet the comparison of Grass with this emblem is misleading in that the latter serves in an official representational capacity whereas Grass only rarely assumed an official role – as, for example, in 1970 when he accompanied Chancellor Brandt to Warsaw on the occasion of the signing of the German-Polish treaty, one of the cornerstones of Brandt's *Ostpolitik*.

In fact, Grass may be said to represent a kind of *Gegenöffentlichkeit*, a literary-intellectual opposition. The impact of this opposition on public discourse can be measured by the reactions of the politicians, which hover between neglect on the one hand and hostility on the other. Unlike Böll, a writer on whom critics bestowed the terms "moral authority" and "conscience of the nation" (see Mews, "Moralist",140), but who refrained from active engagement in politics, Grass's partisan involvement on behalf of the SPD and his insistence, from the 1960s to the 1980s, on a politics of pragmatism made him susceptible to criticism from both the right and the rebellious student left, and hardly supports the assumption of the legitimating function of literature in the (old) Federal Republic as Schirrmacher would have it.

What dirtied the clean linen more than anything else, and prevented the whitewashing of postwar West Germany, was the much discussed literary *Vergangenheitsbewältigung* (coming to terms with the past) that sought to stimulate the process of remembering and mourning *(Erinnerungs- und Trauerarbeit)*. To be sure, Schirrmacher does not ignore literary attempts to come to terms with the Nazi past, but he constructs a contrast between the writers' well-intentioned, subjective endeavors and their objective failure: "It appears as if a large part of West German literature has not opened the space occupied by history but has involuntarily closed it off. The linkage with the past, which it subjectively wanted to establish, it objectively suspended." Paradoxically, as Schütte has noted, in his revaluation Schirrmacher reversed the formerly assumed roles of writers such as Grass and Böll; from *Erinnerungsarbeiter* (those concerned with the task of remembering) they have been turned into virtual *Verdrängungsvirtuosen* (virtuosos of suppression). As a major vehicle for this suspension of the past, its inability to influence the present, Schirrmacher identified the predominance of the child's perspective in major works such as *The Tin Drum*. The child's perspective, Schirrmacher avers, ultimately prevented a full acceptance of the historical continuum of which the Nazi past forms an integral part; rather, the events of that past appeared as "childhood traumas" that were far removed from the present: "Incredulously and endowed with the unambiguous morality of the naive and the innocent, [the figures in novels] witnessed the monstrous catastrophy … . The Third Reich seemed to those born later like a bad childhood memory – but distorted in fairy-tale-like fashion – that had taken place in mythical times and was completely removed from history."

Even a cursory reader of *The Tin Drum* will hardly fail to notice that Oskar Matzerath, the novel's narrator/protagonist, is neither naive nor innocent. Furthermore, he does not confine his role to that of a witness; rather, he uses his guise of both physically and mentally arrested development to hide his active participation in the events depicted in the first two books – a participation that is in part motivated by his realization of his susceptibility to becoming a victim. Although, ultimately, Oskar's role is ambivalent, his professed complicity in the deaths of his "presumable" fathers Bronski and Matzerath, for example, appears to be politically motivated when these deaths are viewed as an inevitable consequence of the fathers' deeds. Thus Grass poses the question of the individual's responsibility – a question that also applies to Oskar himself who, despite his belated growth, does not mature into a physically normal adult and who, in the novel's third book, remains a conspicuous outsider in postwar West German society. Apart from the act of narration that may be viewed as indicative of Oskar's atonement for his sins of both omission and commission, his attempts to start afresh and to assume responsibility have essentially failed – a failure that is shared by an entire society only too eager to forget the past and savor the material blessings of the beginning economic miracle. Grass's fundamental criticism is historically grounded; the intertwining of Oskar's family history and political history is clearly evident, for instance, in the novel's use of significant historical dates as structuring devices. Despite its fairy tale, supernatural, and fantastical elements, *The Tin Drum* is not a text that one could easily mistake, as Schirrmacher does, for taking place in a mythical, prehistorical time devoid of any relevance for the present. On the contrary, Grass's use of mythic structures and mythopeic projections serves to emphasize rather than suppress the significance of the past (Guidry).

One may conclude then that in articulating, as Schirrmacher writes, "the consciousness of the country, its obsessions and its fears," Grass, one of the foremost literary "speakers and representatives of the nation," did not write texts that were designed to serve the above-mentioned function of exonerating society. Nor, for that matter, were these texts perceived or received as legitimating. To be sure, Grass and the members of *Gruppe 47* can be credited with having been one of the "production centers of the consciousness of the Federal Republic." But Schirrmacher's elevation of Oskar Matzerath to chief protagonist and representative of this postwar consciousness is highly dubious: "[Oskar Matzerath is] the figure in which West German consciousness recognizes itself; at a certain stage it has refused to grow. Although it is aging, it continues to assume the role of a child." The novel's drawing attention to manifestations of infantilism, including those in the political realm, seeks to expose the infantile traits of West German society rather than to endorse it. Such a portrayal was hardly conducive to the novel's wholesale acceptance by the reading public.

To be sure, "West German literature ... was the work of one generation" in the sense that it became fully established around 1960 as a consequence of the appearance of a number of significant works, foremost among them *The Tin Drum*. However, Schirrmacher's attribution of an alleged "constant consciousness" to this generation of writers discounts their ability to change and to respond to new challenges via literary texts. Oskar Matzerath's only partially successful attempt to grow physically prior to becoming integrated into society, for instance, does not signify this figure's perennial failure to accept social responsibility. When Grass revived Oskar in his novel *The Rat* (1986), the sixty-year-old protagonist of *The Tin Drum* has taken leave of his spellbinding drumming that evoked the past in the service of *Trauerarbeit* and has resorted to a different but likewise profitable medium, that is, video productions that anticipate the future in all its undesirable consequences. *The Rat*, in fact, offers a primary text on the global "extra-literary" issues that concerned the author Grass in the 1980s and continue to concern him in the 1990s. At the same time, the action of *The Rat* involving the "phony fifties" (200), the period of the 1950s that was dominated by the political figures of Konrad Adenauer in the West and Walter Ulbricht in the East – both of whom enabled Germans to suppress or ignore their past – betrays Grass's "constant consciousness" *not* of a remote, fairy tale-like past but of the uncompleted task of *Vergangenheitsbewältigung*.

Although Schirrmacher is correct in drawing attention to the concept of the so-called zero hour of 1945 that has lately received renewed attention owing in part to the fiftieth anniversary in May 1995 of the end of World War II in Europe , Grass is far from viewing the zero hour as the "unbridgeable beginning of history, the caesura ... the farewell from the holocaust and from everything that has led to it." On the contrary, he has eschewed claiming an exemption from being responsible for the Nazi past on the basis of the "blessing of having been born late" – a phrase coined by Chancellor Helmut Kohl – and has persistently questioned the validity of the concept of *Stunde Null* both in terms of the biography of individual writers and in terms of literary development as a whole. In *Headbirths*, for example, Grass's speculations about the zero hour function as a consciousness-raising device about the liabilities of the past (Mews, *Kopfgeburten*, 512-14).

Grass's stance in the unification debate, his questionable insistence on the concept of *Kulturnation* versus *Staatsnation* (a nation defined by its political institutions and common territory), is based on a moralistic argument derived from the past, that is, the unavoidability of confronting Auschwitz in any major political decision.[5] Grass seemed to argue for a perpetuation of the political status that pertained not *before* the breaching of the Wall but during the short interim period between 9 November 1989 and 3 October 1990 or, rather, 1 July 1990, the beginning of the currency union. As we know, Grass's desire to preserve the GDR and to avoid what has been derogatorily called its *Anschluß* (a reference to the union of Germany with Austria in 1938) was shared by a number of major GDR writers. Yet what distinguishes Grass from many of his colleagues in the GDR is his anti-authoritarian "democratic consciousness" that is reflected in his writing and that developed *not* "forced by a society that felt guilty" (Schirrmacher)" but rather in response to the unwillingness of that society to accept any blame.

The foregoing remarks, which primarily take issue with the misrepresentation of one of postwar West German letters best-known representatives, have sought to demonstrate that Schirrmacher's farewell to the literature of the (old) Federal Republic was, at best, premature. His "rashness in judging" (Schütte) did not result in a profound and convincing revaluation of postwar literature. But implicit in the misguided, speculative, and unsubstantiated evaluation of the *Gesinnungsästhetik* of the leading literary representatives of postwar West German literature – a process more akin to *Abrechnung* (settling of scores) than to *Abschied* (farewell) – is the wish to consider the postwar period that extends from the *Stunde Null* to the *Wende* (turning point) of 1989/1990 an essentially closed chapter.[6] Furthermore, underlying Schirrmacher's "Farewell" is the desire not only to chart but to influence the course of future literary developments with a view to creating a literature that renounces the "extra-literary" topics of the past and, at the same time and somewhat incongruously, expresses a sense of the newly gained nationhood (Stephan 130). In his ambitious 1994 attempt to surmise the "future of German literature," Keith Bullivant has discerned potentially favorable conditions for the "success of the new Conservative Revolution" (197). Yet seen from the vantage point of the mid-1990s, there seem to be no major texts that constitute a radical break with pre-1990 literature and that appear to herald the beginning of a new age of national letters.

5. Grass's major essays on the "national question" have been translated in Grass, *Two States – One Nation?* See also Mews, "Problem," and Peitsch.

6. The desire to use the convenient markers 1945 and 1989/1990 as guide posts in the periodization of literary history is evident, for example, in the title of the anthology by Krauss, *Vom Nullpunkt zur Wende.* As to the problems inherent in such a period concept, see Barner (xx-xxi).

After all, the frequently invoked parallels between 1945 and 1989/1990 are not convincing in that the defeat of Germany and its (re)unfication provided fundamentally different socio-political and economic contexts for literary production. In fact, the immoderate and extensive reappraisal of postwar literature, which during the last few years has been fuelled by the revelations of *Stasi* contacts on the part of leading GDR writers, possibly developed in response to the hesitant and insufficient revaluation of the literature of the Third Reich in the immediate postwar years (Barner, 934).

Even though one may consider Schirrmacher's construct misguided, there is no denying the fact that his premises concerning post-Wall literature are implicitly and explicitly shared by some writers as well as other critics. For example, the 1993 appearance of essays with widely divergent emphases by Botho Strauß, Hans Magnus Enzensberger, and Walser – who "almost single-handedly" (Barner, 936) put the national question on the fictional agenda when he published his novella *No Man's Land* in 1987 – was touted by the influential weekly *Der Spiegel* as a shift to the right on the part of three former participants in or sympathizers of the student movement who now tended to embrace national values ("Hausmitteilung"). Conversely, the publication in 1995 of Grass's latest novel, *Ein weites Feld* (An Expansive Field), proves beyond a doubt that Grass has retained his negative stance towards unification and is intent on perpetuating his accustomed role as an oppositional voice in the new Germany. In his devastating review of the novel, the extraordinarily influential Reich-Ranicki, in the 1970s considered a leftist in the *Feuilleton* section of the *FAZ*, went far beyond justifiable regret about what might be termed Grass's intransigence and singled out his assumed sympathy for the GDR and his criticism of the new Germany as an aberration of major proportions – the novel has indeed been received more favorably in the Eastern part of the country – and proclaimed the failure of a great writer. Voices such Reich-Ranicki's tend to confirm that the prevailing discourse of the critical establishment in the 1990s endorses and promotes a shift in the direction of letters in the new Germany. This shift may be only insufficiently characterized by such terms as nationalism and conservatism, but it is important to note that Schirrmacher's partisan revaluation of postwar literature provided a decisive impetus for the desire to change the direction of postunification letters.

Select Bibliography

Anon. "Hausmitteilung. Betr.: Intellektuelle." *Der Spiegel* 28 June 1993: 3.

Arnold, Heinz Ludwig, and Franz Joseph Görtz. *Günter Grass: Dokumente zur politischen Wirkung.* Munich: Edition Text + Kritik, 1971.

Barner, Wilfried, ed. *Geschichte der deutschen Literatur von 1945 bis zur Gegenwart.* Munich: Beck, 1994.

Bullivant, Keith. *The Future of German Literature.* Oxford: Berg, 1994.

Enzensberger, Hans Magnus. "Ausblicke auf den Bürgerkrieg." *Der Spiegel* 21 June 1994: 170-75.

Görtz, Franz Joseph, ed. *"Die Blechtrommel." Attraktion und Ärgernis.* Darmstadt: Luchterhand, 1984.

Greiner, Ulrich. "Die deutsche Gesinnungsästhetik." *Die Zeit* 8 October 1990.

Grass, Günter. *Aus dem Tagebuch einer Schnecke.* Neuwied: Luchterhand, 1972. Trans. Ralph Manheim as *From the Diary of a Snail.* New York: Harcourt, 1973.

———. *Die Blechtrommel.* Neuwied: Luchterhand, 1959. Trans. Ralph Manheim as *The Tin Drum.* New York: Pantheon, 1962.

———. *Ein weites Feld.* Göttingen: Steidl, 1995.

———. *Kopfgeburten oder Die Deutschen sterben aus.* Darmstadt: Luchterhand, 1980. Trans. Ralph Manheim as *Headbirths: Or, The Germans Are Dying Out.* New York: Harcourt, 1982.

———. *Die Rättin.* Darmstadt: Neuwied, 1986. Trans. Ralph Manheim as *The Rat.* San Diego: Harcourt, 1987.

———. *Two States – One Nation?* Trans. Krishna Winston with A. S. Wensinger. San Diego, CA: Harcourt, 1990.

———. "Vom mangelhaften Selbstvertrauen der schreibenden Hofnarren unter Berücksichtigung nicht vorhandener Höfe." *Werkausgabe in zehn Bänden.* Ed. Volker Neuhaus. Darmstadt: Luchterhand, 1987. 9: 153-58.

Greiner, Ulrich. "Die deutsche Gesinnungsästhetik." *Die Zeit* 2 Nov. 1990. Rpt. *"Es geht nicht um Christa Wolf." Der Literaturstreit im vereinten Deutschland.* Ed. Thomas Anz. Munich: Spangenberg, 1991. 208-16.

Guidry, Glenn A. "Theoretical Reflections on the Ideological and Social Implications of Mythic Form in Grass' *Die Blechtrommel.*" *Monatshefte* 83 (1991): 127-46.

Huyssen, Andreas. "After the Wall: The Failure of German Intellectuals." *New German Critique* 52 (1991): 109-43.

Krauss, Hannes, ed. *Vom Nullpunkt zur Wende. Deutschsprachige Literatur 1945-1990.* Essen: Klartext, 1994.

Krüger, Horst. "Das Wappentier der Republik. Augenblicke mit Günter Grass." *Günter Grass: Auskunft für Leser.* Ed. Franz Josef Görtz. Darmstadt: Luchterhand, 1984. 56-62.

Mews, Siegfried. "After the Fall of the Berlin Wall: German Writers and Unification." *South Atlantic Review* 58.2 (1993): 1-16.

_____. "Grass' *Kopfgeburten*: The Writer in Orwell's Decade." *German Studies Review* 6 (1983): 501-17.

_____. "Günter Grass und das Problem der deutschen Nation." *Zwischen Traum und Trauma - Die Nation. Transatlantische Perspektiven zur Geschichte eines Problems.* Tübingen: Stauffenburg, 1994. 111-27.

_____. "Moralist versus Pragmatist? Heinrich Böll and Günter Grass as Political Writers." *Coping with the Past: Germany and Austria after 1945.* Ed. Kathy Harms, Lutz R. Reuter, and Volker Dürr. Madison, WI: University of Wisconsin Press, 1990. 140-54.

Neuhaus, Volker. *Günter Grass.* 2nd, rev. and enl. ed. Stuttgart: Metzler, 1993.

Peitsch, Helmut. "'Antipoden' im 'Gewissen der Nation'? - Günter Grass' und Martin Walsers 'deutsche Fragen.'" *Dichter und ihre Nation.* Ed. Helmut Scheuer. Frankfurt: Suhrkamp, 1993. 459-89.

Reich-Ranicki, Marcel. "… und es muß gesagt werden. Ein Brief an Günter Grass zu dessen Roman *Ein weites Feld.*" *Der Spiegel* 21 August 1995: 162-69.

Schirrmacher, Frank. "Abschied von der Literatur der Bundesrepublik." *Frankfurter Allgemeine Zeitung* 2 October 1990.

Schneider, Peter. "Man kann sogar ein Erdbeben verpassen." *Extreme Mittellage. Eine Reise durch das deutsche Nationalgefühl.* Hamburg: Rowohlt, 1990. 54-78. Trans. Philip Boehm and Leigh Hafrey as "Some People Can even Sleep through an Earthquake." *The German Comedy. Scenes of Life after the Wall.* New York: Farrar, 1991. 66-91.

_____. *Der Mauerspringer: Erzählung.* Darmstadt: Luchterhand, 1982. Trans. Leigh Hafrey as *The Wall Jumper.* New York: Pantheon, 1983.

Schneider, Rolf. "Von linker Melancholie." *Der Spiegel* 19 August 1991: 46-47.

Schütte, Wolfram. "Auf dem Schrotthaufen der Geschichte. Zu einer denkwürdig-voreiligen Verabschiedung der 'bundesdeutschen Literatur.'" *Frankfurter Rundschau* 20 Oct. 1990.

Stephan, Alexander. "Ein deutscher Forschungsbericht 1990/91: Zur Debatte um das Ende der DDR-Literatur und den Anfang einer gesamtdeutschen Kultur." *Germanic Review* 67.3 (1992): 126-34.

Strauß, Botho. "Anschwellender Bocksgesang." *Der Spiegel* 8 Feb. 1993: 202-07.

Vormweg, Heinrich. *Günter Grass. Mit Selbstzeugnissen und Bilddokumenten.* Reinbek: Rowohlt, 1986.

Walser, Martin. "Deutsche Sorgen." *Der Spiegel* 28 Aug. 1993: 40-47.

_____. *Dorle und Wolf. Novelle.* Frankfurt: Suhrkamp, 1987. Trans. Leila Vennewitz as *No Man's Land.* New York: Holt, 1989.

Wolf, Christa. *Was bleibt: Erzählung.* Frankfurt: Luchterhand, 1990. Trans. Heike Schwarzbauer and Rick Takvorian as "What Remains." *What Remains and Other Stories.* New York: Farrar, 1993. 231-95.

TEXTS AND CONTEXTS

GDR Literature during the 1970s

Carol Anne Costabile-Heming

While politics dictated the socio-ideological structure of the two German states from 1949 to 1990, it also directed the understanding and production of culture. Because these ideologically opposed states shared a linguistic and cultural heritage, one can argue that they also shared one literature. Indeed, Günter Grass claimed that the two German states had literature as a common denominator (8). Yet, the critical literary battle (*Literaturstreit*) carried out in German newspapers in 1990 and 1991 highlighted the very real differences in literary production on either side of the German-German border. After the publication of *What Remains* (Was bleibt), Christa Wolf watched as her reputation as a renowned "German" writer disintegrated; critics scolded her, accusing her of being merely a puppet of the State (Anz). Indeed, this debate forced scholars to re-think the concept of a unified literature as well as to re-evaluate their previous assessments of GDR literature, GDR writers, the role of the State in literary production, and the role of literature in the State. Ultimately, scholars grappled with the question of literature as fictional reality, and its ability to validate assumptions about "real" experiences on either side of the German-German border. Hinrich Seeba's statement that "Germans have always stretched their imagination, inscribing literary fiction – and the story of its imagined history as national literature – with a political mission to both explain and justify the ever-renewed deferral of political redemption" (357), clearly illustrates the extent to which literature was mistaken as a unifying element.

Various factors contributed to the assumption that a unified literature existed. Although the German border did on one level consist of a physical barricade like the Berlin Wall, communication between the two Germanys was able to overcome or at least circumvent any barriers. The common language facilitated dialogue between the two nations; radio and television waves were oblivious to any border structures. The mail, although often searched in the GDR, afforded the opportunity for East and West to enter into unofficial dialogues. Even literary texts crossed borders.

The purpose of this essay is not, however, to debate the extent to which Germany had a unified literature before 1990, but to highlight the problems that political division posed to creative activity. If we assume that literature functioned as a type of ersatz public sphere (Herminghouse, 85), then we need to examine the structures that enabled or hindered literature from entering the public domain. Indeed, in examining specifically texts and writers that have crossed borders, we can draw conclusions about the role that writers in one Germany played in the other, and the way that literature was public in both states. This analysis will focus primarily on the literary careers of Reiner Kunze (1933) and Günter Kunert (1929) because they provide two distinct examples of public discourse *(Öffentlichkeit)* in the GDR. Kunze was all but denied a voice in the GDR. The often exclusive publication of his texts in the West signals him as a true border crosser. Kunert, on the other hand, managed to publish his works on both sides of the German-German border, although variations in the editions often occurred. Both of these artists were "uncomfortable" writers,[1] who did not shy away from criticizing the contradictions and inadequacies of the GDR system. Because of space considerations, I will confine my analysis to the years 1971-1980, a pivotal period for cultural production in the GDR that was characterized by both tolerance and by oppression.

When Walter Ulbricht resigned his post as leader of the Socialist Unity Party (SED) in 1971 because of advanced age, Erich Honecker's succession to that office initially hinted at change. Whereas Ulbricht's cultural policy was based on tight controls and repressive tactics, Honecker seemed to usher in a more relaxed literary landscape. It was in December 1971 that Honecker delivered his now famous speech declaring that there would be no taboos within cultural realms as long as artists approached their topics from the fortified position of socialism (198). While this statement appeared to relax the restrictions imposed on writers, a new period of ideological crisis for GDR writers occurred. The qualifying phrase, "from the fortified position of socialism," enabled editors, outside readers, and even Party members to suppress any texts they

1. I have borrowed this term from the description of Wolf Biermann in the protest letter following his expatriation (*Sachen,* 70).

deemed too controversial. Additionally, this clause implied that any writer who was loyal to Party doctrine would represent critical topics appropriately. Indeed, as Kurt Hager's speech before the Central Committee in July 1972 emphasized: "if we choose the magnitude and multitude of possibilities offered by socialist realism, favoring the large freedom of creativity this guidance offers, then we exclude all concessions to bourgeois ideology and imperialistic interpretations of art" (Rüß, 508). Such qualifications and implied threats negated the outward emphasis on tolerance. Thus, the cultural policy of the 1970s vacillated between periods of tolerance and repressive tactics.

Initially, Honecker's promise of relaxed control seemed promising. As a first step, several of Stefan Heym's critical works, *The Lampoon or the Queen against Defoe* [Die Schmähschrift oder die Königin gegen Defoe (1970), *Lasalle* (1969) and *The King David Report* (Der König David Bericht, 1972) received their first GDR printing. At this time, the magazine *Sinn und Form* became the vehicle for public debates about literature and its function in socialist society. In 1971 Adolf Endler ignited a discussion by suggesting that *Germanistik* in the GDR was too provincial and unable to view its poetry in the context of world literature. Indeed, the magazine served as a catalyst for the debate surrounding Ulrich Plenzdorf's *The New Sufferings of Young W.* when it first published the controversial text in 1972. While the text and the adapted play found resounding acceptance among GDR youth ("Der neue Werther", 139), adults characterized it as alienating. Perhaps most biting was Friedrich Karl Kaul's reaction which decried the portrayal of such a disturbed teenager as the positive hero of socialist society ("Diskussion um Plenzdorf", 220). Yet, stories such as Plenzdorf's are indicative of the struggle brewing between cultural politicians who emphasized the adherence to socialist realism, and writers interested in focusing on the individual's interaction with society.

The controversy surrounding Plenzdorf's text illustrates the disparity between Honecker's understanding of tolerance and the writers' practical attempts at openness. During the 7th Congress of the Writers' Union (November 1973) discussions focused on the necessity of finding a middle ground for this "new" tolerance, which entailed abandoning both the Bitterfeld Way and the New Economic System as guidelines for aesthetic production. Party loyalists and liberals alike struggled to set policy: writers loyal to the Party apparatus claimed their allegiance to dogma. Erik Neutsch, for example, declared that literature was part of the ideological field and therefore was not open to compromise (qtd. in Jäger, 158). Volker Braun proposed that literature could portray life as part of the historical process. Yet, at least in Braun's eyes, literature should not solely rely on its heritage, but should be free to contribute to the development of society. For Braun and others like him this meant an openness and freedom of expression that went far beyond what Honecker had originally intended. Indeed, the cultural politicians quickly realized that a push for liberalization had found too much resonance among the writers. Honecker himself acknowledged that texts such as Plenzdorf's *New Sufferings* enabled interpretations that were contrary to the real socialist understanding (Rüß, 777).

External political factors, particularly relations and negotiations between East and West Germany, contributed to an atmosphere of openness. The partial relaxation of tension between East and West prompted GDR writers to strengthen their contacts with West German publishers and colleagues. These contacts fostered a type of open dialogue for which there was no "real" possibility within the context of literary production in the GDR. Indeed, writers' contacts with the West made East German politicians increasingly nervous and served as yet another reason to enforce restrictions on writers living in the GDR. The cases of Reiner Kunze and Günter Kunert serve as representative examples of the repressive tactics of GDR cultural functionaries.

Kunze's place in official GDR literary history is almost non-existent. As a show of solidarity with Czechoslovakian reformers during the Prague Spring, Kunze resigned from the SED in 1968, provoking the GDR to prohibit his publications. In 1969, the West German publishing house Rowohlt printed *Sensitive Paths* (Sensible Wege). The text's publication in a "Western" context prompted open attacks against Kunze for its content. At the 6th Writers' Congress, Max Walter Schulz decried the content of the poetry. Heiner Feldkamp has argued that this denunciation of Kunze in the GDR contributed to the start of his critical reception in West Germany ("Einleitung", 11). Hans Dieter Schäfer has concluded that Schulz's attack on Kunze was the start of an attempt to declare Kunze persona non grata in the GDR (169). Despite the GDR's reactions, the majority of poems in *Sensitive Paths* had been translated and published earlier in the then Czechoslovakia, where Kunze was also a constant contributor to literary journals. Indeed, Kunze confirmed in an interview with Ekkehart Rudolph that Czechoslovakia had served as a psychological asylum and literary homeland for him (18). In time, the controversy surrounding Kunze in the GDR also had an adverse effect on his publications in the West. Hans Dieter Schäfer has reported that two West German publishing houses rejected the volume *Room Volume* (Zimmerlautstärke), because Kunze no longer reflected the atmosphere of tolerance developing between the two Germanys (169). Eventually, S. Fischer published the volume. Kunze's contact with Western publishers did not occur without problems or without risks. Because the GDR controlled and regularly opened the mail, Kunze was forced to exercise caution in sending manuscripts. In one instance, he used very thin typing paper, divided his manuscript into twenty one-gram lletters, and mailed it from various cities in the GDR to a number of places in West Germany. It was then forwarded to the publishing house, which reconstructed the entire manuscript.

A momentary thaw in the GDR's restrictive policy toward Kunze occurred in 1973 when Reclam (Leipzig) published 30,000 copies of *Letter with the blue seal* (brief mit blauem siegel), a volume containing a large number of texts that had previously appeared only in the West. Shortly thereafter, in the spring of 1974, Kunze gave an officially sanctioned public reading of his poetry during the Leipzig book fair. Until that time, Kunze was prohibited from appearing publicly, yet another example of the cultural politicians' attempts to prevent his works from reaching their intended audience. Prior to 1974, Kunze had held "public" readings in churches, which did not have to obtain permission for religious gatherings. In order to maintain the air of legality, a pastor would say a brief prayer before the reading and offer a blessing at its conclusion. The existence of this unofficial public caused *Letter with the blue seal* to sell out almost immediately, confirming Kunze's large following. Peter Horst Neumann writes of the numerous letters Kunze received from readers and describes them as a type of literary criticism, a productive underground (221).

Kunze is most famous for *The Wonderful Years* (Die wunderbaren Jahre), which S. Fischer published in 1976. This collection of short prose pieces describes momentary aspects of life for the "typical" young person in the GDR. Combining miniatures, anecdotes, quotations, and discussions, Kunze created an ironic portrayal of the contradictions inherent in the GDR's totalitarian system. In addition, the book contained texts reflecting Kunze's solidarity with colleagues in Czechoslovakia, still repressed because of their participation in the Prague Spring eight years earlier. As a result of the publication of this text (for which Kunze had received the required permission from the GDR's licensing bureau), Kunze was expelled from the Writers' Union. Subsequently, he applied for and received permission to move to West Germany with his family.

In this highly acclaimed volume, Kunze depicts inquisitive children and youth, searching for their identities. He skillfully contrasts the youthful optimism of children with the steadfast adherence of adults to the State approved propaganda. "Heritage" (Erbe), just one example, employs a Goethe quote to symbolize the extent to which the State suppressed the expression of individuality. Kunze reduces each experience to its most essential element, and presents it as protocol, dialogue or report without comment or generalizing remarks of any kind. (Neumann, 224). Although a text such as *The Wonderful Years* provides insight into everyday life in the GDR, Peter Horst Neumann concluded that any Western critic who would employ Kunze's criticism as a "weapon" in the German-German controversy would do more harm than good (222).

The Wonderful Years reached a large audience. Although the first edition was limited to a mere 8,000 copies, a 1994 printing registers 437,000 copies, clearly indicating that the text resonated in a West German context. In an interview with Jürgen P. Wallmann, Kunze indicated that the reception of *The Wonderful Years* in West Germany did not surprise him because the political divisions of countries, in his view, do not prevent people from understanding the societal peculiarities that a text contains ("Gespräch",191). Despite restrictions on Kunze's access to the public sphere in the East, many of the texts from *The Wonderful Years* were read on the radio; others were passed along in handwritten and photocopied reproductions (Linn,70). Indeed, one former East German reported to me that, among his peers, *The Wonderful Years* was one of four essential underground books. A copy of Kunze's text, which someone's grandmother had smuggled into the GDR, circulated among a group of friends. The book resonated among GDR youth because it represented the truth; for every experience described in the book, people knew someone whose life it resembled. Unsanctioned readings further fueled the "unofficial reception" of Kunze's texts. Heiner Feldkamp, commenting on Kunze's "unofficial" readings in churches and for youth groups, surmises that Kunze was indeed able to reach and sustain an audience because of the critical and communicative quality of his texts. More important, however, was Kunze's self-understanding, his view of his readers as partners in a dialogue ("Einleitung", 20). This is further played out his extensive exchange of letters that he had with readers.

While the Western media praised the book's publication in 1976, they denounced Kunze and the film a few years later. Although Kunze was awarded the Bavarian Film prize in 1979 for his adaptation of the book, the media questioned Kunze's motivation, denouncing him for his membership in the SED. As a citizen of West Germany, Kunze had somehow lost his right to criticize the GDR. Sabine Brandt has theorized that West German critics could only tolerate opposition to the GDR when the opponent still lived in the GDR. Once this opponent crossed the border, any oppositional statements appeared directed at all Germans (245).

In the case of *The Wonderful Years*, the question of contexts is clouded. The crossing of borders occurs on several levels: the initial transport of the manuscript to the West and its subsequent publication, the illegal smuggling and copying of the text in the GDR, unsanctioned public readings, and Kunze's emigration to Bavaria. Officially, Kunze's text was only allowed to reach an audience in the West. Through an underground, however, *The Wonderful Years* created its own public sphere. Indeed, Kunze was aware that handwritten copies of the text circulated in the GDR, although he himself did not have a copy (Wallmann, "Gespräch", 193). East German official literary history does not account at all for the fact that the text was able to reach its intended audience secretly. In the West the critical reception accorded Kunze focused more on his texts as social criticism than as poetry (Heise, 188-89). Today, the text is valuable for its historical perspective, that grants us a look at the GDR quotidian as young people experienced it. While the social criticism is an essential part of Kunze's *oeuvre*, the literary-artistic nature of his texts deserves recognition, particularly the use of metaphors, the interrelatedness of Kunze's and Czech texts, and the musical influences (such as "Organ Concert"). Furthermore, many of the texts in this volume possess a pedagogical value that has added to the work's long life (Eigenwald).

Günter Kunert assumes an unusual position in German literary history. As early as 1963 West German readers were introduced to Kunert's poetry through newspaper reviews of his texts. Furthermore, Kunert established a profitable working relationship with the West German publishing house of Hanser in Munich early in his career. Unlike many of his East German contemporaries, Kunert managed to exert a great deal of control over the direction his literary career would take. Of singular importance was his decision in the 1950s to retain ownership of the rights to his texts. The majority of writers at that time turned their rights over to East German publishing houses, in an effort to demonstrate solidarity with and confidence in the newly developing socialist society. In Kunert's case, the East German publishing house Aufbau retained the rights to his works in the GDR and other East Bloc countries. This business decision proved significant for Kunert's place in German literary history, because it prevented the GDR government from interfering with the publication of his texts in the West. Kunert partially attributes the reasoning for the different treatment he received to his half-Jewish heritage. Since he had already suffered under the Nazis, the GDR could not suppress him further. Indeed, Kunert never paid any fines for his Western publications, was never arrested, and was generally granted permission to travel, although his Stasi files indicate that he was officially prohibited from touring. The possibility of publishing in the West guaranteed Kunert an audience there. Yet, like Kunze, authorities did not permit Kunert to conduct readings in schools or at universities, denying him access to part of the public sphere in the East.

A comparison of Kunert's publications in East and West indicates that a majority of the lyrical texts published in the West also eventually appeared in the East. This is not to say that Kunert was free from government repression. During the 1960s several of his texts were prohibited. The tolerance of the 1970s brought a relaxation of the restraints placed on him. Records of the publication permission procedures *(Druckgenehmigungsverfahren)* for several of Kunert's books from this time indicate, however, that Kunert's practice of offering his manuscripts to the West did indeed influence the publication of those texts in the East. The file on *An English Diary* (Ein englisches Tagebuch) contains documents tracing a controversy that beset the text "Dream." According to Kunert, this text was an accurate representation of a dream he had in which Erich Honecker was arrested. Fully aware that he could not use the full name of the GDR's leader, Kunert abbreviated it to "Erich H." The publisher requested that Kunert delete the reference to Honecker, deeming it too provocative for publication. The authorities that granted permissions referred the controversy to Klaus Höpcke, the administrative authority for publishing and book trade. Ultimately, Kunert agreed to amend the text to read that "H." was arrested. The publisher reasoned that because Kunert had referred to Michael H. (Michael Hamburger) as his English host throughout other parts of the book, a singular reference to "H". would imply to the reader that the same individual was intended. Clearly, the administrative authorities attempted to alter the context in which this particular text would be received. Thus, this case illustrates the extent to which governing powers interfered in both the writing and reception processes.

In 1978, Kunert published a volume of poetry entitled *Along the Path to Utopia* (Unterwegs nach Utopia) in West Germany. In July of that same year, Kunert presented a slightly different manuscript for publication permission in the GDR. Two poems had previously been published in the GDR; six additional poems were added. Although the permissions office originally granted permission in August 1978, the volume was not published until 1980. (Ironically, this occurred after Kunert had chosen to emigrate to West Germany with his spouse in 1979.) Originally, East German reactions to the book focused on several poems that reviewers deemed inappropriate for a GDR audience because they reflected Kunert's historical pessimism too sharply. Numerous discussions between Aufbau and Kunert took place, as the two parties tried to reach an agreement on the content of the text. Ultimately, the publishing house consulted with Klaus Höpcke before a final agreement was reached. Once again, Kunert made concessions on the final product, removing several poems that the publishing house found objectionable.

In both of these examples, we find that the publishing house called on various authorities to aid in determining whether texts should be published. In this way publishers, administrative authorities, and the Ministry of Culture played a role in determining the context in which a given text could appear. Indeed, the role of West German publications was particularly important to this process. Included in the permissions file for *Along the Path to Utopia* is a copy of a memo (January 1980), that specifies the particulars of a confiscation of the West German edition. A private East German citizen attempted to transport the third edition across the border into the GDR. Because this edition contained the four poems deemed inappropriate for GDR audiences, the citizen's copy could not be returned to him. At the time the transgression took place, Kunert's GDR volume had been printed but not delivered; a note in the file indicates that no decision had been reached about the final disbursement of copies. The ultimate distribution of the GDR text came with the provision that the publisher would neither advertise the book, nor provide complimentary copies for review.

Following unification, Kunert learned the details of the publication history of this text. Additional information in Kunert's *Stasi* files revealed the extent to which the State Security System also influenced literary production. Kunert discovered a review of the West German edition of *Along the Path to Utopia* in which "IM Uwe" (Uwe Berger) wrote that more than one third of the poems in the volume contained hateful attacks on the GDR, as well as the Party and its leaders. "Uwe" categorized Kunert as an enemy of socialism, attacked the literary-aesthetic quality of individual poems, and asserted that the poems could have no place in the literary traditions of the GDR and should therefore not be published. In 1993 Kunert rebutted "Uwe's" assessment ("Lesehilfe").

Following his emigration to the West, the official reception of Kunert in the GDR ceased (Sahner 78) and his texts were no longer published. In 1988, however, the GDR reconsidered the appropriateness of Kunert's poetry for GDR audiences and in 1989 granted permission to publish *The defiled Conception* (Die befleckte Empfängnis) , an assortment of poems taken from three West German publications: *The Process of Mortification* (Abtötungsverfahren , 1980); *Still Life* (Stilleben, 1983); *Berlin in Good Time* (Berlin beizeiten, 1987). According to the permissions file, cultural politicians now deemed it necessary to reclaim former GDR writers for the GDR tradition. Although Kunert had not altered the message in his poetry, the Aufbau publishing house considered this message significant. The publisher found that topics such as existentialism, nature, and the environment were also valuable to GDR audiences. The outside reviewers, Silvia and Dieter Schlenstedt, also emphasized Kunert's antifascist roots, citing them as an important element of the GDR's literary tradition.

This discussion of Kunze and Kunert illustrates the manner in which government control of and interference in literary production varied. Both Kunze and Kunert opted to live in West Germany, a wish that governing authorities granted. Other writers did not enjoy the same treatment. Wolf Biermann was also denied access to the GDR public sphere. Born in Hamburg, Biermann consciously chose to emigrate to the GDR in 1953. Like Kunze, he acted as a constant thorn in the sides of GDR cultural policy makers. No complete volume of his texts and songs was ever published in the GDR, although several poems, mostly love songs, did appear in selected anthologies. Even though Biermann was allowed to perform in concerts during the early 1960s, he was not permitted to broadcast on radio or television. Following the publication of *The Wire Harp* (Die Drahtharfe) in West Berlin in 1965, colleagues and political functionaries attacked him at the 11th plenary session of the SED Central Committee in the same year with accusations of anarchy and pornography. Immediately thereafter, Biermann was forbidden to publish and perform in the GDR. Biermann continued to publish his texts in the West, an act that repeatedly angered those in power in the GDR. In an effort to remove Biermann from the GDR cultural scene, the government granted his application for a visa to travel to West Germany in 1976 for a concert tour. Both television and radio broadcast his initial performance in Cologne (13 November 1976), which made it possible for Biermann to reach an audience in the GDR as well. The GDR government, interpreting Biermann's criticisms as an attack on socialism in general and the GDR in particular, revoked his citizenship (16 November). Indeed, this action seems to have been pre-planned by the SED. In May 1974, when Biermann applied for a travel visa to Cologne so that he could claim the Offenbach Prize personally, it was suggested to him that he surrender his East German citizenship (*Biermann*, 69). Biermann refused and his visa was denied. Having learned their lesson, the authorities were able successfully to spring the trap two years later.

Biermann's expatriation came as a surprise to most in the GDR (*Biermann*, 127), and it reminded artists and writers of similar repressive tactics employed under National Socialism. This political action unleashed an avalanche of protests, as writers and artists felt compelled to object to the SED decision. *Neues Deutschland*, the official party newspaper, refused to print the letter of protest signed by twelve prominent writers; eventually 84 other artists and writers added their signatures. The letter's publication in the West resulted in further repressive actions against the writers. The Party was not only unwilling to rescind its decision but also not open to any discussion. Those writers who signed the letter were subject to punishment: forbidden to publish, expelled from the Writers' Union or the Party or both (*Sachen*, 68-236), penalties normally inflicted on agents of enemy powers (Kunert, "Exil", 106). Many writers requested and received travel visas to leave the GDR. The departure of so many prominent writers (Emmerich, 251-54) changed the literary landscape on both sides of the German-German border. Indeed, this mass exodus of writers further complicates the issue of "GDR writers" and their contexts, as literary scholars confronted the development of a new exile literature. This unusual situation prompted Günter Kunert to edit a collection of texts from "exiled" writers in 1988. Kunert has, however, argued that he and those like him did not really live in exile, because they were neither forced to abandon their language, their people, and their traditions, nor were they in physical danger ("Exil", 100).

The GDR's reaction to and handling of the Biermann affair clearly illustrate that the official sanctioning of repressive tactics was once again the norm for dealing with "uncomfortable" writers. Following the mass exodus of writers to the West, both the political and cultural climates worsened. According to Joachim Walther, four societal structures combined to exert pressure on the remaining writers to conform: the Ministry of Culture within the SED Central Committee, led by Ursula Ragwitz; the administrative authority for publishing houses and book trade, led by Klaus Höpcke; the Writers' Union, led by Hermann Kant and Gerhard Henniger; and the *Stasi* (7-8). Because he published *Collin* in West Germany without obtaining prior permission, authorities slapped Stefan Heym with a monetary penalty of 9,000 Marks. Furthermore, Heym was defamed publicly. While GDR authorities intended the treatment of Heym as scare tactic, it only served to incense the writers further. This form of punishment once again prompted a written response from eight writers. In a letter addressed to Erich Honecker, the writers (Kurt Bartsch, Jurek Becker, Adolf Endler, Erich Loest, Klaus Poche, Klaus Schlesinger, Dieter Schubert, and Martin Stade) alleged that the combination of censorship and penal law aided the State to prohibit the publication of critical works. Once again, the Writers' Union met to censure its own members. Ultimately, the signatories (except Becker and Stade, who were no longer members), as well as Heym, Karl-Heinz Jakobs, Rolf Schneider and Joachim Seyppel, were expelled from the Writers' Union. With this measure, the GDR denied yet another group of writers access to its intended audience by interceding in the contextual dialogue between writer and reader.

Since unification, numerous debates have occurred about the possibilities and problems of GDR literature. Literary scholars are still seeking contexts for these texts. With each passing year, new information about the conditions under which writers lived and worked in the GDR reveals the complexities of literary production within a totalitarian state. The difficulties that writers faced in bringing their message into the public sphere should function as the basis for any examination of texts and their context in the East. Revelations in recent years about the cooperation between writers and the *Stasi* further cloud discussions about the public sphere there. The presence of the *Stasi* in the Prenzlauer Berg counter-culture calls into question the potential for a viable alternative artistic scene. By examining the publication histories of texts, we can learn more about the lengths to which the State was willing to go to prevent texts from reaching their intended audiences, and writers to permit them to do so. The presence of Kunze, Kunert, and Biermann in West Germany contributed to their official absence in GDR contexts, while appraisal of their role in the literary and cultural world in the West has to take account of their special status as 'dissident' writers before their move to the Federal Republic, and of their changed reception there afterwards. A particularly intriguing case in this context is represented by Günter Kunert. While Kunze and others lost status after arriving in the West, and Biermann seemed to have lost a thematic focus to his work before the opening up of the Berlin Wall, Kunert built on, and enhanced, the status he had enjoyed since the 1960s up to and beyond unification. The place of this particular border crosser in German literary history since 1945 has still to be adequately defined.

Select Bibliography

Anz, Thomas, ed. *"Es geht nicht um Christa Wolf." Der Literaturstreit im vereinten Deutschland.* 2. Auflage. Frankfurt: Fischer, 1995.

Biermann und kein Ende. Eine Dokumentation zur DDR-Kulturpolitik. Eds. Dietmar Keller und Matthias Kirchner. Berlin: Dietz, 1991.

Brandt, Sabine. "Politische Polemik um einen deutschen Film." *Reiner Kunze. Materialien zu Leben und Werk.* 241-48.

Braun, Volker. "Literatur und Geschichtsbewußtsein." *Texte in zeitlicher Folge 4.* Halle: Mitteldeutscher Verlag, 1990. 305-14.

"Diskussion um Plenzdorf. *Die neuen Leiden des jungen W."* *Sinn und Form* 25 (1973): 219-52.

Eigenwald, Rolf. "Verstummen oder sich äußern. Reiner Kunze, der Schul- und Literaturbetrieb." *Reiner Kunze. Werk und Wirkung.* 55-64.

Emmerich, Wolfgang. *Kleine Literaturgeschichte der DDR.* 5. erweiterte Auflag. Frankfurt: Luchterhand, 1989.

Endler, Adolf. "Im Zeichen der Inkonsequenz. Über Hans Richters Aufsatzsammlung *Verse Dichter Wirklichkeit."* *Sinn und Form* 23 (1971): 1358-66.

Feldkamp, Heiner. "Einleitung." *Reiner Kunze. Materialien zu Leben und Werk.* 10-32.

_____. *Poesie als Dialog. Grundlinien im Werk Reiner Kunzes.* Regensburg: S. Roderer, 1994.

_____, ed. *Reiner Kunze. Materialien zu Leben und Werk.* Frankfurt: Fischer, 1987.

Grass, Günter. *Kopfgeburten oder Die Deutschen sterben aus.* Darmstadt and Neuwied: Luchterhand, 1980.

Heise, Hans-Jürgen. "Verlust der poetischen Unschuld." *Reiner Kunze. Materialien zu Leben und Werk.* 187-92.

Herminghouse, Patricia. "Literature as 'Ersatzöffentlichkeit'? Censorship and the Displacement of Public Discourse in the GDR." *German Studies Review. Special Issue: Totalitäre Herrschaft – totalitäres Erbe* (1994): 85-99.

Honecker, Erich. *Die Rolle der Arbeiterklasse und ihrer Partei in der sozialistischen Gesellschaft.* Berlin: Dietz, 1974.

In Sachen Biermann. Protokolle, Berichte und Briefe zu den Folgen einer Ausbürgerung. Eds. Roland Berbig et al. Berlin: Christoph Links Verlag, 1994.

Jäger, Manfred. *Kultur und Politik in der DDR. 1945-1990.* Cologne: Verlag Wissenschaft und Politik, 1995.

Kunert, Günter. *Abtötungsverfahren.* Munich: Hanser, 1980.

_____, ed. *Aus fremder Heimat. Zur Exilsituation heutiger Literatur.* Munich: Hanser, 1988.

_____. *Die befleckte Empfängnis.* Berlin: Aufbau, 1989.

_____. *Berlin beizeiten.* Munich: Hanser, 1987.

_____. "Deutsch-deutsches Exil." *Aus fremder Heimat. Zur Exilsituation heutiger Literatur.* 100-12.

_____. *Ein englisches Tagebuch.* Berlin: Aufbau, 1978.

_____. "Lesehilfe." *Neue Deutsche Literatur* 41.3 (1993): 127-34.

_____. *Stilleben.* Munich: Hanser, 1983.

_____. *Unterwegs nach Utopia.* Munich: Hanser, 1978.

Kunze, Reiner. "Konsequenz Leben – Schriftsteller sein im geteilten Deutschland." *Deutschunterricht* 43 (1990): 506-13.

_____. *Sensible Wege.* Reinbeck bei Hamburg: Rowohlt, 1969.

_____. *Die wunderbaren Jahre.* Frankfurt: S. Fischer, 1976.

Linn, Marie Luise. "Reiner Kunzes *Die wunderbaren Jahre:* Analyse der literarischen Form." *Der Deutschunterricht* 30.6 (1978): 70-81.

"Der neue Werther. Ein Gespräch." *Neue Deutsche Literatur* 21.3 (1973): 139-49.

Neumann, Peter Horst. "Wertsache Buch: *Die wunderbaren Jahre* von Reiner Kunze." *Reiner Kunze. Materialien zu Leben und Werk.* 219-30.

Rudolph, Ekkehart. "Gespräch mit Reiner Kunze." *Reiner Kunze. Materialien und Dokumente.* 12-21.

Rüß, Gisela, ed. *Dokumente zur Kunst-, Literatur- und Kulturpolitik der SED. Band 2: 1971-74.* Stuttgart, 1976.

Sahner, Christoph. "Kunert-Rezeption in der DDR? Einige Beobachtungen zu einem Un-Thema." *Text und Kritik* 109 (Januar 1991): 78-81.

Schäfer, Hans Dieter. "Zimmerlautstärke." *Reiner Kunze. Materialien zu Leben und Werk.* 169-78.

Schulz, Max Walter. "Das Neue und das Bleibende in unserer Literatur." *Neue Deutsche Literatur* 17.9 (1969): 24-51.

Seeba, Hinrich C. "'Germany – A Literary Concept': The Myth of National Literature." *German Studies Review* XVII (1994): 353-69.

Wallmann, Jürgen P. "Gespräch mit Reiner Kunze." *Reiner Kunze. Materialien und Dokumente.* 191-96.

_____, ed. *Reiner Kunze. Materialien und Dokumente.* Frankfurt: Fischer, 1977.

Walther, Joachim et al, eds. *Protokoll eines Tribunals. Die Ausschlüsse aus dem DDR-Schriftstellerverband 1979.* Reinbeck bei Hamburg: Rowohlt, 1991.

Wolff, Rudolf, ed. *Reiner Kunze. Werk und Wirkung.* Bonn: Bouvier, 1983.

LITERATURE AND CONVERGENCE

The Early 1980s

Stephen Brockmann

With the unexpected collapse of the German Democratic Republic in 1989 and German reunification in 1990, literary debates in Germany have revolved around two interconnected problems: 1) the demise or continued existence of GDR literature; and 2) closely connected to the first problem, the post-unification status of the literature of the Federal Republic. The belief that GDR literature no longer serves a useful social function is seen as a corollary to the death of the GDR state itself: what sense does it make to speak of the continued existence of GDR literature when the GDR no longer exists? Jurek Becker, for instance, suggested in 1990 that "GDR literature in its previous form will cease to exist."[1] The second problem is somewhat more subtle, but makes sense in the same framework. To the extent that the "old" Federal Republic, sometimes referred to in German political shorthand as the *Bonner Republik*, has ceased to exist, it seems to follow that the literature of the "old" Federal Republic no longer serves a useful literary purpose. The most famous statement of this last position is literary critic Frank Schirrmacher's influential essay "Abschied von der Literatur der Bundesrepublik" (Farewell to the Literature of the Federal Republic), in which Schirrmacher, also in 1990, declared that the literature of the Federal Republic had ceased to exist.[2]

---

1. Jurek Becker, "Die Wiedervereinigung der deutschen Literatur," *The German Quarterly*, v. 63, n. 3/4 (Summer/Fall 1990),359-66; here, 363. Unless otherwise noted, translations from German sources are my own.

2. Frank Schirrmacher, "Abschied von der Literatur der Bundesrepublik," *Frankfurter Allgemeine Zeitung* 2 October 1990: L1-2.

At the root of both beliefs is an unarticulated assumption: that literature itself reflects more or less unproblematically and without mediation existing social and political conditions. Thus the "literature of the Federal Republic" reflects the existence of the Federal Republic itself, while the "literature of the GDR" reflects the existence of the GDR. Upon the demise of a political state, it therefore follows that the literature associated with that state ceases to be produced. While crude, such a belief is not without all merit, since it is demonstrably true that "West German literature" is somehow connected to West Germany, while "East German literature" is somehow connected to East Germany. It is the precise nature of the "somehow" that is at issue, however. Recent research into the history of literature and of *Germanistik* demonstrates that the very concept "German literature" is at root connected to the existence of a nation-state called Germany. There were, of course, no German departments before there was a Germany. On the contrary: German departments emerged with Germany itself as a nation-state, which only then needed *Germanistik* as a science of differentiation and identity. And when Germany the nation-state was divided, so too was the study of German literature: there was GDR Studies, and there was the study of the literature of the Federal Republic. National literary studies always provide not only analyses of but also justifications for political and cultural boundaries. If the European Union ever becomes a political reality, replacing individual nation-states, then that development, too, will no doubt be reflected in literary studies by the elimination of separate French, German, Italian, and Spanish departments.

However, it is also true that the abstractions "West German literature" and "East German literature" dissolve upon closer examination into a multitude of individual writers, each with his or her own style, obsessions, and areas of expertise. The demise of East Germany or even of West Germany does not, of itself, imply the demise of the writers previously associated with those states. Thus Christa Wolf and Volker Braun continue to publish in spite of the GDR's non-existence, and a writer like Günter Grass has gone on to publish two lengthy works of fiction in violation of Schirrmacher's declaration that the literature of the Federal Republic has come to an end. Such persistence reminds one of previous writers' continued publication in spite of pronouncements of the "death of literature."

It is useful in this context to recall the debate about a "zero hour" in German literature that occurred in the early 1970s. At that time critics like Frank Trommler and Hans Dieter Schäfer suggested that the year 1945 did not represent a literary "zero hour" in the way that post-1945 writers and literary critics had previously claimed. Trommler showed that, far from beginning in 1933 and ending in 1945, German literature of the 1930s and 1940s in fact represented a continuity of non- or antipolitical existentialist humanism that emerged in the late 1920s and did not end until the late 1950s: a thirty-year period in which the years 1933 to 1945 played an important political and social role but did not represent an absolute literary boundary.[3] Trommler's intervention was a useful reminder that what Peter Bürger calls the "institution literature" has its own laws of inertia that frequently cause it to remain unaffected, at least in the short run, even by the most far-reaching political changes. Such a statement does not require adherence to an autonomous view of literature as *l'art pour l'art*. Writers are affected by and in turn have an influence on political events, but one should not imagine the interrelationship between writers and politics as unproblematic, crude, or obvious. If one accepts Trommler's suggestion that the period from 1930 to 1960 marks a literary continuity and that 1945 was therefore not a literary "zero hour" – and most Germanists probably do – then it should follow that there is no reason why the years 1989 or 1990 must mark a second postwar German literary "zero hour." To assert the contrary is to imply a crude view of literature as the unmediated mapping of the political that recalls the excesses of the Marxist theories of reflection and base-superstructure. What is especially peculiar about the recent discussions of a new "Zero Hour" in German literature is that they come precisely from conservatives who see themselves as champions of aesthetic autonomy. Karl Heinz Bohrer, Frank Schirrmacher, and Ulrich Greiner do not even seem to be aware that their "Zero Hour" interventions contradict the idea of aesthetic autonomy.[4]

3. See the following articles by Frank Trommler: "Der 'Nullpunkt 1945' und seine Verbindlichkeit für die Literaturgeschichte," *Basis: Jahrbuch für deutsche Gegenwartsliteratur* I (1970): 9-25; "Der zögernde Nachwuchs: Entwicklungsprobleme der Nachkriegsliteratur in Ost und West," in *Tendenzen der deutschen Literatur seit 1945*, ed. Thomas Koebner (Stuttgart: Alfred Kröner, 1971): 1-116; "Emigration und Nachkriegsliteratur: Zum Problem der geschichtlichen Kontinuität," in Reinhold Grimm and Jost Hermand, eds., *Exil und innere Emigration* (Frankfurt: Athenäum, 1972): 173-97; "Nachkriegsliteratur – eine neue deutsche Literatur?" *Literaturmagazin*, v. 7 (1977): 167-86. See also Hans Dieter Schäfer, *Das gespaltene Bewußtsein: Über deutsche Kultur und Lebenswirklichkeit 1933-1945* (Munich: Hanser, 1981), particularly the chapter "Zur Periodisierung der deutschen Literatur seit 1930", 55-71. For a recent reassessment, see Keith Bullivant, *The Future of German Literature* (Oxford: Berg, 1994).

4. See Ulrich Greiner, "Die deutsche Gesinnungsästhetik," *Die Zeit* 9 November 1990, 15-16; and Karl Heinz Bohrer, "Die Ästhetik am Ausgang ihrer Unmündigkeit," *Merkur* 44 (1990), 851-65. Many of the contributions to the Christa Wolf debate were later collected in Thomas Anz, ed., *"Es geht nicht um Christa Wolf: Der Literaturstreit im vereinten Deutschland* (Munich: Spangenberg, 1991). See also Karl Deiritz and Hannes Krauss, eds. *Der deutsch-deutsche Literaturstreit oder "Freunde, es spricht sich schlecht mit gebundener Zunge"* (Hamburg: Luchterhand, 1991).

In what follows, I wish to step back from the debates of the 1990s about "East German" and "West German" literature and ask instead about "German" literature. What I would like to suggest is that in spite of Germany's lack of political unity from 1945 to 1990 there was nevertheless a larger cultural unity that belied the political situation and had deep roots in German cultural history. While it is not my intention to explore those roots here, it is important to remember that the concept of "Germany" existed prior to Bismarck's political unification of 1870/71, and that "Germany" was to a not inconsiderable extent constituted during the nineteenth century as a cultural and literary construct prior to its constitution as a political construct. The nation, in other words, was first seen as a cultural unity and only later created as a geopolitical reality, a place travelers could find on a map. In Germany, therefore, the relative autonomy of the "institution literature" has a national political significance that has enabled "German literature" and "German culture" to survive even the most profound political shocks. In this sense, German political disunity is more the historical norm than German political unity, and in the face of that political disunity German culture serves the ideological function of preserving a unity no longer (or not yet, or imperfectly) existent in the political realm. The years 1945 to 1990 are therefore part of a much older tradition.

My argument is that during the years of German political disunity following World War II there was a continuing sense of German cultural unity, and that literature played a major role in the maintenance of that sense. Such an argument does not negate the existence of "GDR literature" and "literature of the FRG;" it suggests merely that such a bipartite division does not exhaust the possibilities for understanding German literature during the period 1945 to 1990. I further wish to suggest that within the postwar period the early 1980s, and writers' active involvement with the pan-German peace movement, were particularly important as a moment in which the sense of cultural unity increased in a German literature that understood itself as the primary locus of national identity.

In order to make my claim about the 1980s, however, I need to back up and revisit the immediate postwar period and the literary situation that prevailed then. The two German states that emerged out of the wreckage of the Third Reich in 1949 began with quite different literary preconditions. In the West a small and relatively isolated group of non-conformist writers associated with Hans Werner Richter's Group 47 proclaimed a complete break with the past that has since – with the objections raised above – come to be understood as a literary "zero hour," while, in spite of the younger writers' proclamations, older writers such as Gottfried Benn and Ernst Jünger retained primary control of the literary sphere for at least a decade and a half. A sign of the strength of this older, apolitical generation was one of the first major debates in West German letters: the attack on Thomas Mann – and on other writers who had left Germany during the Third Reich – by members of the so-called "inner emigration," who accused Mann of spiritual desertion and inability to understand the real situation in Germany. Both of the major groups in post-1945 West German letters – the dominant inner emigrants and the nonconformist younger authors of the "Zero Hour" – largely rejected exiles like Thomas Mann, who had left Germany during the Third Reich and functioned in exile as the locus for a "better" or "truer" Germany in which culture was precisely the positive "other" opposed to a negative Hitlerian politics. However, in spite of Mann's and other exiles' understanding of themselves as guarantors of a continuing German unity, and in spite of Mann's own agitation for an overcoming of German division in the late 1940s and early 1950s, the concerns of exiles fell largely on deaf ears in West Germany during the first fifteen years after 1945.

In the East the situation was quite different. Exile writers like Anna Seghers, Bertolt Brecht, Arnold Zweig, Johannes R. Becher, and many others were immediately welcomed to the GDR and became the dominant force in GDR letters for over a decade, until the middle of the 1960s, when a new generation of writers such as Heiner Müller and Christa Wolf began to come to prominence. However the older generation of exile writers retained its literary and moral power until many decades later; Anna Seghers was still alive and influential into the early 1980s.

This divergent approach toward exile writers strongly affected the future of literary politics in the two Germanys. In the East there was no literary "zero hour" myth, and since literature during the 1940s and 1950s was already thoroughly politicized, there was also no need to politicize literature in the 1960s. The exile writers were all well aware of the political and moral role of literature, and they understood their work in the GDR as a continuation of their previous work in exile and in the Weimar Republic. In the West, on the other hand, there was no sense of continuity with exile, and the continuity with the Weimar Republic was largely an apolitical continuity dominated by the inner emigration. It was not until the early 1960s that this continuity was overcome in a repoliticization of literature, which, significantly, incorporated major exile figures into the West German canon for the first time. The primary example is Bertolt Brecht.

In both the West and the East it was the so-called "Flakhelfer" (anti-aircraft volunteer) generation of writers born in the late 1920s and early

1930s that began to achieve dominance by the mid 1960s: in the West people like Günter Grass, Martin Walser, Hans Magnus Enzensberger, and in the East Heiner Müller and Christa Wolf. However, the different preconditions for these writers' work continued to affect them for decades: while Müller and Wolf explicitly understood their own work in the light of the previous work of Brecht and Seghers, their West German counterparts had no such role models. One cannot imagine an East German writer uttering the following words of Wolfdietrich Schnurre: "It was not easy for us to write; we were left completely to our own devices. Because there was no ethical support system, there was no literary model, there was no tradition."[5] In a sense, literature in the GDR had an excess of role models, while authors in the West complained about a lack of father figures.

The period of vociferous official insistence on the goal of German unity came to an end in the West with the beginning of Willy Brandt's Ostpolitik in 1969, one of whose results was the quasi-diplomatic recognition of the German Democratic Republic in the Basic Treaty of 1972. While West German politicians after 1972 continued to proclaim national reunification as their ultimate goal, these claims and protestations began to have a hollow ring in a country that maintained ongoing diplomatic and economic relations with a sovereign communist neighbor recognized by most of the world's governments. In the East Erich Honecker's accession to power resulted in the banning of the words to Johannes R. Becher's national anthem, which included the words "Deutschland, einig Vaterland" (Germany, united fatherland), and the proclamation that the GDR had achieved fully developed socialism. Throughout the 1970s and 1980s the relationship between the GDR and the FRG was "normalized" to the extent that Erich Honecker's 1987 visit to Bonn was treated as an official state visit. It would not be an exaggeration to state that until the late fall of 1989 the very word "reunification" was politically taboo in both Germanies.

Meanwhile literature developed in a very different direction. At the beginning of the postwar period the two literatures were massively separated by the unequal prestige awarded to exile writers in the two countries, as well as by an explicitly apolitical view of writing in the West and an overtly political view of writing in the East. Significantly, in spite of Walter Ulbricht's post-Stalinist oppression of the 1950s and 1960, few major authors publicly left East Germany for the West during those decades. It was not until 1976, with Wolf Biermann's loss of GDR citi-

5. Uwe Schultz, *Fünfzehn Autoren suchen sich selbst*, ed. Uwe Schultz, 27, cited in Frank Trommler, "Der zögernde Nachwuchs", 13.

zenship, that a major flow of East German writers began to move West. In other words, it was only after Honecker's liberalizations of the 1970s that writers who had weathered the worst excesses of Stalinism became dissatisfied enough to leave the GDR. How can one explain this paradox?

Probably the most convincing explanation involves the relative prestige of communism among German writers. Immediately after 1945, the Soviet Union's defeat of the German Wehrmacht in World War II and German communists' resistance to Hitler during the Third Reich lent communism an unparalleled prestige in both parts of Germany – a prestige that it had never enjoyed before and has never enjoyed since. It was for this reason that so many exile writers returned not to the Federal Republic but to the GDR. Many Germans believed that the primary reason for Germany's descent into fascism had been the capitalist system itself. For them, National Socialism was neither a third entity different from both capitalism and socialism nor a mix between the two; rather, National Socialism was simply an extreme form of capitalism, "the open, terrorist rule by violence of the most reactionary, chauvinist and aggressive forces of finance capital," as a blue-ribbon team of East German historians was to refer to it in the mid-1980s, and World War II was not a German, but rather an imperialist war.[6] When Heiner Müller insisted during the 1980s that "German fascism was simply a particularly bloody episode ... in the capitalist world war that has been going on now for four hundred years," he was stating the primary element in an East German anti-fascist consensus that enjoyed great prestige throughout the postwar period.[7]

In addition to its status as *the* anti-fascist ideology in Germany, communism during the 1940s and 1950s also enjoyed an economic prestige that derived from Stalin's largely successful – albeit brutal – drive for industrialization of the Soviet Union in the 1930s, from the Soviet ability to develop atomic and thermonuclear weapons at a rate only slightly behind that of the leading economic and military superpower, the United States, and from well-publicized Soviet successes in the aerospace industry, particularly the first earth satellite (Sputnik) missions in 1957, during which the Soviet Union actually stole a march on the United States. It is important to remember that during this period the Cold War was at its height, and western fears of Soviet supremacy were based on at least the impression – however mistaken that impression

6. This statement was part of the thesis put forward by East German historians in honor of the 750th anniversary of the city of Berlin: "750 Jahre Berlin: Thesen," *Berliner Zeitung*, 14/15 December 1985, 11.

7. Heiner Müller in Ulrich Dietzel, "Gespräch mit Heiner Müller," *Sinn und Form* n. 6, November/December 1985, 1205.

subsequently turned out to be – of an efficient, successful, and powerful Soviet economy. It is no coincidence that the two major international incidents in Christa Wolf's first novel, *Der geteilte Himmel* (The Divided Heaven), are the building of the Berlin Wall in August 1961, and the success of Soviet Cosmonaut Yuri Gagarin as the first man in space four months earlier. In Wolf's novel the latter event changes the world itself:

> Was not the shadow of that blazing capsule up there moving like a scalpel horizontally over all the meridians and opening the earth's crust down to its boiling, red-hot core? Was this still the round, careful earth comfortably promenading through space? Hadn't the earth suddenly become younger, angrier because of the challenge of her son [Gagarin]?[8]

It is my contention that during the 1940s, 1950s, and part of the 1960s major authors in the GDR continued to support the East German regime at least in part because of their genuine belief that the communist system as it had developed in that country was ultimately more efficient, productive, successful, and humane than the economy of the Federal Republic. Such a view may seem irrational or illogical in a post-1989 context, but one must instead understand it in a post-1945 context. After all, Hitler had always claimed that the people of the Soviet Union were "Untermenschen" (subhumans). And yet Hitler's Germany, his "Herrenvolk" (master race) had been defeated militarily precisely by these "Untermenschen." Such defeats leave permanent scars. In Christa Wolf's short story "Blickwechsel" (Liberation Day), which describes the German "liberation" of 1945, the scar is evident in the very first sentence, in which the victorious Russians are referred to by one character as Asiatic beasts.[9] Franz Fühmann's instructive short story "Regentag im Kaukasus" (A Rainy Day in the Caucasus) illustrates precisely the mechanisms by which former German "supermen" came to "learn" from the Soviet Union.[10] One should not forget one of the major slogans of post-war East German propaganda: "Von der Sovietunion lernen heißt siegen lernen" (To Learn from the Soviet Union Means to Learn Victory). By adherence to communism and to the Soviet Union East Germans were able, after the war, to become ex post facto "victors." "The people of the GDR are among the victors of history and honor the 8th of May as their

8. My translation, from Christa Wolf, *Der geteilte Himmel* (Munich: dtv, 1973 [originally 1963], 143.

9. Christa Wolf, "Blickwechsel," in Wolf, *Gesammelte Erzählungen* (Hamburg: Luchterhand, 1993), 5-19. Translated by Heike Schwarzbauer and Rick Takvorian as "Liberation Day," *Granta* 42 (winter 1992), 55-64.

10. Franz Fühmann, "Regentag im Kaukasus," in Fühmann, *Das Judenauto* (Leipzig: Reclam, 1987 [originally 1962]), 136-42.

holiday," said Werner Scheler, President of the Academy of Sciences of the German Democratic Republic in April 1985 at a scholarly conference in commemoration of the end of World War II forty years earlier.[11] The word *Sieg* (victory), already overused during Hitler's Nuremberg rallies, was here used to underline the essential credo of historical ideology in East Germany: *this* Germany, unlike Hitler's Germany, had won World War II. Of course there was a similar mechanism at work in West Germany, which had aligned itself with its own victorious superpower, but my point is that after 1945 many East Germans were able, because of their embrace of communism, to see themselves as "winners."

Beginning in the 1960s, a picture of the Soviet Union specifically or the East bloc in general as "victorious" became increasingly untenable because of the evident onset of long-term economic stagnation in the communist bloc. If Americans and Western Europeans during the 1950s and 1960s had still given credence to Soviet and East German threats that they would soon "bury" or "pass by" the capitalist west, they were no longer able to do so in the 1970s and 1980s, a period during which the economies of the East bloc were actually declining relative to the economies of western nations. This relative decline made it increasingly unlikely that the East bloc would prove itself *economically* superior to the West bloc. Of course it was still possible for communists to view East bloc economies as *ethically* superior to western economies because of a socialist morality that guaranteed every human being the right to work and a minimum standard of living. But Marxism was primarily an economic, not a moral theory, and therefore the relative decline in eastern economies meant that the west was beating the east on its own materialist turf.

Can it be a coincidence that it was precisely during this period of stagnation and lethargy that East German writers began to abandon the production plays and socialist realist novels of the 1940s, 1950s, and early 1960s, and to move toward a less economically driven, more humanistic literature? I think not. Let us take the two major emerging East German writers of this period as our prime examples. Heiner Müller's "production plays" of the 1950s and early 1960s are by no means unproblematic glorifications of the communist economy. In the most famous of these plays, *Der Lohndrücker* (The Lowerer of Wages), Müller honestly depicted problems of postwar socialist reconstruction and production: the need to rely on Nazi and bourgeois "experts," the problem of socialist work norms, worker rivalry, lack of enthusiasm, etc. Nevertheless, in spite of these problems, production itself went forward

11. Quoted from a paraphrase in the official press organ of the Socialist Unity Party of Germany, *Neues Deutschland*, 18 April 1985, 3.

in this play; indeed, the entire play revolved around economic production as the central aspect of all human life. By the end of the 1960s, however, Müller had abandoned the theme of production in Communist society and had, significantly, moved on to pan-German and common human problems. A play such as *Die Schlacht* (The Battle), for instance, dealt with a Nazi past that was indivisible: it was as valid for the Federal Republic as for the GDR. Müller's plays of the 1970s and 1980s were no longer meditations specifically on the East German situation; rather, they were screams of despair at the pointlessness of history.

Wolf took a substantially similar path. Her debut novel, *Der geteilte Himmel*, was still primarily socialist realist. Like Müller's production plays, *Der geteilte Himmel* revolved around the problem of socialist production. It would be just as unfair to accuse Wolf's first novel of slavish whitewashing of the problems of socialism as it would be to accuse Müller's *Lohndrücker*. Like *Der Lohndrücker*, *Der geteilte Himmel* also addressed issues of fascist continuity, East-West tensions, worker rivalry, etc. However for all its honesty and daring, Wolf's first novel was still very much in the socialist realist tradition, still centered around production as the central act of human life. Wolf's next novel, the famous *Nachdenken über Christa T.* (The Quest for Christa T.), was fundamentally different: it dealt with the intensely personal problems of its main character, her inability to live in an advanced socialist society in which conformism had become the primary human virtue. The problems of conformism were just as profound in an advanced western society as in an eastern one. Moreover, because of its unconventionality and daring, *Nachdenken über Christa T.* was largely unavailable to ordinary East German readers in an East German edition. Instead, it became well known in West Germany as one of the founding texts of a new feminism and a new subjectivity, and Wolf's increasing fame in the West translated itself into increased influence in the East. By the 1970s writers of the stature of Müller and Wolf were no longer *simply* East German writers; rather, they were writers living in East Germany and convinced of the superiority of the communist system who nevertheless played a major role in an increasingly pan-German literary context. In this pan-German context, major East German writers abandoned socialist realism and the specificity of the communist system in general and instead dealt with general German and even human problems; at the same time, critics and audiences in West Germany began to accept such East German writers as major German authors in their own right. The increasing politicization of the West German literary sphere in the 1960s, followed by the growth of the new subjectivity in the 1970s, made possible a literary convergence between GDR and FRG literature that would have been unthinkable in the 1950s, when even such major figures as Thomas Mann had contended in vain against German division.

The word "convergence" here has a specific history. During the 1960s, with the liberal West at the height of its postwar economic boom and the East seeking to correct failures of its command economies via cautious liberalization, economists and political scientists began to speak of a "convergence" between the two systems, suggesting that the West was becoming increasingly social democratic and oriented toward a welfare state, while the East was gradually moving from Stalinism toward more political and economic freedom. The father of convergence theory was the Dutch economist Jan Tinbergen, who, in a 1961 article entitled "Do Communist and Free Economies Show Converging Patterns?", suggested that indeed the two economies did have a tendency to converge in a number of key areas: bureaucratization, social welfare guarantees, and pricing.[12] Tinbergen argued that the various changes occurring in the two systems were "in many respects converging movements," and that "the systems begin to influence each other more and more," suggesting that ultimately the two systems would move toward some sort of optimum mix of free market and command elements.[13] Tinbergen's work proved to be immensely influential and spawned an entire branch of comparative economics known as "convergence theory."[14] Moreover, convergence theory soon spread beyond the relatively narrow realm of economic theory to become part of broader cultural debate about postwar industrial society. Soviet dissidents such as Andrei Sakharov referred precisely to the theory of "convergence" in suggesting that "the development of modern society in both the Soviet Union and the United States is now following the same course of increasing complexity of structure and of industrial management," and that there would be a general "socialist convergence" in the future.[15] Sakharov and others argued for a democratization of socialism while at the same time maintaining the superiority of the socialist system over its ideological and economic competitor. By the 1970s, when the disappointing performance of Soviet and East bloc economies had led growing numbers of economists to

12. Jan Tinbergen, "Do Communist and Free Economies Show a Converging Pattern?", *Soviet Studies* v. XII, n. 4 (April 1961),333-41.

13. Tinbergen, 333, 337.

14. For a pre-1989 summary of convergence theory, see Michael Ellman, *Collectivisation, Convergence and Capitalism: Political Economy in a Divided World* (London: Academic Press, 1984); for a post-1989 critique, see Bruno Dallago, Horst Brezinski and Wladimir Andreff, eds., *Convergence and System Change: The Convergence Hypothesis in the Light of Transition in Eastern Europe* (Aldershot: Dartmouth, 1991).

15. Andrei D. Sakharov, *Progress, Coexistence & Intellectual Freedom* (New York: W. W. Norton, 1968), 76, 83.

doubt the validity of "convergence theory" as an economic model, others in the East and West welcomed the theory as part of a more general climate of détente, ideological moderation, and coexistence in the face of common problems. The 1970s, as the decade of détente, were also the heydays of dreams of convergence, which the German writer Alfred Andersch, in a 1975 open letter to the Soviet writer Konstantin Mikhailovich Simonov, described as the theory "that our two technocracies will ultimately level out the differences between our social systems and spawn a unified, computerized human being."[16] Andersch's definition is particularly useful because it shows that by the mid-1970s the idea of convergence had gone far beyond a relatively specific set of predictions about economic organization and performance to encompass entire societies and the human beings within them. While Andersch distanced himself from this version of the theory of convergence, he nevertheless declared that "we have now reached a point in time at which the dialectic has entered into the condition of synthesis," and that even Alexander Solzhenitsyn "will not be able much longer to slow down the process that is overcoming our alienation. Our alienation is outdated, done for, ridiculous."[17] By the mid-1970s the ideological distrust of the Cold War had given way to a growing recognition of shared human problems.

Given the parallel developments in East and West German literature during the late 1960s and 1970s, there were very good reasons for the respected literary critic Hans Mayer to declare in 1979 that "there is a movement of convergence in German-language literature of our day." Mayer stated that "the convergences are obvious" and "amazing," and he spoke of contemporary German literature as a "concrete totality."[18] Likewise, Trommler suggested five years later that there was only one German literature, irrespective of national boundaries.[19] Working with specifically literary criteria, as opposed to national and political ones, Trommler identified areas of commonality and convergence in all German-language literatures. While Trommler's declaration seemed shocking given the institutionalization of literary studies in the 1980s, it is much more reasonable in a post-unification framework. As Trommler

---

16. Alfred Andersch, *Öffentlicher Brief an einen soujetischen Schriftsteller, das Überholte betreffend: Reportagen und Aufsätze* (Zurich: Diogenes, 1977), 208.

17. Andersch, 208.

18. Hans Mayer, "Stationen der deutschen Literatur: Die Schriftsteller und die Restauration, die zwei Deutschlands und die Konvergenz," *Frankfurter Allgemeine Zeitung* 16 June 1979, in the unpaginated glossy insert "Bilder und Zeiten."

19. Frank Trommler, "Auf dem Wege zu einer kleineren Literatur: Ästhetische Perioden und Probleme seit 1945," in Thomas Koebner, ed., *Tendenzen der deutschen Gegenwartsliteratur* (Stuttgart: Alfred Kröner, 1984), p. 29.

wrote in 1984, "The thesis that there are two separate German literatures is now showing its historical and political function, as well as its
limitations."[20] During the 1970s and 1980s, as the permanence of German political division became increasingly self-evident, German literature – paradoxically – moved in a very different direction. What
primarily characterized the literature of the 1970s and 1980s was its
lack of ideological specificity and its applicability to pan-German or
even general human problems. It was not surprising that in the treaty
on German reunification signed in 1990 between the Federal Republic of Germany and the German Democratic Republic politics made a
bow to culture in the following words: "During the years of division art
and culture – in spite of separate developments in the two states in
Germany – were a basis for the continuing unity of the German
nation."[21] Literature and politics in Germany had developed in opposite directions: at the beginning of the postwar period, it was the two
states that publicly proclaimed national unity, while the literatures of
the two states were very far removed from each other. During the
1960s, 1970s, and 1980s, however, as the political division between the
two Germanys began to seem increasingly permanent, the two literatures began coming closer together.

West German literature of the 1980s stood under the sign of two
seemingly opposing trends: politicization and national identity on the
one hand and postmodernism and poststructuralism on the other. The
politicization of West German literature emerged to a large extent out of
the tense geopolitical situation of the early 1980s. The election of
Ronald Reagan as President of the United States in 1980, as well as the
1979 NATO "two-track decision" to station intermediate range Pershing
II and Cruise missiles in West Germany, caused fears in the FRG of a
renewed cold war and spurred the emergence of a new consciousness of
national identity under the threat of nuclear destruction. That these
political events had a profound effect on writers as well is evidenced by
the two writers' conferences against nuclear war which were held in East
and West Berlin in 1981 and 1983. While these two conferences had no
direct impact on the political situation in either of the two Germanys,
they nevertheless demonstrated East and West German writers' feelings

20. Trommler, "Auf dem Wege zu einer kleineren Literatur: Ästhetische Perioden und
Probleme seit 1945", 17.
21. Cited by Peter Peters, "'We are One Book,': Perspectives and Developments of an
All-German Literature," in *The Individual, Identity and Innovation: Signals from Contem-
porary Literature and the New Germany*, ed. Arthur Williams and Stuart Parkes (Berne:
Peter Lang, 1994), 297-314; here, 298, from: *Verträge zur deutschen Einheit* (Bonn:
Bundeszentrale für politische Bildung, 1991) 69.

of togetherness and mutual responsibility. Out of the political situation of those years came a number of major works dealing with the German-German and the world-political situation. Peter Schneider's *Der Mauerspringer* (The Wall Jumper), for instance, told the story of Germans who refused to recognize the Berlin wall as a permanent symbol of German division.[22] Rolf Hochhuth's *Judith* explicitly compared the American President to a Nazi politician, and ended with the assassination of the President as an understandable, perhaps even justifiable act of human self-defense against political evil.[23] (The play appeared several years after John Hinckley's failed attempt to assassinate Reagan in 1981.) Stefan Heym's novel *Schwarzenberg* depicted a utopian moment in the history of the German defeat in World War Two when one small area in East Germany remained unoccupied by troops from the Allied powers for about a month.[24]

Significantly, writers from both the East and the West contributed to this political and national literature of the 1980s. Perhaps the most popular of the writers was Wolf, who published highly successful novels about common German problems in the 1980s. Wolf's *Cassandra* retold the ancient story of the fall of Troy from the perspective of a previously marginalized voice, that of the doomed Trojan prophet Cassandra. The East-West confrontation between Trojans and Greeks became for Wolf a model of the same kind of arrogance and stupidity on both sides that led, several millennia later, to the East-West confrontation between the Russians and the Americans (and the East and West Germans). Unlike her model Homer, Wolf glorified neither the two sides nor the male warriors seeking victory in war; her heroine was the woman in the middle, a feminist Third Path between the two male extremes. Wolf's 1987 story *Störfall* (Accident) dealt with the reactor explosion in the Ukraine a year earlier. For Wolf, the explosion at Chernobyl rendered the East-West border insignificant, since radioactivity knew no ideological boundaries. It threatened East and West Germans and Europeans alike. A passage from this story captures the spirit of Wolf's rejection of both sides in the 1980s Cold War:

> I was feeling superior to the agents of both world systems because they did not know and would not – for a long time, perhaps too long – catch on to the fact that their profession had become redundant. One, two, three radioactive clouds from one, two, three reactors in different parts of the world and the governments would be forced to change their policies out of

22. Peter Schneider, *Der Mauerspringer* (Hamburg: Luchterhand, 1982). Translated into English by Leigh Hafrey as *The Wall Jumper* (New York: Pantheon, 1983).
23. Rolf Hochhuth, *Judith* (Reinbek: Rowohlt, 1988 [originally 1984]).
24. Stefan Heym, *Schwarzenberg* (Frankfurt: Fischer, 1987 [originally 1984]).

the instinct for self-preservation, and proceed to downright press their secrets upon the other side.[25]

The themes of politicization and national identity were of course not the only or even the primary literary movement of the 1980s. Just as important was the belated emergence of a "postmodern" literature in the two Germanys. This is not the place to engage in an explicit attempt to define what is meant by a "postmodern" German literature or to defend the use of the term. It should suffice for the purposes of my present argument to point out that, regardless of the accuracy or usefulness of the term "postmodernism," some West German writers of the 1980s explicitly understood their project as postmodern. The novelist Hanns-Josef Ortheil, for instance, wrote in 1990 that "The literature of the 1980s is inconceivable without the larger experiences of post-history, post-modernity, and poststructuralism which accompanied it and, over the years, gained more and more contour."[26] Associated with literary post-modernism were phenomena such as: 1) the loss of teleology; 2) randomness; 3) a blurring of the boundary lines between "high" and "low" culture; 4) increasing playfulness and self-referentiality; 5) narrative instability; 6) increasing doubts about the non-textual nature of reality; 7) an obsession with subject positions; 8) relativism; and 9) pluralism. Participating in these developments were not only Ortheil himself but also Patrick Süskind, whose *Perfume* became one of the most successful novels of the 1980s, as well as writers such as Gert Jonke, Sten Nadolny, and Bodo Kirchhoff.

However, "postmodernism" was not limited simply to West Germany. In East Germany, too, a group of authors emerged in the 1980s who specifically and loudly distanced themselves from their "modern" fathers and mothers and adopted many of the theories of poststructuralism and postmodernism. This group was largely centered around the "Prenzlauer-Berg scene," named after a working-class area of Berlin where many neo-avant-garde East German writers of the younger generation began settling in the late 1970s and early 1980s. The works of these writers were largely banned in East Germany during the 1980s, but banned writers were nevertheless able to publish in samizdat editions in the GDR and in the West. The first major anthology of these writers'

25. Christa Wolf, *Accident: A Day's News*, trans. Heike Schwarzbauer and Rick Takvorian (New York: The Noonday Press, 1991),104. First published as *Störfall* (Darmstadt: Luchterhand, 1987).

26. Hanns-Josef Ortheil, "Perioden des Abschieds: Zum Profil der neuen und jüngsten deutschen Literatur," *The German Quarterly* v. 63, n. 3/4 (Summer/Fall 1990), 367-76; here, 375.

work to appear in the west was the 1986 *Berührung ist nur eine Rander-scheinung* (Touching Is Only a Marginal Phenomenon), edited by Sascha Anderson and Elke Erb. Significant members of this younger group of writers were Jan Faktor, Bert Papenfuß-Görek, Rainer Schedlinski, Kurt Drawert, Uwe Kolbe, Durs Grünbein, and of course Anderson himself, who later proved to have been an agent for the *Stasi*. In both West and East Germany, the "postmodernism" of literature of the 1980s implied a certain depoliticization in which a younger, post-"Flakhelfer" generation distanced itself from what it saw as the excessively political work of its literary elders.

For both the postmodern literature and the national-political litera-ture of the 1980s, it is important to recognize that "East German" and "West German" literature of the 1980s functioned as part of a larger pan-German system. This was not true simply because West German law made all East German writers also potential West German writers, although the latter was certainly the case, and the post-1976 period saw a major exodus of literary talent from the GDR: Wolf Biermann, Sarah Kirsch, Jurek Becker, Günter Kunert, Monika Maron, Wolfgang Hilbig, Hans Joachim Schädlich, Lutz Rathenow, and, later, Anderson and Kolbe. Beyond the very significant impact of West German citizenship laws that treated all East Germans as West Germans, however, the West German public sphere also functioned as a substitute sphere for an inad-equate East German public sphere. Thus most GDR citizens were avid consumers of West German media, and GDR writers needed success in the West even more than they needed success in the East. By the late 1970s the East and West German economies had become inextricably intertwined due to the Federal Republic's loans to the GDR and the GDR's "secret" participation, via its ties to the FRG, in the European Common Market. The East German literary sphere was similarly depen-dent on West Germany for publication possibilities, critical acceptance, and institutional prestige. To take just two prominent examples, Müller's plays were staged primarily in the west during the 1980s, even though Müller himself remained a GDR citizen until the end; and while Stefan Heym lived in East Berlin, his novels and stories could be published only in the West because of their oppositional content. It would be difficult to find even a single major East German writer who did not, by the 1980s, have crucial institutional links to the West German literary sphere. But one should not view these ties as a one-way street. West Ger-man literature was also significantly enriched by the contributions of writers from the East, and the East German literary situation had its effect on public and critical opinion in the West. Writers persecuted in the East, for instance, could count on support in the west, and one of the reasons for the West German success of writers like Biermann and Maron was precisely their status as persona non grata in the East. As a character in Wolfgang Hilbig's brilliant 1994 novel *Ich* (I) declares, "There was not a single person in the West ... who did not repeat without resistance judgments about literary quality that in the end were judgments of the *Stasi* (or the KGB)."[27]

If East and West German literature were in fact two parts of a larger pan-German system by the early 1980s, then our understanding of recent German literary history is somewhat changed. Looking back to the early 1980s as the moment of the emergence of a new German nationalism in the wake of the peace movement, we can view the concept of literary "convergence" in a slightly different light. The two major works of German literature to come out of the peace movement and the two pan-German writers' conferences of the early 1980s were Wolf's *Kassandra* and Günter Grass's *Die Rättin* (The Rat). In *Kassandra* the vision of a community that went beyond the bipolar East-West division was embodied in the feminist collective; in *Die Rättin* it was embodied by rats who managed to survive a nuclear catastrophe that destroyed all human beings on the planet Earth, and who represented a positive alternative to human aggression. In these works of literature and in the socialist writings of GDR dissidents Robert Havemann and Rudolf Bahro we already have the vision of a Third Path that rejects the instrumental rationality and aggression of both the West and the East. Here the concept of convergence was a negative, not a positive idea: convergence as the fundamental identity of two social systems that were, at root, equally destructive. Such a view of convergence equated the social systems of the two superpowers as both representing instrumental rationality and posited a Third Path beyond the constraints of such rationality.

While the original positive economic convergence theory of the 1960s and 1970s had envisioned convergence as the gradual approach of two fundamentally opposite systems toward each other, the negative ideas of convergence developed by German writers and intellectuals in the late 1970s and especially the early 1980s saw convergence, on the contrary, as the essentially static identity of two systems, both characterized by instrumental rationality and scorn for human beings. Such a view of convergence fed into powerful currents in German ecologism, feminism, and national political and cultural history, including the concept of *Mitteleuropa*.

From a post-1989 perspective the original economic convergence theory is now passé. This convergence theory, which encompassed a specific

27. Wolfgang Hilbig, *Ich* (Frankfurt: Fischer, 1993), 288.

prediction about how the Soviet and American economies would function in the future, was proven wrong by history itself. However the ideas of convergence of German writers in the 1980s did not experience the same kind of refutation in 1989. On the contrary, the collapse of socialism into capitalism made the opposition between the Third Path and the First and Second Paths even clearer by eliminating the Second Path altogether. What remained for disgruntled literary intellectuals was an opposition between an actually existing capitalism based on materialism and an as-yet unrealized Third Path that was "no place, nowhere": *Kein Ort. Nirgends* – the title of one of Christa Wolf's novels. But in German ideology since the late eighteenth century that utopian "no place, nowhere" had always been somewhere in the sky above Germany. In Schiller's famous statement on the German nation, Germany is precisely the question that cannot be answered, the nation that cannot be located: "Germany? But where is it? I don't know where to find the land."[28] Or, as the narrative voice in one of Martin Walser's national-political characters from the 1980s expresses a character's longing for a lost German unity: "Wolf wanted the whole unity, even if it was lost."[29]

Christa Wolf's *Was bleibt* (What Remains) in a sense marks the end, not the beginning, of a specific literary convergence. If the Wolf of the late 1960s, the 1970s, and the 1980s had moved increasingly toward pan-German problems, the Wolf of the 1990s had once again returned to her specifically GDR identity. In this sense it is, paradoxically, true that 1989/90 probably marks the beginning of a new "GDR literature" in the sense of a literature that comes to terms with the now historical reality of the GDR. In *Was bleibt* Wolf returned once again to East German concerns that had little applicability to either the contemporary or the historical West German scene. *Was bleibt* was followed by a number of other noteworthy literary treatments of the GDR in its socialist specificity: Uwe Saeger's *Die Nacht danach und der Morgen* (The Night After and the Morning), Kurt Drawert's *Spiegelland* (Mirror Land), Christoph Hein's *Exekution eines Kalbs* (The Execution of a Calf), and Wolfgang

---

28. Friedrich Schiller, "Das Deutsche Reich," *Gesamtausgabe*, v.2 (Munich: dtv, 1965), 30. Compare Schiller's statement to the following statement by Peter Schneider, who, with reference to the sentence "I come from Germany," says: "Either the concept makes no sense, or I am talking about a country that is not listed on any political map. As long as I speak about a country called Germay, I am talking about neither the GDR nor the FRG but rather about a country which exists only in my memory or imagination. Asked where it lies, I know of no other place to name than its history and the language which I speak." Comparing the two statements, one feels onself in a historical hall of mirrors. Peter Schneider, *Der Mauerspringer*, 124.

29. Martin Walser, *Dorle und Wolf* (Frankfurt: Suhrkamp, 1987), 149. Translated into English by Leila Vennewitz as *No Man's Land* (New York: Henry Holt, 1989).

Hilbig's short story collection *Grünes, grünes Grab* (Green, Green Grave) and novel *Ich*. Paradoxically, German reunification allowed for a renewed literary coming-to-terms with the era of German separation. That Wolf should have been attacked by West German critics for *Was bleibt* was in a sense logical. She became the butt of a pan-German attack at the very moment when, as a writer, she was returning to East German themes and thus opening herself up to criticism as a specifically East German writer. But Wolf's West German critics used her East German specificity primarily as a veil for their larger concern with post-unification German culture as a whole. What was at stake for them was not East German literature or culture, as Wolf's defenders mistakenly believed. That battle was long since over. Christa Wolf's 1990 attackers had already recognized convergence as a *fait accompli*. Like Martin Walser's character, they wanted everything – not as a lost, but as a regained unity.

CRITICAL INTERVENTIONS

German Women Writing after 1945

Barbara Kosta and *Helga Kraft*

The prospect of writing about literature by women since 1945 in Germany is a daunting one. The complexity of the project lies in the abundant and varied contributions women have made to the literary landscape since the infamous "zero hour" (1945). It lies also in the need for a reflective look at the advances women writers have made, particularly since the late 1960s, at the questions that have stirred the literary imagination and at the remarkable literary movements they have initiated. Owing to the immense contributions women have made since the postwar era, not only in the area of literature, but also in film and theater, a retrospective can provide a scant series of snapshots of authors, issues, and themes that represent only partially the expansive register of works by women in Germany. In part, this essay retains the divide between the literary developments of East and West Germany because of a belief in the embeddedness of literature within a specific cultural, political, and social context. Admittedly, however, there are points at which the borders between East and West blur, especially in the case of former East German authors who were either widely read in the West or had relatively easy access to "foreign markets" and borders.

This survey begins with the women's movement in West Germany that grew out of the politicized climate of the late 1960s. The desire to affect social change and introduce institutional reform provoked questions that primarily concerned the distribution of power along lines of gender and the organization of life spheres. At the same time, the theoretical shifts regarding authorship and the function of literature opened new avenues for women writers. In defiance of the male-dominated literary market of West Germany's restorative postwar period, the writers who rode the second wave of feminism challenged the literary establishment and published their own narratives.

A review of the 1950s produces merely a handful of names, of which only a few are mentioned here: Marie Luise Kaschnitz (1901-1974), Luise Rinser (1911), Nelly Sachs (1891-1970), Anna Seghers (1900-1983), and Rose Ausländer (1901-1988). Among this list of writers, the name of poet and novelist Ingeborg Bachmann (1926-1973) stands out for her sensational literary success at the age of 27. Recognized for her poetry by one of the most prestigious literary cliques at the time, *Gruppe 47*, Bachmann's career was launched by their support. Established as a poet, Bachmann expanded her literary repertoire to include the writing of prose. However, the alleged transgression of genre boundaries was viewed as a scandalous violation, for which the literary establishment strongly criticized Bachmann. Of the three novels of Bachmann's *Todesarten*, only *Malina* (1971) was completed and published before her death in 1973. Even though the women's movement did not immediately embrace Bachmann's work because of its own initial commitment to a prescriptive feminist agenda, Bachmann was transformed later into an icon. Her keen and subtle exploration of power relationships within traditional gender arrangements, in particular, anticipated some of the issues that would later be taken up by feminism.

The move to politicize the private sphere, which became the mantra of the women's movement of the late 1960s, cast a light on the spheres of experience that public discourses conventionally overlooked or even dismissed. Yet for women, the private sphere was an essential part of the political equation, since it was the sphere in which the majority of women resided, and that consequently defined their identities. The introduction of the private realm called for working through the publicly invisible, if not the repressed arena of human activity, and turning inside out what Foucault referred to as "subjugated knowledges." With the spotlight on the private sphere, the first questions that most haunted literature were those of the formation of gendered identity.

Interventions: Questions of Identity

A difficult project awaited the growing number of women writers who were new arrivals on the literary scene in West Germany. These writers, bereft of models, stumbled into a no- woman's land with questions concerning subjectivity, the workplace, family, female sexuality, and female identity as configured within a patriarchal system, as well as the possibility of a female aesthetic. In Elfriede Jelinek's play *Was geschah, nachdem Nora ihren Mann verlassen hatte?* (What happened after Nora left her husband? 1977), Ibsen's Nora expresses the *Aufbruchsstimmung* that accompanied the venture into the new topographies of self-expression. Nora tells her employer: "I am immensely curious. I slammed the door behind me which means that there is no going back, just forward." Although Jelinek's Nora, impeded by the social structures, eventually returns home, a further sense of curiosity led women writers, if not their protagonists, to the exploration of uncharted territories and to a critical confrontation with the social conventions that silenced women as social actors. The deluge of protocols, interviews, and journals bore witness to a struggle for voice and the desire to work through the deeply ingrained psychological structures that inhibited self-realization. These texts served to create a counter- public sphere, in the Habermasian sense of a forum for narratives that resist dominant social narratives and that seek to empower the disenfranchised. These texts furnished a counternarrative to an ideologically fermented understanding of gender. Erika Runge's interviews in *Frauen: Versuche zur Emanzipation* (Women: Attempts toward Emancipation, 1969) were exemplary in their documentation of women's preliminary reflections on their position within the patriarchal order.

With the advent of the 1970s, a shift occurred from a documentary mode of representation to more subjective explorations of gendered identity. The growing emphasis placed on subjectivity reflects a decisive development in the literature of both East and West German women writers, although each political context evoked specific considerations. Authors in the former GDR frequently addressed the role of women within a socialist society that promoted equality in the public realm, but tacitly perpetuated traditional gender relations within the home. In Gerti Tetzner's *Karen W.* (1974), the protagonist candidly evaluates her marriage and describes the deadening, claustrophobic routine from which she longs to break out.[1]

In the West, *Verständigungsliteratur*, a genre of experiential literature, flooded the market. It purposively engaged writers and readers in an experiment of self-discovery and a process of consciousness-raising. Identified as *Frauenliteratur* (women's literature), which implies litera-

---

1. See Nancy Lukens and Dorothy Rosenberg, ed. and trans., *Daughters of Eve: Women's Writing from the German Democratic Republic* (Lincoln, NB.: University of Nebraska Press, 1993).

ture by women and for women, this aggregate of works was prescriptively authentic, uncensored and confessional in its ideological postings. The most remarkable evidence of this genre, in terms of its resonance, is Verena Stefan's pastiche of autobiographical reflections in *Häutungen* (Shedding, 1975). As the title of this immediate best-seller suggests, the protagonist attempts to shed the various layers of discourse that have held female identity hostage. The first barrier Stefan faces in her desire to configure an identity, i. e. to create a protagonist outside of patriarchy, is language itself. In an analytical preface to her work, Stefan succinctly identifies the difficulty of articulating female sexuality without drawing upon medical jargon or derisiveness that reduce the female body to a sexualized object. She writes: "Language fails me as soon as I wish to convey new experiences." Stefan's realization echoes Christa Reinig's much quoted observation that "Literature is a tough male business that has been around for three thousand years. Every woman must experience it when she uses the word *I*. From that point on, nothing works."[2] The theoretical conundrum many writers faced in producing a female subject outside of the descriptors of hegemony found a response in the works of such French feminists as Luce Irigaray, Hélène Cixous, and Monique Wittig, who experimented with the concept, based on psychoanalysis, of writing the body. Their project posed a subversive practice of claiming the female body and of exploring new subjective languages in order to cast experience and identities anew. Still, a number of authors like Reinig (*Entmannung*. Emasculation, 1976) found other means to deconstruct traditional gender norms and engage in literary experiments that range from satirical to surreal, to autobiographical representations. Among them are Margot Schroeder (*Der Schlachter empfiehlt noch immer Herz*, The butcher still recommends heart, 1976), Jutta Heinrich (*Das Geschlecht der Gedanken*, The gender of thought, 1977), Brigitte Schwaiger (*Wie kommt das Salz ins Meer?*, Why is there salt in the sea?, 1977) and Svende Merian (*Der Tod des Märchenprinzen*, The death of a fairy tale princess, 1980). In the case of novelist Karin Struck (*Die Mutter*, The mother, 1975), the venture of a "new femininity" called for elevating the experience of motherhood and female sexuality in response to the denigration of the female body and the devaluation of the maternal.

The programmatic reflex of women's literature *(Frauenliteratur)*, popularized in the 1970s, incited a polarization of male and female identity that often essentialized gender differences and hypostasized a universally victimized "woman," subjected to patriarchal oppression. With time these representations became insufficient to probe the dynamics of gen-

2. Christa Reinig, "Das weibliche Ich." *alternative* 108/109: 119.

der, just as gender, as the sole analytical category, became inadequate to explain the multiple vectors of identity. While the analysis of gender became more nuanced, so too did the question, which Silvia Bovenschen explores in her collection of essays entitled *Die imaginierte Weiblichkeit* (Imagined femininity, 1979), of how a unique female aesthetic evolved into an investigation of the alternate means of representing female subjectivity practiced by many women authors. The exclusionary posture of a univocal, that is, hyphenated feminism, based on the concerns of an all-white, middle-class population, unwittingly created its own margins and erased the complex and often contradictory positioning of the subject in terms of class, ethnicity, sexual preference, national identity and race. The voices of Afro-German women in the collection *Farbe bekennen: Afro-deutsche Frauen auf den Spuren ihrer Geschichte* (Showing Our Colors: Afro-German Women Speak Out, 1986) edited by Katharina Oguntoye, May Opitz, and Dagmar Schultz, were among the first to challenge radically the assumptions that fixed identity within the discourses of mainstream feminism and to unsettle the ethnocentric equation of Germanness with white. Much like the experiential literature that preceded the publication of *Showing Our Colors,* these essays drew upon personal experiences within a larger sociohistorical context, with the exception that these testimonies unmasked the racism that has yet to be dealt with in Germany.

Questions of identity continue to pose new challenges and gain a dizzying complexity with each border crossing and subsequent displacement, especially for those authors who write in German, but who are not German per constitutional law. Libuše Moníková, who left Czechoslovakia in 1972, describes in her novel *Pavane für eine verstorbene Infantin* (Pavane for a dead princess, 1983), the travels of an academic between her native Prague and Göttingen, where she teaches a seminar on Kafka and Arno Schmidt. The displacements the protagonist encounters are reflected in the disjointedness of the text, in the constant allusion to both figurative and literal amputations, in the representation of exile, as well as in such banal formulations as "Good day, who do you think you are" (15). Although Moníková's protagonists are emotionally rooted in the Czech Republic, they are cast as disabled and ailing. In *Pavane*, the main character, who harbors a fascination for the literary representation of disabilities, takes to a wheel chair to play out the role of a physically challenged person so as to free herself symbolically of the dependencies that have inhibited her as a writer. Her injured hip, an outward symptom of her psychic impairment, encumbers mobility. It is only once she burns the wheelchair in a ritual-like exorcism, along with her sister's photograph, a doll, and a box of tablets that suppress appetite, that the protagonist frees herself from the traditions that have governed her productivity.

While in Moníková's novel it is the body that manifests the experienced displacements, it is the loss of language that reflects a metaphorical "homelessness" in Emine Sevgi Özdamar's collection of short stories entitled *Mutter Zunge* (Mother tongue, 1993). Lamenting the loss of her native language as a symbol of the "in-betweenness" of identity, the protagonist attempts to recall: "If I would only know, exactly when I lost my mother tongue" (7). The figures Özdamar presents are all strangers to their native and adopted countries. They are shown as trafficking back and forth from Turkey to Germany through what the author refers to as the "Germany Door." It marks a point of entry and departure through bureaucratic turnstiles where identities are reconfigured and negotiated with each border crossing. For authors like Moníková, Özdamar, Herta Müller, Sahilia Scheinhardt, to name only a few, the dislocations portrayed within the text resonate with the critical discussions of attribution surrounding literature by non-German citizens, and the inclusion of their texts to the body (*ius sanguinis*) of German literature.[3]

Dialogues with the Past

The explorations of subjectivity and interpersonal relationships in many narratives of the 1970s were situated in the immediate present. With the increasing interest in the relationship of the subject to history and as part of a genealogy, a turn toward autobiographically inflected narratives appeared. The mother/daughter relationship ranked as a principal theme in protocols and interviews with such titles as Barbara Franck's *Ich schaue in den Spiegel und sehe meine Mutter* (I look in the mirror and see my mother, 1979), or more dramatically, Erika Schilling's, *Manchmal hasse ich meine Mutter* (I sometimes hate my mother, 1981). These texts reveal a progression from a rejection of the mother as a model symbolic of a dramatic performance of separation, and the desire for autonomy sought by daughters during the early phases of feminism, to the onset of a dialogue and an exploration of the constraints that have informed traditional mothers' lives. In the fictional setting, but in most cases still autobiographically motivated, the narrative gestures toward a working through of a damaging symbiotic relationship that has a pow-

---

3. See Leslie Adelson, "Migrants' Literatur or German Literature? TORKAN's *Tufan: Brief an einen islamischen Bruder*," *German Quarterly* 63.3/4 (1990): 382-387, and Fritz J. Raddatz, "In mir zwei Welten," *Die Zeit* 26 (1994): 45-46. Noticeably, Raddatz's article does not feature one woman writer except within a passing note.

erful grip on the daughter's psychic development. The mother/daughter relationship figures prominently in Gabriele Wohnmann's, *Ausflug mit der Mutter* (An excursion with mother, 1976), Helga Novak's *Die Eisheiligen* (The ice saints, 1979), Ingeborg Drewitz's *Eis auf der Elbe* (Ice on the Elbe, 1982), Elfriede Jelinek's *Die Klavierspielerin* (The piano teacher, 1986), and Waltraut Anna Mitgutsch's *Die Züchtigung* (The punishment, 1985). Of prime significance in these arduous confrontations with the mother is her function in the formation of the daughter's gendered identity. These narratives also make manifest that the past, as it is embodied in the relationship between generations, cannot be separated from the present. Indeed, it is an integral part of the fabric of the present and future.

For a number of writers who belong to the postwar generation, the exploration of identity led to personal investigations of Germany's fascist past. With the inclusion of the experiences of women and children and the dynamics of the private sphere, the general discourses about the Nazi regime and its consequences achieved new insights. These works called for a confrontation with personal experiences, with the making of subjectivity, with the cultivation of selective memories and with the wounds of history. The recognition of the intersection of personal and national identity called into being a genre of *Väterliteratur* (literature of the fathers) that highlighted the father as a traditional representative of history, the public sphere, and the state. The deep psychological wounds left by parents whose unresolved traumas imprinted themselves on the psychic structures of an emotionally ambivalent postwar generation became the topic in Jutta Schütting's *Der Vater* (The father, 1980) and Brigitte Schwaiger's *Lange Abwesenheit* (Long absence, 1983). It is interesting to note that many works that belong to this genre are engaged in the process of mourning because the father's death releases many of the questions that have burdened the younger generation. These narratives often substituted for a rebellion against the father and then, through him, against the politics of the fatherland. Of particular interest as the first to reflect critically upon the relationship between daughter and father in order to understand her development within the historical context of fascist Germany, is Elisabeth Plessen. As a member of the SDS, the League of Socialist German Students in Berlin in the 1960s, the protagonist Augusta, in Plessen's novel *Mitteilung an den Adel* (Such Sad Tidings, 1976), renounces her aristocratic name and privileges in an initial break with the father and all for which he stands. More importantly, she demands to know why her father did not resist Hitler's regime. In the course of her autobiographical reflections, she recognizes her father's willingness to give and obey orders, his uncontested acceptance of tradition, his vague, stereotypical perception of human nature, the need for male bonding and heroism in war, and an inability to develop close relationships.

On the way to her father's funeral, Plessen contemplates a new approach to the narration of history that allows her to criticize the intolerable generalizations that informed her father's world view. She demands an honest confrontation, a method she employs in scrutinizing her own past. This approach to documenting the past may also be seen in Plessen's novel *Kohlhaas* (1979), which features the historical sixteenth-century rebel from Heinrich von Kleist's famous novella of the same name. Here Plessen experiments with a new kind of historical narrative that self-consciously merges fiction and fact, a technique that leads her to position herself as "the writer" within the text. Instead of assuming a false objectivity, Plessen struggles with her biases, reveals the inevitable gaps in reconstructing history, and admits to a lack of knowledge at times. She revives the Kleistian setting to work through the charged debates among the Left of the 1970s in West Germany, who sought to define political engagement and weigh its extreme expression in the terrorist activity of Baader-Meinhoff group. Plessen meticulously traces the personalities of various types of revolutionaries, and concludes that the activities of those like Ulrike Meinhoff cost too many people their lives – a price too high to pay. At the root of the narrative, however, is the question of resistance and the specter of Germany's fascist past.

A number of writers like Ingeborg Drewitz (1923-1986), Ruth Rehmann (1922), and Christa Wolf (1929) who experienced wartime and fascism also responded to the much delayed and perilous need to remember. Ruth Rehmann's novel *Der Mann auf der Kanzel: Fragen an einen Vater* (The Man in the Pulpit, Questions for a Father, 1980), for one, takes issue with her father's role as pastor during the Nazi period and his proverbial conformist stance *vis à vis* the insidious racial politics which the Church adopted and openly supported. Yet despite the biographical focus of the work, the primary motivation and underlying interest is the subjectivity of the author herself, and the desire to identify the ways in which parents' lives, their experienced histories, write themselves, often unconsciously, onto the bodies of the generations that follow. The questions that inform and structure the dialogue with the past, indeed, reveal the present concerns of those who pose them.

The autobiographical excavation of the past in Christa Wolf's *Kindheitsmuster* (Patterns of Childhood, 1976) is a search for the missing pieces of the puzzle of "how did we become the way we are?" (145). With her inquiry, Wolf sets out to counter the willful erasure of historical memory from present day consciousness and insists upon recognizing that "what is past is not dead; it is not even past. We cut ourselves off from it; we pretend to be strangers" (3). She engages in a dialogue with a past self that Wolf calls Nelly to signal the simultaneous distance and proximity of the past and its voices. As a work of memory, the narrative retraces the locations of childhood to reflect on Nelly's development and review the activities and gestures of daily life that were signs of repressed knowledge and the potential resistance. In addition to providing a textual surface to maneuver dialogically between past and present in order to work through the past, these "documents" serve another purpose. They provide an opportunity to pursue alternatives and resist the compulsion to repeat a horrifying history when faced with choices similar to those of Wolf's generation. Ground breaking in its intense self-reflexivity, *Patterns of Childhood* is in a unique position as one of the first works to deal with the fascist past as part of the GDR's own history, in contrast to its official location within the borders of West Germany.

On stage, Gerlind Reinshagen traces a family history that reveals not only the development of fascist tendencies but also a potential for resistance in the same character in the trilogy *Sonntagskinder* (Sunday's children, premiered 1976), *Das Frühlingsfest* (The spring party, 1980) and *Tanz, Marie* (Dance, Marie, 1987). Reinshagen was among the first to show that the home was not innocent of ideology and that women participated in the war machinery and the beliefs that fueled it. The dramatist shows how women can become collaborators. In *Sonntagskinder,* the traditional socialization of girls fosters dependencies that perpetuate relationships of domination and subservience. The limitations placed upon women by traditional expectations of their roles robs many women of their dreams, which makes them susceptible to Nazi propaganda. As the mother figure in the play, who represents a typical fellow traveler, admits: "I still had the dreams that I used to have in my childhood … But they are poison … They prevent us from adapting to things" (Reinshagen, 336). Reinshagen avoids one-dimensional stereotypes by giving her protagonists multifacetted identities that often produce a change of mind or allow for resistance to the status quo. Perhaps a more direct implication of women's complicity is the book *Judasfrauen* (Judas Women, 1990) in which Helga Schubert documents ten women's accounts of collaboration and denunciation. Interestingly, most of these women engaged in betrayal for reasons of love, rather than a desire to further their careers, as was often the case with men. Both of these works seem to respond to a widely held view that women remained outside of history as its victims rather than as participants or agents. Both of these roles must be taken into account in order to reveal the makings of history.

The project of many of the works discussed here invariably recalls Alexander and Margarethe Mitscherlich's often cited study *The Inability to Mourn,* a psychoanalytical résumé of the historical amnesia that screened out the trauma of World War II and its atrocities. Many women writers reviewed the symptoms that suggested the denial of knowledge and the missed opportunities to intervene or remember, as well as an unacknowledged pain or trauma. The works thus serve to mourn the loss of the potential for change. They seek to illuminate what Christa Wolf refers to as the blind spots that consciously or not, obstruct utopian visions. Given that many of the narratives that initiated the work of memory and mourning first appeared in the mid-1970s, it may be said that the repression of the past in official public memory is an agenda shared by both East and West Germany.

It is the overwhelming reception of Ruth Klüger's recollection of her childhood experiences as a survivor of Ausschwitz in *weiter leben. Eine Jugend* (continuing on. A Childhood, 1992) that manifests the ongoing need to remember the Holocaust, to work through the brutal crimes against humanity that Germany staged, and to resist the impulse to bury the past. The author recalls her aunt's advice when she emigrated to the United States to erase the memories of the past. As she realized then, "I thought, she wanted to take away from me the only thing I had, namely the life that I had already lived. One can't throw that away, as if I had others stashed away in a closet" (Klüger 228). Yet, Klüger describes in numerous interviews her long avoidance of the memories of the past and the ways she sought to outmaneuver recollections. She ends up struggling with the reliablity of memory, the desire to reconstruct the suffering she experienced as a child, and self-reflexively grapples with her own subjectivity in reporting the events of history. She writes: "Yesterday I wrote these sentences, they appear false today, wrong. I want to erase them but hesitate" (Klüger, 166). It is the difficult process of looking a horrific history in the face in order to pass on this knowledge to the generations to come. Klüger dedicates her book to friends who live in Göttingen.

The work of remembering and mourning continues in the literature of post-unification, particularly in those works by authors of the former GDR. In contrast to the close attention paid to Germany's fascist past in much literature since the 1960s, these works specifically address the history of the GDR since its inception in 1949 and its ideological foundations. In Monika Maron's novel *Stille Zeile Sechs* (No. 6 Stille Zeile, 1991) the main character Rosalind Polkowski quits her job as historian and refuses to place her intellectual capabilities in the service of anyone but herself. She meets Herbert Beerenbaum, a Communist of the old guard and powerful GDR functionary, who hires her to take down his memoir while he dictates the significant moments of the past. As his memoir, which serves not only to legitimate the official history of the GDR but his own life, unfolds, the protagonist is faced with her conflict-ridden relationship to her own father and his biography, in addition to the history of the GDR. With Beerenbaum's death, the protagonist inherits the hated manuscript. To open it would mean to accept his history which she refuses to do. This novel may be the beginning of a new "literature of the fathers".

An insightful and challenging dialogue with the past in the works of women writers has proceeded along numerous lines. A search for role models and the need recognize and to counter the exclusion of pioneering female artists and scientists from the canon has produced a series of works within the past twenty-five years. (Books have appeared on Luise Gottsched, Lily Brown, Rosa Luxemburg). In *Respektloser Umgang* (Irreverent Discourse, 1987), Helga Königsdorf imagines a meeting with the physicist Lise Meitner, who was denied recognition of her contributions in the study of radioactivity, which were credited mainly to Otto Hahn, who won the Nobel Prize. Such historical omissions, now referred to as "gender censorship" were not uncommon experiences for a woman and a Jew, especially during the Hitler period. Yet, as Königsdorf, who is a trained physicist herself, shows, many important women denigrate their own achievements in order to be accepted into male dominated fields. To indicate that Meitner did not expect fame, Königsdorf's character states: "I will leave a trace in people around me which will become a new message when it is united with all the other traces, even when my name is long forgotten." (Königsdorf, 114). With this imaginary dialogue, Königsdorf provides a much needed role model for women, particularly in the sciences, and secures Meitner her rightful place in history.

Reaching back into the history of music, Elfriede Jelinek transports the nineteenth century composer Clara Wieck Schumann (1819-1896) into the 1920s and onto the modern stage in her play *Clara S*. Clara visits the Italian writer d'Annunzio, who embodies the fascist and capitalist tendencies of men who consume women and art. This postmodern pastiche critiques the mode of production of male artists and caustically takes to task the historical reasons for women's absence from the field of music. Clara, not only a composer and a famous concert pianist, but the mother of eight children, complains about the straight jacket of her existence in her marriage to the famous classical composer Robert Schumann: "The female artist pays. If she is an artist, her limbs rot away one by one from her living body as a result of the artistic production of man" (Jelinek, 95). In the end, Jelinek allows Clara to strangle her husband as a belated gesture of poetic justice.[4]

4. For a comprehensive study of women dramatists and the German stage, see Helga Kraft, *Ein Haus aus Sprache: Dramatikerinnen und das andere Theater*, Stuttgart: Metzler,

Deconstruction of Myths and Tentative Utopias

While until very recently literary historians regarded myths as conveyors of universal truths, the works of many twentieth century women writers contributed significantly to changing this perception. Their interest in myth expresses a desire to intervene in traditional historical narration and in representations of the past and to rewrite the narratives that have traditionally defined culture.

Many authors seem to share Roland Barthes's definition of myth as "depoliticized speech" that "has the task of giving an historical intention a natural justification, and making contingency appear eternal" (Barthes, 142). It is to the credit of cultural materialists and the postmodern practice of debunking unquestioned eternal values that a major revision of mythology has taken place. Women writers especially have developed a keen sense for the need to deconstruct absolutes since their experiences as females in a patriarchal society contradicted the "universal truths" that defined them. In the process of deconstructing myths, fairy tales, and archetypes, women writers challenged notions that naturalized gendered roles, and that locked women away in towers and into a disenfranchised mode of existence. In revisiting the "canon", contemporary authors found that concepts of "woman's nature" were based on naturalized historical, cultural constructions (as described by Judith Butler) that assured the continuation of privileges for a certain portion of the population and sustained power relations that disadvantaged women. As women writers deconstructed popularized myths, they simultaneously reconstructed their own versions of female existence and identity.

One of the first writers to pioneer the deconstruction of myth was Ingeborg Bachmann. In her short, lyrical story *Undine geht* (Undine goes, 1961), Bachmann touches upon the experience of women who have been socialized to depend on the love of men, a practice that leaves them open to exploitation. Undine, who represents a self-sacrificing mermaid – this imagery recalls the fluid "feminine" element of creativity – refuses to surrender to her traditionally assigned role. The impossibility of self-definition in a male dominated society causes her to leave for good. Bachmann opts to break with an existence that objectifies women, even if it is painful.

More than Bachmann, Irmtraud Morgner lavishly highlights the magical elements of mythology. In her book *Leben und Abenteuer der*

1996. It should be noted that an increasing number of women playwrights beginning in the 1970s were able to conquer the stage, thus contributing to a public discourse on their own terms.

Trobadora Beatriz nach Zeugnissen ihrer Spielfrau Laura (Life and Adventures of the Trobadora Beatriz as Chronicled by her Minstrel Laura, 1973), the GDR author virtually rewrites the magical tale of Sleeping Beauty. Here, "Sleeping Beauty" is no longer a passive, young girl, but rather a mature, married troubadour of medieval times, who actively produces literature and songs. She induces her own sleep to last from the twelfth to the twentieth century, since she no longer wants to live in the male-dominated cosmos of the dark ages, in which her own desires have no chance of fulfillment. Contrary to the Grimms's version of the fairy tale, Morgner's Sleeping Beauty is not awakened by the kiss of a prince, but by the dynamite of an engineer, who blasts through the prickly rose hedge. Instead of carrying her off to his castle to make her his bride, the "anti-prince" tries to use her for a lucrative business deal. Morgner's humorous dynamiting of the traditional fairy tale reveals that there is nothing universal about women's condition as traditional interpretations of fairy tales would make one believe happily ever after.[5] Morgner's Marxist training in historical materialism, and her initial belief in the imminent success of a great communist society, made her one of the first writers to question mainstream assumptions about women that circulated within the literary canon. Indeed, Morgner demonstrates that women can be writers and even active heroes in picaresque novels. Her work is populated with many mythological women figures. For instance, through "the beautiful Melusine," Morgner etymologically corrects the association of this figure with water, since the name derives from the medieval Luisinia, which means the "Lady of the Light" (*Women's Encyclopedia*, 630). Hence, Morgner furnishes an alternative to Bachmann's murky feminine water symbolism. By contrast, Melusine writes things down in an attempt to bring light to the dark ages, to which she still belongs. When asked why her book became an instant success, even in the FRG, Morgner answered: "I believe the reason lies in its subject matter. Both socialism and women's emancipation are on the agenda. This is the subject matter of an epoch" (Gerhart, 24).

Through Morgner's method of intertwining and contrasting epochs in *Life and Adventure*, it becomes clear that mythological structures supply meanings that are ideologically based. The thorny hedge, which actually traps women, has literally been blasted away to make way for an improvement in the future. The productive powers at work here, as

---

5. Klaudia Heidemann Nebelin's new book *Rotkäppchen erlegt den Wolf. Marieluise Fleisser, Christa Reinig und Elfriede Jelinek als satirische Schriftstellerinnen* reveals that the aggressive humor especially in Reinig and Jelinek is directed against men who usually misunderstand or fail to see the humor. The author contends that women have learned to laugh at men's jokes even if it is directed toward them.

Morgner's female troubadour maintains, are desire and eroticism. However, Morgner theoretically considers a feminist utopian goal secondary to an economic goal of general betterment that is considered reasonable, through the socialist political structure of the GDR (Gerhardt, 26). The hope to achieve a "concrete utopia" in the GDR, in the sense of Bloch's *Das Prinzip Hoffnung* (The Principle of Hope), was dashed by the collapse of the communist government in 1989. It is difficult to gauge whether Morgner – despite her public pronouncements – anticipated the destruction of this utopia and surreptitiously critiqued the patriarchal structures of her country (Gerhardt, 198).

In the 1970s, women writers in the FRG also took an interest in probing and rewriting traditional mythic representations. Both Christa Reinig and Christine Brückner, for instance, selected the figure of the vilified, "unfaithful" Greek queen Clytemnestra, who kills her husband Agamemnon and is murdered by her son Orestes. The figure of Clytemnestra may have attracted many writers as one of the very few strong women in mythology. The depiction of Clytemnestra in Reinig's *Entmannung* and Brückner's *"Bist Du nun glücklich, toter Agamemnon?"* (Are you finally happy, dead Agamemnon?, 1981) challenges early versions of the female "other'" and invites society to view this type of female, embodied in Clytemnestra, anew (Komar, 20). While Brückner lends a modern voice to the ancient queen and retains the historical context, Reinig gives a modern woman the ancient name: "Reinig's 1970s Klytemnestra struggles for survival as a person rather than for dominion over a kingdom. She can only wound her husband, not kill him. Her children are lost to abortions, not to ritual sacrifices." (Komar, 24) Yet the present day woman is still punished for her desired autonomy and must go to prison.

Unlike Reinig and Brückner, a number of feminist writers undertook the exploration of a matriarchal mythology, hoping to find a non-aggressive model of communities that allegedly preceded the institutionalization of patriarchy. One of the results was a concept of femininity that was based on the inherently different and superior nature of women. A major theoretical debate about essentialism emerged that, for the most part, was resolved by the late 1980s. It was widely recognized that such essentialism introduced a new dichotomization of the sexes that merely reversed poles. The creation of a new mythology that retained asymmetrical power structures could hardly produce a better society.[6]

Another representation of a strong mythological woman may be found in Grete Weil's novel *Meine Schwester Antigone* (My sister

---

6. See Sonja Distler, *Mütter, Amazonen und dreifältige Göttinnen: Eine psychologische Analyse der feministischen Matriachatsdebatte*, (Wien: Picus Verlag, 1989).

Antigone, 1980). Here, the writer reflects on the experience of being Jewish and a survivor of the Holocaust. Weil's mistrust of mythology stems from its exploitation by fascism, which served to obfuscate Nazi demagoguery. Her project is to expose the abuse of myth. As a result, Antigone, who resists the law of the land, becomes a model in her fierce struggle for the freedom that she gains by refusing to comply with state law. The female narrator plans to write a book about Antigone, who progressively becomes her imaginary companion and a symbol of uncompromising resistance. The book leaves open the question of whether the narrator has the courage to fight for freedom, or whether she falls short of her model because she has been socialized against engaging in confrontation.

It does not come as a surprise that Christa Wolf too turned to the realm of mythology. In 1983, Wolf published the well-received novel *Cassandra*, along with four theoretical lectures she had delivered at Frankfurt University (*Poetik-Vorlesungen*) in 1982, on the making of the novel. Not only did the temporal displacement offer her a way to go beyond her own experiences (which she had explored substantially in *Patterns of Childhood*), but the setting in antiquity gave her the opportunity to mask her growing criticism of the communist regime. Unlike Morgner, Wolf only indirectly infuses contemporary historical and political realities into her story. In writing this book, she also became aware of the legitimacy of a feminist agenda. In order to understand women's situations, she revisits the original scripts of patriarchal society and fills in the voids by imagining the voices of women that have been stifled throughout history. With the prophetess Cassandra, who in the classical myth is cursed by Apollo and fated never to be believed, Wolf shows that there are other motives behind wars other than the righteous agendas often proclaimed. At the same time, her various descriptions of Amazons, nymphs, king's daughters, and female slaves demonstrate the significance of context in the construction of gender and contradict the notion of a feminine essentialist ontology.

Wolfs' interest in mythology continues on into the 1990s. Her book *Medea, Stimmen* (Medea, Voices, 1995) turns the commonly transmitted Medea myth on its head: Medea neither kills her brother nor her sons, nor does she love Jason. Instead, she enjoys a satisfying non-binding relationship with another man. In Wolf's version, sexuality has no hold over Medea's life. Yet it is her shedding of traditional female characteristics that precipitates her down fall and constitutes her tragic flaw. Jealousy and fear of the powers she develops through her knowledge of medicine, her love of people, and her courage to follow her own desires lead to her exploitation as a political pawn. Wolf is not shy in implying that it is no picnic to be an independent thinker. Cynically, Medea maintains that human beings too easily surrender to the dominant discourses of society that determine what a person may be. In a less than disguised form, Wolf evokes her own situation after the fall of the Berlin wall and the fierce criticism against her for her role as an unofficial *Stasi* informer, however brief and inconsequential. It may be added that she drew much more criticism than a number of male writers who had even stronger ties to the East German secret police. As Medea, Wolf may see herself cast as a scapegoat, an image which is not only politically but also artistically denigrating.

A quite different reworking of myth can be found in Gerlind Reinshagen's play *Medea bleibt* (Medea stays, 1996). The author does not return to antiquity but chooses, as Christa Reinig did, a modern setting for a mythological story.[7] She inquires: How would people nowadays react to a Medea? Reinshagen draws conclusions that address the present historical situation. The modern Medea, who is called Jana, leaves her drinking husband, Wolf, for another man. He takes her back, however, after Jana's new live-in boyfriend finds a younger, richer mate. Medea does not kill her children, but rather a neighbor does, who can no longer take present day, superficial tendencies to come to arrangements. Despite the contemporary context, Reinshagen has observed in conversation (March 1996) that age-old emotions, such as those played out in the Medea story, continue to lay the foundation of Western culture. This points either to a renewed interest in the revival of transhistorical truths or to a need for a more refined analysis of the influence of history on the way we have become who we are.

It will be the work of contemporary authors, as it has been for those authors who have been writing for the past four decades, to challenge the myths and narratives of identity that hinder discovery, the knowledge of history, and the potential for change.

---

7. Marianne Fritz created a "new Medea" in 1978 in her novel *Die Schwerkraft der Verhältnisse*. Her fate follows more closely that of the mythical Medea. Fritz describes the life of a *petit-bourgeois* Medea , Berta Schrei, between 1945 and 1963. She wants to save her children from a damaging post-war society by killing them. After a failed suicide she lives on in a mental asylum.

Select Bibliography

Adelson, Leslie, "Migrants' Literature or German Literature? TORKAN's *Tufan: Brief an einen islamischen Bruder,*" *German Quarterly* 63, 1990.

Appelt, Hedwig . *Die leibhaftige Literatur. Das Phantasma und die Präsenz der Frau in der Schrift,* Weinheim und Berlin: Quadriga Verlag, 1989.

Bachmann, Ingeborg. "Undine Goes," in: *The Thirtieth Year: Stories.* New York: Holmes & Meier, 1987. (First published as: *Das dreißigste Jahr.* Munich: R. Piper, 1961.)

_____. *Malina: A Novel.* New York: Holmes & Meier, 1990.

Barthes, Roland. *Mythologies,* New York: Hill and Wang, 1987.

Brandes, Ute, ed. *Zwischen gestern und morgen. Schriftstellerinnen der DDR aus amerikanischer Sicht,* Berne: Peter Lang, 1992.

Brückner, Christine. "Bist du nun glücklich, toter Agamemnon?" *Wenn du geredet hättest, Desdemona: ungehaltene Reden ungehaltener Frauen.* Hamburg; Hoffmann und Campe, 1983 (first published in *Mein schwarzes Sofa,* Frankfurt/Berlin: Ullstein, 1981).

Brügmann, Margret. *Amazonen der Literatur. Studien zur deutschsprachigen Frauenliteratur der 70er Jahre,* Amsterdamer Publikationen zur Sprache und Literatur, vol. 65, Amsterdam: Rodopi, 1986

Butler, Judith P. *Gender Trouble: Feminism and the Subversion of Identity.* New York: Routledge, 1990.

Distler, Sonja. *Mütter, Amazonen und dreifältige Göttinnen: Eine psychologische Analyse der feministischen Matriachatsdebatte.* Wien: Picus Verlag, 1989.

Drewitz, Ingeborg. *Eis auf der Elbe, Tagebuchroman.* Düsseldorf: Claassen, 1982.

Ewering, Cäcilia. *Frauenliebe und -literatur. (Un)gelebte (Vor)Bilder bei Ingeborg Bachmann, Johanna Moosdorf und Christa Reinig,* Essen: Die Blaue Eule, 1992.

Franck, Barbara. *Ich schaue in den Spiegel und sehe meine Mutter: Gesprächsprotokolle mit Töchtern.* Hamburg: Hoffmann & Campe, 1979.

Fritz, Marianne. *Die Schwerkraft der Verhältnisse.* Frankfurt: Fischer, 1978.

Gerhardt, Marlis, ed. *Irmtraud Morgner. Texte, Daten, Bilder.* Frankfurt/M.: Luchterhand, 1990.

Habermas, Jürgen. "Concerning the Public Use of History." *New German Critique* 44 (1988): 40-50.

Heidemann-Nebelin, Klaudia. *Rotkäppchen erlegt den Wolf. Marieluise Fleisser, Christa Reinig und Elfriede Jelinek als satirische Schriftstellerinnen.* Bonn: Holos Verlag, 1994.

Heinrich, Jutta. *Das Geschlecht der Gedanken.* Munich: Frauenoffensive, 1977.

Jelinek, Elfriede. *Was geschah nachdem Nora ihren Mann verlassen hattte.* Munich: Deutscher Taschenbuch Verlag, 1982.

_____. *Clara S.* In: *Theaterstücke.* Reinbeck/Hamburg: Rowohlt, 1992

_____. *Die Klavierspielerin..* Reinbeck/Hamburg: Rowohlt, 1983.

Klüger, Ruth. *weiter leben. Eine Jugend.* Munich: Deutscher Taschenbuch Verlag, 1994.

Knapp, Mona und Labroisse, Gerd, ed. *Frauen-Fragen in der deutschsprachigen Literatur seit 1945.* Amsterdamer Beiträge zur Neueren Germanistik, Amsterdam, Atlanta: Rodopi 1989.

Komar, Kathleen, L. "Klytemnestra in Germany: Re-visions of a Female Archetype by Christa Reinig and Christine Brückner." *The Germanic Review,* LXIX (1994): 20-27.

Königsdorf, Helga. *Respektloser Umgang.* Berlin, Weimar: Aufbau-Verlag, 1986.

Koonz, Claudia. *Mothers in the Fatherland. Women, the Family and Nazi Politics,* New York: St. Martin's Press, 1987.

Kosta, Barbara. *Recasting Autobiography. Women's Counterfictions in Contemporary German Literature and Film.* Ithaca and London: Cornell University Press, 1994.

Kraft, Helga. *Ein Haus aus Sprache. Dramatikerinnen und das andere Theater.* Stuttgart: Metzler, 1996.

Kraft, Helga und Liebs, Elke, eds. *Mütter, Töchter, Frauen. Weiblichkeitsbilder in der Literatur,* Stuttgart: Metzler, 1993.

Lukens, Nacy and Dorothy Rosenberg, ed. and trans. *Daughters of Eve: Women's Writing from the German Democratic Republic.* Lincoln, NB: University of Nebraska Press, 1993.

Maron, Monika. *Stille Zeile Sechs.* Frankfurt/M: Fischer, 1991.

Merian, Svende. *Der Tod des Märchenprinzen.* Reinbeck/Hamburg: Rowohlt, 1983. (copyright: Merian, 1980).

Mitscherlich, Margarethe and Alexander. *The Inability to Mourn: Principles of Collective Behavior.* New York: Grove Press, 1984.

Moffit, Gisela. *Bonds and bondage: Daughter-father Relationships in the Father Memoirs of German-speaking Women Writers of the 1970s.* New York: Peter Lang, 1993.

Moníková, Libuše. *Pavane für eine verstorbene Infantin.* Munich: Deutscher Taschenbuch Verlag, 1988.

Morgner, Irmtraud. "Die täglichen Zerstückelungen. Gespräch mit Ursula Krechel," in: Gerhardt, Marlis.

———. *Leben und Abenteuer der Trobadora Beatriz nach Zeignissen ihrer Spielfrau Laura. Roman in dreizehn Buchern und sieben Intermezzos.* Darmstadt und Neuwied: Luchterhand, 1976 (First published: Berlin, Weimar: Aufbau-Verlag, 1974).

Novak, Helga. *Die Eisheiligen.* Darmstadt: Luchterhand, 1979.

Oguntoye, Katharina and May Opitz and Dagmar Schultz, eds. *Farbe bekennen: Afro-deutsche Frauen auf den Spuren ihrer Geschichte.* Frankfurt/M: Fischer, 1986.

Özdamar, Emine Svegi. *Mutter Zunge.* Berlin: Rotbuch, 1993.

Plessen, Elissabeth. *Mitteilung an den Adel.* Zürich, Köln: Benzinger Verlag, 1976.

———. *Kohlhaas.* Zürich/Köln: Benzinger Verlag, 1979.

Puknus, Heinz, ed. *Neue Literatur der Frauen. Deutschsprachige Autorinnen der Gegenwart,* München: C.H. Beck, 1980.

Rehmann, Ruth. *Der Mann auf der Kanzel: Fragen an einen Vater.* München/Wien: Hanser, 1979.

Reinig, Christa. *Entmannung. Roman.* Darmstadt: Luchterhand, 1977 (first published: Düsseldorf: Eremiten-Presse, 1976).

Reinshagen, Gerlind. *Medea bleibt.* Unpublished, 1995.

Reinshagen, Gerlind. *Sonntagskinder, Das Frühlingsfest, Tanz, Marie!* in: *Gesammelte Stücke.* Frankfurt: Suhrkamp, 1986.

Richter-Schröder, Karin. *Frauenliteratur und weibliche Identität. Theoretische Ansätze zu einer weiblichen Ästhetik und zur Entwicklung der neuen deutschen Frauenliteratur,* Frankfurt: Verlag Anthon Hain, 1986.

Runge, Erika. *Frauen: Versuche zur Emanzipation.* Frankfurt: Fischer, 1969.

Schäffer-Hegel, Barbara and Wartmann, Brigitte, eds. *Mythos Frau. Projektionen und Inszenierungen im Patriarchat,* Berlin, 1984.

Schilling, Erika. *Manchmal hasse ich meine Mutter.* Münster: tende Verlag, 1981.

Schmitz-Köster, Dorothee. *Trobadora und Kassandra und ... Weibliches Schreiben in der DDR,* Köln: Pahl-Rugenstein, 1989.

Schroeder, Margot. *Der Schlachter empfiehlt noch immer Herz.* Munich: Frauenbuchverlag, 1976.

Schubert, Helga. *Judasfrauen.* Frankfurt: Luchterhand, 1990.

Schütting, Jutta/Julian. *Der Vater: Erzählung.* Salzburg: Residenz, 1980.

Schwaiger, Brigitte. *Lange Abwesenheit.* Wien/Hamburg: Zsolnay, 1980.

_____. *Why Is There Salt in the Sea?* Lincoln: University of Nebraska Press, 1988.

_____. *Wie kommt das Salz ins Meer?* Wien/Hamburg: Zsolnay Verlag, 1977.

Stefan, Verena. *Shedding and Literally dreaming.* New York: Feminist Press at the City University of New York, 1994. (First published as: *Häutungen: Autobiografische Aufzeichnungen, Gedichte, Träume, Analysen,* Munich: Verlag Frauenoffensive, 1975.

Struck, Karin. *Die Mutter.* Frankfurt: Suhrkamp, 1975.

Tetzner, Gerti. *Karen W.* Halle/Leipzig: Mitteldeutscher Verlag, 1974.

Walker, Barbara C. *The Women's Encyclopedia of Myths and Secrets.* San Francisco: Harper & Row, 1983.

Weigel, Sigrid. *Die Stimme der Medusa: Schreibweisen in der Gegenwartsliteratur von Frauen.* Dulmen-Hiddingsel: Tende, 1987.

Weil, Grete. *Meine Schwester Antigone. Roman.* Zurich/Cologne: Benzinger, 1980.

Williams, Arthur and Parkes, Stuart, ed. *The Individual, Identity and Innovation. Signals from Contemporary Literature and the New Germany,* Berne: Peter Lang, 1994.

Wohmann, Gabriele. *Ausflug mit der Mutter.* Darmstadt, Luchterhand, 1976.

Wolf, Christa. *A Model Childhood.* New York: Farrar, Straus, & Giroux, 1980. Subsequently republished under the title *Patterns of Childhood.* First published as *Kindheitsmuster,* Darmstadt/Neuwied: Luchterhand, 1977.

Wolf, Christa. *Kassandra. Vier Vorlesungen. Eine Erzählung.* Berlin/Weimar: Aufbau-Verlag, 1983.

_____. *Medea. Stimmen.* Munich: Luchterhand, 1996.

Additional Notable Post-WW II Writers

Katja Behrens (1942). Elisabeth Borchers (1926), Barbara Bronnen (1938), Brigitte Burmeister (1940), Daniela Dahn (1949), Eva Demski (1944), Hilde Domin (1912), Elke Erb (1938), Fless Bettina (1961), Barbara Frischmuth (1941), Kirsten Hensel (1961), Hanna Johansen (1939), Sarah Kirsch (1935), Ursula Krechel (1947), Ilse Langner (1899), Christine Lavant (1915), Gertrud Leutenegger (1948), Friederike Mayröcker (1924), Angelika Mechtel (1943), Johanna Moosdorf (1911), Christine Nöstlinger (1936), Birgit Pausch (1942), Erica Pedretti (1930 - 1994), Renate Rasp (1935), Brigitte Reimann (1933-1973), Friederike Roth (1948), Erika Runge (1939), Herrad Schenk (1948), Helga Schubert (1940), Helga Schuetz (1937), Jutta/Julian Schutting (1937), Brigitte Schwaiger (1949), Ginka Steinwachs (1942), Marlene Streeruwitz (1950), Eva Zeller (1923).

"THOU BLEEDING PIECE OF EARTH"

The Affinity of Aesthetics and Ethics and
Erich Fried's Poems

Walter Pape

1. After Virtue

"**E**verything that exists is an analogue of all things that exist; our existence therefore seems to be divided and related at the same time. If one follows too much analogy, everything becomes identical; if one avoids analogy, everything is scattered into infinity. In both cases reflection is stagnant; it is either too lively, or it is deadened."[1] What Goethe thematizes in this maxim from *Wilhelm Meister* is the problematical relation between the complexity of perception and rational order and explanation of multi-faceted impressions. It is the central issue of modern rational scientific discourse: How can an approach that is itself abstract and generalizing at once do justice to a phenomenon, its various aspects, and the requirements of rational judgment? And secondly: In what way does ratio-

---

1. Goethe, *Wilhelm Meisters Wanderjahre.* 2. Buch, Betrachtungen Nr. 115 *Sämtliche Werke. Briefe, Tagebücher und Gespräche,* ed. Hendrik Birus et al. Vol. I, 10. Ed. Gerhard Neumann and Hans-Georg Dewitz (Frankfurt: Deutscher Klassiker Verlag 1989), 575: "Jedes Existierende ist ein Analogon alles Existierenden; daher erscheint uns das Dasein immer zu gleicher Zeit gesondert und verknüpft. Folgt man der Analogie zu sehr, so fällt alles identisch zusammen; meidet man sie, so zerstreut sich alles in's Unendliche. In beiden Fällen stagniert die Betrachtung, einmal als überlebendig, das andere Mal als getötet."

nalistic separation and isolation of specific parts, traits, and qualities affect our perception? The dilemma is comparable to the question as to how language controls and influences our perception of "reality".

Habermas is right in pointing out that in "everyday communication, cognitive interpretations, moral expectations, expressions, and evaluations cannot help overlapping and interpenetrating."[2] Even the different modes or parts of communication are often linked by analogy and metaphors of the different realms. To "everyday communication" Habermas, following Max Weber, opposes the "expert cultures" of science, morals, and art. These "autonomous sectors,"[3] which Kant tried to separate in clarifying the different modes of perception and judgement, in modern times indubitably tend to model cultural phenomena according to their individual perspectives. Kant tried to disentangle the modes of perception in his discussion of analogy. He tried to explain, as Marian Hobson put it, "the deep and mysterious way we connect together what we perceive."[4] Kant posed as a cardinal question how we position an object for our ideas (Vorstellungen)[5]. But that did not mean that Kant intended to separate aesthetic, moral, and rational or scientific judgment in order to claim clearly separated *objects* of reference for them. Aesthetic, moral and political judgments can be theoretically discerned, but none of them have specific objects. Thus aesthetic judgment does not depend on the subject of the work of art, nor did Kant or his followers claim peculiar works of art for a "non-interested pleasure."[6] Even the "Ausdifferenzierung des Kunstsystems" (differentiation of the art systems)[7], as Luhmann never tires of observing, cannot but systematize the question of the actual participation of art (its form, its objects, its reception) in other social systems; yet, reading the "history" of aesthetics and literary or art history as a, if not straight, nevertheless irreversible process towards a "reflecting form of self-reference",[8] ignores

2. Habermas, *Moral Consciousness and Communicative Action*. Transl. by Christian Lenhardt and Shierry Weber Nicholson. Introduction by Thomas McCarthy (Cambridge, MA: MIT Press, 1990), 18.

3. Ibid, 19.

4. Cf. Marian Hobson, "What Is Wrong with Saint Peters's: Or, Diderot, Analogy, and Illusion in Architecture,"in *Reflecting Senses: Appearance and Perception in Literature, Culture, and the Arts*, Walter Pape and Frederick Burwick (Berlin, New York: de Gruyter, 1995), 53-74. here 73.

5. Kant, *Kritik der reinen Vernunft, Werke in zehn Bänden*. Sonderausgabe, ed. Wilhelm Weischedel. (Darmstadt: Wissenschaftliche Buchgesellschaft, 1983), vol. 3, 232 (A 197).

6. Immanuel Kant, *Kritik der ästhetischen Urteilskraft*, ibid., vol. 8, 288 (A 17, 18) and 319 (A 61).

7. Cf. now Niklas Luhmann, *Die Kunst der Gesellschaft* (Frankfurt: Suhrkamp, 1995), esp. 244-392.

8. Ibid., 498.

the fact that "art" is no way a homogeneous phenomenon, either in the eighteenth century or today[9].

Why something is regarded as beautiful does not depend on its moral qualities, but nevertheless the piece of art can be judged morally. Art is embedded in more than one culture, in everyday culture, where moral, scientific, and aesthetic spheres are not separated, and in professional cultures. But even an expert in aesthetics can never read a text, listen to a piece of music, look at a painting, or view a film or a video only according to his aesthetic expertise. Pure aesthetic judgment needs a process of refinement of actual perception. There certainly are realms of art that try to comply with that pure aesthetic judgement, but there is no reason why these works should not have moral or social functions, and even overt or hidden moral or social intentions. Marlies Janz in her study on Paul Celan (1976) has demonstrated that there is no definite contradiction between aesthetic absolutism and social and political engagement.[10] No wonder that for Fried Hölderlin is the poet who combines both in an archetypical way.

Discussing the relationship between ethics and aesthetics has been a central issue in postmodern aesthetics, even in public discourse.[11] Lothar Bredalla used a series of eight articles on *Ethics and Aesthetics*, published from April to September 1992 in the *Frankfurter Rundschau,* as a forum for his recent discussion of this crucial relationship. He not only reveals the ethics behind the arguments of the advocates of a strict separation of ethics and aesthetics, he also asks the decisive question as to "why it is good to protect art from ethics." He muses: "Do we appreciate horror, cruelty and pain in the aesthetic experience, but reject them when we judge them ethically? Do we live in completely separate worlds? Is it not an impoverishment of the aesthetic experience if we exclude ethical evaluations from it?"[12]

The collapse of the GDR as a political system seemed to be also the ultimate termination of a literature that follows some dubious *Gesin-*

9. Cf. Walter Muschg, "Dichtertypen," *Gestalten und Figuren*. Auswahl von Elli Muschg-Zollikofer (Berne, Munich: Francke, 1968), 7-27, here 7.

10. Marlies Janz, *Vom Engagement absoluter Poesie: Zur Lyrik und Ästhetik Paul Celans* (Frankfurt: Syndikat, 1976), 7. On the relation between ethics and autonomous art see Klaus Günther, "Das gute und das schöne Leben. Ist moralisches Handeln ästhetisch und läßt sich aus ästhetischer Erfahrung moralisch lernen?" in *Ethik und Ästhetik: Nachmetaphysische Perspektiven,* ed. Gerhard Gamm and Gerd Kimmerle (Tübingen: edition discord, 1990) (Tübinger Beiträge zu Philosophie und Gesellschaftskritik. 2), 11-37.

11. Cf. the very substantial volume ed. by Gerhard Hoffmann and Alfred Hornung, *Ethics and Aesthetics: The Moral Turn of Postmodernism.* (Heidelberg: Winter, 1996).

12. Bredella, "Aesthetics and Ethics: Inommensurable, Identical or Conflicting?" Ibid., 27-51, here 30.

nungsästhetik (aestheticized morality)[13]. But in spite of the various funerals of this aesthetics celebrated in some newspapers and journals, the end of the GDR and the end of communism as a state ideology, together with the postmodern debate about the contingency of values and the deconstructionist belief in the self-referentiality of language, have proved that relativism and skepticism are of no use in understanding the post-1989 cultural condition.

Against this background of a post-postmodern critique of modern rational professional cultures and against the background of the latest discussion of ethics and aesthetics there are definitely some arguments to be added to the discussions about autonomous literature and *littérature engagée* in Germany after World War II. The request for pure literature is no longer the latest craze, as it seemed to be shortly after German unification. The debate about Christa Wolf proved that the central issue is due less to different kinds of literature – one that follows aestheticized morality and politics, the other sticking to a concept of autonomous literature – than it is the offspring of a rigorous claim to the isolation of professional cultures. Literature and the arts, of course, can theoretically be differentiated into a system of their own. But the primary goal of the "inventors" of artistic autonomy was not to create an independent system that only may have contact to other systems at its outer margins, but to make art the "system" whereby isolated social systems can be reunified through different modes of perception and judgement.

The relation between the beautiful on the one hand and morality and ethics on the other has been blurred by the reception of Kant in German aesthetics; Kant's definition of beauty as an object of pleasure without interest, as form without the idea of any purpose, was only later used as a legitimation of a morally indifferent *l'art pour l'art*. Kant, like Schiller, connects the morally good with the beautiful, though not directly by theme or by form as did the aesthetics of the enlightenment, but by metaphor: " beauty is a symbol of ethics (des Sittlichguten)."[14] A precondition of recognizing these metaphorical transformations of the good into the beautiful for the reader of a text or the viewer of a piece of art is the "development of ethical ideas and the culture of moral sentiment."

13. Cf. Greiner, "Die deutsche Gesinnungsästhetik. Noch einmal: Christa Wolf und der deutsche Literaturstreit. Eine Zwischenbilanz," in *"Es geht nicht um Christa Wolf": Der Literaturstreit im vereinten Deutschland,* ed. Thomas Anz (Munich: Spangenberg, 1991) (edition Spangenberg), 208-16, here 213. See also the contributions of Terence James Reed and Karl-Heinz Schoeps in *1870/71 – 1989/90: German Unifications and the Change of Literary Discourse,* ed. Walter Pape (Berlin, New York: de Gruyter, 1993) (European Cultures. 1).

14. Kant, *Kritik der ästhetischen Urteilskraft, Werke,* vol. 8 (see note), 461.

Kant deliberately describes the nexus of perception and judgment as a process of analogy: aesthetic judgment (taste) is nothing but "the ability of judging the sensualization (Versinnlichung) of ethical ideas by a certain analogical reflection (Analogie der Reflexion) on both", that is on the beautiful as a symbol (or metaphor) of ethical ideas.[15] Going back to Kant and Schiller in this case does not mean to redefine modern aesthetics by going back to its roots.[16] It could mean rereading Kant by using his concept of analogy as a means of remembering modern art's forgotten complexity and its amalgamation with ethical discourse.

However Nietzsche's skepticism in questions of truth and morality contributed to the impact of professional cultures on cultural practices. If one part of an analogical process becomes dubious, the other part has to free itself from these doubts. As in many other cultural discourses the metaphor lost its metaphorical quality;[17] thus art *(pour l'art)* is also a metaphor of which the reference tends to be forgotten. Kant's concept of aesthetic judgment could become so widely accepted because this kind of judgment seems to be free from any cultural, social, and moral implications. The concentration on the mode of symbolization blurred the symbolized cultural phenomena.

Alasdair C. MacIntyre's *After Virtue* (1981, translated into German in 1987 as *Der Verlust der Tugend: Zur moralischen Krise der Gegenwart*), to which Habermas refers in his discussion of ethics, no longer seems to represent the actual state of the arts: Nothing but a consistent philosophical concept of ethics is lost, not its omnipresence in cultural and political discourses. MacIntyre also made clear in his *History of Ethics* as early as 1966 why communication in ethics is so difficult.[18] There still is a somewhat homogeneous moral vocabulary, but the contrast between the language of moral judgment with its firm set of valid moral rules backing it, and the language of predelection and interest has vanished not only because "in our society the acids of individualism have for four centuries eaten into our moral structures, for both good and ill," but because "we live with the inheritance of not only one, but of a number of well-integrated moralities. Aristotelianism, primitive Christian simplicity, the puritan ethic, the aristocratic ethic of consumption, and the

15. Ibid., 465.

16. See e.g. the various ways of approximation of ethics and aesthetics Herbert Grabes describes in his essay "Ethics, Aesthetics, and Alterity," in *Ethics and Aesthetics,* ed. Hoffmann and Hornung (see note), 13-28, here 14-16: "Approximation via Re-definition."

17. Cf. e. g. Nietzsche, "Über Wahrheit und Lüge im außermoralischen Sinne," *Sämtliche Werke.* Kritische Studienausgabe in 15 Bänden, ed. Giorgio Colli and Mazzino Montinari (Munich: Deutscher Taschenbuch Verlag; Berlin: de Gruyter, 1980), vol. 1, 883.

18. For the following see MacIntyre, *A Short History of Ethics* (New York: Macmillan 1966), esp. 265-69.

traditions of democracy and socialism have all left their mark upon our moral vocabulary."[19] For some postmodern philosophers, skepticism seems to be the latest craze: as no reasons can be given for a "secularized morality free of metaphysical and religious assumptions," the notion of the capacity for truth of practical questions has to be abandoned.[20]

Following the questionable notion discussed above, modern aesthetics has freed art from its references to life (Lebensbezüge)[21] and thus from all practical function and responsibilty. Waiving "extra-literary themes" as non-aesthetic,[22] sticking to a mere magic of abstraction (Zauber der Abstraktion) after World War II, were termed by Walter Muschg, an admirer and pioneer in literary criticism of the avant-garde, a "flight from reality" and "literary industry" as early as 1964.[23]

From these premises I want to look back on Erich Fried, who died in November 1988, one year before the much debated November of 1989, from a perspective of postmodernism as basically being the "modern label of mannerism as a meta-historical category."[24] In this retrospective I want to show, with a few examples from Erich Fried's poems, that the realm of art, especially in modernity (1800 and after) is not (only) the beautiful, but the sublime (which does not fall within a disinterested pleasure); and secondly, that Erich Fried (and others, of course) tries to open the isolated spheres of moral and art and "mediate," as Habermas would call it, "between the everyday world and cultural modernity with its autonomous sectors."[25]

It was Christa Wolf who in her early essay *Tagebuch. Arbeitsmittel und Gedächtnis* (Diary. Tools and Memory, 1964) posited the "banality of the good" (Banalität des Guten) against Hannah Arendt's "banality of evil", and thus pointed to the importance of everyday communication and its values in a world that grows more and more violent, more and more labyrinthine for the individual; she goes so far as to say that "the ordinary, the common, the obvious – they alone form security against Treblinka."[26] Erich Fried's verses were very often accused of being trite, and he may

19. Ibid. 266.

20. Habermas, *Moral Consciousness* (see note), 43.

21. Helmut Kuhn, "Ästhetik," in *Literatur II*, ed. Wolf-Hartmut Friedrich and Walther Killy, Part 1. 7th ed. (Frankfurt.: Fischer Taschenbuch Verlag, 1974), 53.

22. Greiner, "Die deutsche Gesinnungsästhetik. Noch einmal: Christa Wolf und der deutsche Literaturstreit. Eine Zwischenbilanz," in *"Es geht nicht um Christa Wolf,"* ed. Anz (see note), 208-16, here 213.

23. Muschg, "Der Zauber der Abstraktion," *Studien zur tragischen Literaturgeschichte* (Berne, Munich: Francke, 1965), 9-30, here 28.

24. Umberto Eco, *Nachschrift zum "Namen der Rose"* (Postille a "Il nome della rosa", dt.) Transl. Burkhart Kroeber. 4th ed. (Munich: Hanser, 1984), 77.

25. Habermas, *Moral Consciousness* (see note), 19.

26. Wolf, "Tagebuch – Arbeitsmittel und Gedächtnis," *Lesen und Schreiben: Aufsätze und Prosastücke* (Darmstadt, Neuwied: Luchterhand, 1972) (Sammlung Luchterhand.

serve as a somewhat extreme example of an writer who adheres to aestheticized morality. But unlike most modern writers he does not accompany his work with explicit theoretical reflections, which makes him even more suitable for a concise discussion of the problem at hand.[27] There is no necessity here to discuss the intricate, yet very German question of political poetry as such;[28] the analysis will show that even in radical (post)modern aesthetics and arts, as Terence James Reed puts it, "'aesthetic' and 'political' " cannot be set against each other because they cannot be neatly separated, either in acts of creation or in acts of judgement."[29] The "object" of Erich Fried's *littérature engagée* is taken from a political context, but the poem's discourse transcends it.

2. "You can't do that … "

One year before he died, Erich Fried recalled in a dialogue with Heiner Müller that "Biermann once sung a poem, a song – 'Enfant Perdu' – on Flori's [Florian, Robert Havemann's son] marching off, that he now is corrupted in the West. What he ought to know.is that Flori, unfortunately, was so rigid that he can't be corrupted at all. But when he met him again in the West, he said: 'O dear, I'm glad to see now that I did wrong you.' And some weeks later he recorded this song. You can't do that …"[30] Even when Wolf Biermann sang this song, knowingly based on erro-

90), 61-75, here 67-68: "Gewöhnliches, Durchschnittliches, Selbstverständliches – das allein ist wirksame und dauerhafte Garantie gegen Treblinka."

27. On Fried's aesthetics and his poetological poems see also Michael Zeller, *Gedichte haben Zeit: Aufriß einer zeitgenössischen Poetik* (Stuttgart: Klett, 1982) (Literaturwissenschaft, Gesellschaftswissenschaft. 57), especially 186-95.

28. On this topic see my "'Die Wüsten- und Löwenpoesie war im Grunde auch nur revolutionair': Ästhetischer Ursprung und ethische Legitimation von politischer Lyrik im 19. Jahrhundert am Beispiel Ferdinand Freiligraths," *Kontroversen, alte und neue. Akten des VII. Internationalen Germanistenkongresses, Göttingen 1985*, (Tübingen: Niemeyer, 1986) vol. 8, 66–77; and my "'Ein Orpheus – mit den Liedern Andrer!' Ferdinand Freiligraths Anthologie poetologischer Lyrik *Dichtung und Dichter*," *Grabbe-Jahrbuch*, 6 (1987), 82–104.

29. Reed, "Another Piece of the Past,.." *1870/71 – 1989/90: German Unifications and the Change of Literary Discourse*, ed. Pape (see note), 234-50, here 248.

30. Erich Fried and Heiner Müller, *Ein Gespräch geführt am 16.10.1987 in Frankfurt/Main*. Mit sechzehn Fotos von Cornelius Groenewold (Berlin: Alexander, 1989), 13: "Der Biermann hat ein Gedicht, ein Lied gesungen – ,Enfant Perdu' – über den Abmarsch vom Flori, daß der jetzt da im Westen korrumpiert wird. Was er eigentlich hätte wissen müssen, ist, daß der Flori, Gott sei's geklagt, dermaßen verkrampft war, daß er gar nicht korrumpierbar ist. Und als er ihn im Westen wiedertraf, sagte er: ,Du, ich bin froh, daß ich jetzt sehe, daß ich Dir Unrecht getan habe.' Und ein paar Wochen später hat er dieses Lied auf einer Platte gesungen. Das darf man doch nicht".

neous presuppositions, in 1976 on the occasion of the (in)famous concert in Cologne that was to initiate his expatriation, he did not sing the whole song, but "some verses that are still important to me."[31]

"You can't do that ...": no other phrase could characterize Fried's morality better than this one. His statement also reveals that Fried is not interested in the political issue of Biermann's song the refrain of which ambiguously mourns that Flori Havemann is "gone" ("hinüber," meaning both "to the other side" and "dead"): "From East to West – a German case" (Von Ost nach West – ein deutscher Fall; "Fall" meaning also "downfall"), whereas the last three stanzas assert that the GDR in the long run needs neither prison nor wall. Erich Fried, who was always convinced of the communist party's miserable deprivation under Stalinism,[32] seems less interested in Biermann's brave utopian belief than in individual moral behavior. His verdict is based upon unmediated moral sentiment: "You should not repeat statements that have been shown to be not in accordance with facts"; without long consideration in everyday life we know: "You can't do that ...". Erich Fried concentrates on moral behavior, Biermann on political issues and a good performance of a piece of his art.

P. F. Strawson has investigated moral intuition in everyday life, especially indignation and resentment, and Habermas says: "Feelings seem to have a similar function for the moral justification of action as sense perceptions have for the theoretical justification of facts." Sentiments are preconditioned by a cultural and biographical context; hence Fried is not interested in a "feeling-neutral assessment of means-ends relations,"[33] but in what Habermas calls, in contrast to the normative principles of a moral system, *Sittlichkeit* (ethical substance of life), which can hold its ground against even the most ferocious rationalist: "In a word, the skeptic may reject morality, but he cannot reject the ethical substance of the life circumstances in which he spends his waking hours, not unless he is willing to take refuge in suicide or serious mental illness."[34] Advocats of discourse ethics like Habermas or Odo Marquard or the American communitarists are thus revitalizing the Aristetolian and Hegelian concept of *Sittlichkeit* and its foundation in customs, manners, institutions, forms of life and the use of language.[35] For that reason *Sittlichkeit* is a form of

---

31. Phonograph Recording: *Das geht sein' sozialistischen Gang.* CBS 88 224. 1977.

32. Fried, "Mißtrauen lernen," *Gesammelte Werke*, ed. Volker Kaukoreit and Klaus Wagenbach, vol. 1-4 (Berlin: Wagenbach, 1993), vol. 4, 612.

33. Cf. Habermas, *Moral Consciousness* (see note 2), 45-50.

34. Ibid., 100.

35. Cf. *Moral und Sittlichkeit: Das Problem Hegels und die Diskursethik*, ed. Wolfgang Kuhlmann (Frankfurt: Suhrkamp, 1986) (Suhrkamp Taschenbuch Wissenschaft. 595), 8 and Habermas' essay "Moralität und Sittlichkeit. Treffen Hegels Einwände gegen Kant auch auf die Diskursethik zu?" ibid., 16-37, esp. 24-25. See also Wolfgang Kersting,

ethics that has no need to refer to transcendence or religion; there is no need for ultimate reasons.

Consequently, with the loss of transcendence modern literature can be the symbol of the ethical substance of life, not of a moral system; thus it is only indirectly linked with politics. Before the eighteenth century no moral science was recognized outside the contexts of society and state, because they alone made it possible to speak of ethics, as Thomas Hobbes argued.[36] The eighteenth century, however, introduced the idea of the dualism of the modern world which divided the political and social reality of man from his individuality.[37] Politics, especially in the German tradition, is equated with the state, not with a society of communicative individuals. Thus even today Max Weber's definition is regarded as the German notion of politics: "In our terms, then, 'politics' would mean striving for a share of power or for influence on the distribution of power, whether it be between states or between the groups of people contained within a single state."[38] Erich Fried, like many other writers on "political topics", again attaches politics to the ethical substance of life circumstances; his political poems thus do not illustrate rational moral principles by example, as did the political fable of the Enlightenment, and as did minor socialist or other political poets up to the present. Basically his work, and the works of other authors concerned about "aestheticized morality", is aesthetic in an older sense of the word: politics is absorbed by ethics expressed in aesthetic representations of sensual perceptions in order to incite feelings (of moral justification).

Günter Grass, however, without mentioning Fried's name, in his poem "Zorn, Ärger, Wut" (Wrath, Anger, Rage) consigned Fried's poems ... *und Vietnam und* ..., originally published between 1964 and 1966 in *konkret*, to the category of poems of protest: "Helpless I protest against the protesting poems ... Like steel has its economic trend, poetry has its economic trend. / Armament opens the markets for anti-war poems. / Production costs are low. / Take: one eighth of righteous anger, / two eighths of daily nuisance / and five eighths, to get a foretaste of it, of helpless rage."[39] At a

---

"Sittlichkeit, Sittenlehre," *Historisches Wörterbuch der Philosophie,* ed. Joachim Ritter and Karlfried Gründer, [thus far:] vol. 1-9 (Darmstadt: Wissenschaftliche Buchgesellschaft, 1971-95), vol. 9. cc. 907-23, here cc. 921-22.

36. The following according to Joachim Ritter, "Ethik," Ibid., vol. 2, cc. 759-95, esp. cc. 770ff.

37. Ibid., c. 772.

38. Weber, "The Profession and Vocation of Politics," *Political Writings,* ed. Peter Lassmann and Ronald Speirs (Cambridge: Cambridge University Press, 1994) (Cambridge Texts in the History of Political Thought), 309-69, here 311.

39. Günter Grass, *Werkausgabe in zehn Bänden,* ed. Volker Neuhaus, (Darmstadt und Neuwied: Luchterhand, 1987), vol. 1, 183: "Ohnmächtig protestiere ich gegen

closer look it becomes evident that "Zorn, Ärger, Wut" may offer an image of an ordinary member of the peace movement, but neither the content nor the intent of Fried's poems. It would be too simple to regard Fried as nothing but a "rasenden Verworter" (manic wordsmith).[40] Unlike Günter Grass, Karl Heinz Bohrer in 1968 aligned Fried with the German Romantic poets and the metaphysical poets of the English Renaissance, pointing at the tension between "actual information and hermetic expression." Even in Fried's political poems of … *und Vietnam und* …, according to Bohrer, "the terrifying had been expressed in a far too beautiful, far too parabolic manner,"[41] whereas Heiner Müller reproached Fried for the transparency of his poems.[42]

Twenty-two years later Karl Heinz Bohrer would not have criticized Fried's poem for their beauty but rather for their *Gesinnung* (moral principles), because he certainly belonged to the "alte Garde der für den Sinn zuständigen" (the Old Guard of those responsible for sense and significance.)[43] After the end of power-politics and of the confrontation between communism and capitalism, neo-conservatism in asethetics became influential on the literary scene. Though in 1990 Bohrer, in his essay "Die Ästhetik am Ausgang ihrer Unmündigkeit" (Aesthetics at the close of its immaturity),[44] summarized only his former aesthetic concept, this essay can serve as an example of an aesthetic shift among the trendy literary coterie after 1989. The alleged tradition of an anti-moralistic aesthetics (Schlegel, Nietzsche, Baudelaire etc.) is seen in his essay as a mere construction; with regard to a "philosophy of poetry" Schlegel indeed advised beginning with the independence of the beautiful and separating it from truth and ethics;[45] but that did not mean that truth or moral-

---

ohnmächtige Proteste" – : "Wie der Stahl seine Konjunktur hat, hat Lyrik ihre Konjunktur. / Aufrüstung öffnet die Märkte für Antikriegsgedichte. / Die Herstellungskosten sind gering. / Man nehme: ein Achtel gerechten Zorn, / zwei Achtel alltäglichen Ärger / und fünf Achtel, damit sie vorschmeckt, ohnmächtige Wut."

40. Walter Hinck, "Erich Fried, der rasende Verworter: Drei Bände mit seiner Lyrik und Prosa," *Frankfurter Allgemeine Zeitung* No. 12, 14. 11. 1984, "Bilder und Zeiten", 5. Hinck's title is a pun on "rasender Reporter", the title of a book by the famous reporter Egon Erwin Kisch.

41. Bohrer, "Befreiung von der Flucht? Erich Fried's 'Gedichte und Gegengedichte'," *Frankfurter Allgemeine Zeitung*, No. 172, 27.7.1968.

42. Fried/Müller, *Ein Gespräch* (see note), 27.

43. Bohrer, "Kulturschutzgebiet DDR?" *Merkur* 44 (10/1990), No. 500, 1015-18, here 1016.

44. Bohrer, "Die Ästhetik am Ausgang ihrer Unmündigkeit." *Merkur* 44 (10/1990) H. 500, 851-65.

45. Schlegel, "Athenäums-Fragmente". *Schriften zur Literatur*, Hrsg. von Wolfdietrich Rasch. 2. Aufl. Munich: Deutscher Taschenbuch Verlag, 1985 (dtv-Taschenbuch. 2148), 25-83, here 53: "Eine Philosophie der Poesie überhaupt aber würde mit der Selb-

ity were excluded from the *work of art* and its reception. Schlegel deliberately pointed at the connection of the beautiful and ethics in the work of art: "essential aesthetic *Sittlichkeit* (*Sittlichkeit* as such is the preponderance of pure humanity over animality in desire) thus is a necessary part of the perfect beauty."[46] And in his essay on Lessing he turns against the "trendy aestheticians who make no difference and are full of contempt against everything that might be called moral or actually is moral."[47] Even in the discussion of the sublime, Bohrer tries to identify modern disinterested and non-metaphysical aesthetics with the sublime. For Kant the "sense for the sublime" was made possible only by "a frame of mind similar to the moral,"[48] whereas Bohrer only uses arguments in favor of a sublime which is nothing but a surprisingly innovative interruption of a context of expectations, aiming neither at truth nor at advocating life.[49] A sublime, in Bohrer's sense, reduced to some rhetorical device, to some contingent aesthetic phenomenon of difference with regard to the non-identical[50] is, like the end of history, "nothing but the dream of satiated elites."[51] Likewise, the aesthetics of literary autonomy never did free art from ethics; Schiller, who very clearly distinguished the aesthetic *judgement* from the moral *judgment*, was well aware that it is "a commendable characteristic of mankind that it at least in aesthetic judgments stands up for the good thing" (achtungswerter Charakterzug der Menschheit [ist], daß sie sich wenigstens in ästhetischen Urteilen zu der guten Sache bekennt).[52]

In contrast to participants in the discussion of aesthetics after 1989 like Bohrer, I want to re-read aesthetic theory and Fried's poems by asserting that poetry did not lose its function as a cultural memory. The

---

ständigkeit des Schönen beginnen, mit dem Satz, daß es vom Wahren und Sittlichen getrennt sei und getrennt sein sollte"; Bohrer, "Die Ästhetik am Ausgang ihrer Unmündigkeit" (see note), 856.

46. Schlegel, "Über das Studium der griechischen Poesie". *Schriften zur Literatur* (see note) 84-192, here 166: "wesentliche ästhetische Sittlichkeit (Sittlichkeit überhaupt ist das Übergewicht der reinen Menschheit über die Tierheit im Begehrungsvermögen) ist daher ein notwendiger Bestandteil der vollkommenen Schönheit."

47. Schlegel, "Über Lessing". Ibid., 215-49, here 219: "modische, nichts unterscheidende Verachtung der Ästhetiker gegen alles, was moralisch heißen will oder wirklich ist."

48. Kant, *Kritik der Urteilskraft. Werke in zehn Bänden* (see note), vol. 8, 358 (A 115): "in der Tat läßt sich ein Gefühl für das Erhabene der Natur nicht wohl denken, ohne eine Stimmung des Gemütes, die der zum Moralischen ähnlich ist, damit zu verbinden."

49. Bohrer, "Die Ästhetik am Ausgang ihrer Unmündigkeit," (see note), 864-65.

50. Ibid. 864 and 862.

51. Heiner Müller, "Bautzen oder Babylon," *Sinn und Form*, 43 (1991), 664: "das Ende der Geschichte ist ein Wunschtraum saturierter Eliten."

52. Schiller, "Vom Erhabenen" . *Sämtliche Werke*, ed. Gerhard Fricke und Herbert G. Göpfert, 4th ed., vol. 1-5 (Munich: Hanser, 1967), vol. 5, 512.

abandoning of mimesis and imitatio (in the Romantic era and other-wise) did not leave "the poet to the solitary task of self-examination and personal anamnesis",[53] or free poetry from transcendence and meta-physics, for literature and poetry can hardly be imagined without some reference to the divine, be it even through negation.

3. "Help to Harden Hearts"

Erich Fried's most controversial poem, "Auf den Tod des Generalbunde-sanwalts Siegfried Buback",[54] may well serve as an example of sublimity in the tradition of the enlightenment, Schiller, and Adorno, which I want to oppose to the one favored by some aestheticians of postmodernism:

1	1
Was soll ich sagen	What shall I say
von einem toten Menschen	about a dead man
der auf der Straße lag	lying in the street
zerfetzt von Schüssen	ripped apart by shots
den ich nicht kannte	whom I did not know
und nur wenig zu kennen glaubte	and whom I thought to know but little
aus einigen seiner Taten	for some of his deeds
und einigen seiner Worte?	and for some of his words?
2	2
Dies Stück Fleisch	This piece of flesh
war einmal ein Kind	once was a child
und spielte	and played
Dieses Stück Fleisch	This piece of flesh
war einmal ein Vater	once was a father
voll Liebe	full of love
Dieses Stück Fleisch	This piece of flesh
glaubte Recht zu tun	thought to do right
und tat Unrecht	and did wrong
Dieses Stück Fleisch	This piece of flesh
war ein Mensch	was a man
und wäre wahrscheinlich	and probably
ein besserer Mensch	would have been
gewesen	a better man
in einer besseren Welt	in a better world

53. This is the argument of Michel Beaujour, "Memory in Poetics," in *Memoria: Vergessen und Erinnern*, ed. Anselm Haverkamp, Renate Lachmann, and Reinhart Herzog (Munich: Fink, 1993) (Poetik und Hermeneutik. 15), 9-16, here 16.

54. Fried, *Gesammelte Werke* (see note), vol. 2, 316-18, first published in: Fried, *So kam ich unter die Deutschen: Gedichte* (Hamburg: Association 1977), 103-06.

3
Aber genügt das?
Könnte man nicht dasselbe
von anderen Menschen sagen
die eingingen in die Geschichte
befleckt und verurteilt
vom Nachruhm
ihrer Unmenschlichkeit?

4
Was er für Recht hielt
hat Menschen
schaudern gemacht

Was er für Recht hielt
hat dieses Recht
in Verruf gebracht

Seine Nachrufe waren
nur so
wie Nachrufe sind

5
Was er getan hat
im Leben
davon wurde mir kalt ums Herz

Soll mir nun warm ums Herz werden
durch seinen Tod?

6
Der Abscheu vor ihm
half Herzen
verhärten wie seines

sein Tod
wird helfen
sein Lebenswerk fortzusetzen

Sein Tod
wird helfen
das Denken auf ihn abzulenken

und so verdecken das Unrecht
von dem dieser Mensch
nur ein Teil war

Schon darum
kann ich nicht ja sagen
zu seinem Tod

vor dem mir
fast so sehr graut
wie vor seinem Leben

3
However, is that enough?
Couldn't that also be said
of other men
who became part of history
sullied and condemned
by the fame
of their inhumanity?

4
What he thought right
made men
shiver

What he thought right
brought the law
into disrepute

His obituaries
were just
as orbituaries are

5
What he did
during his lifetime
made my heart freeze

Why should my heart be warmed
by his death?

6
The abhorrence of him
Help to harden
Hearts like his own

his death
will help
to continue his lifework

His death
will help
to divert thoughts of him

and thus conceal the wrong
of which this man
was but a part

And that is why
I cannot say yes
to his death

of which I am
terrified almost as much
as of his life

7	7
Es wäre besser gewesen	It would have been better
so ein Mensch	if such a man
wäre nicht so gestorben	had not died this way
Es wäre besser gewesen	It would have been better
ein Mensch hätte	if a man had
nicht so gelebt	not lived this way

During a debate in the German Bundestag on 28 October 1977 the then Secretary of Justice Hans Jochen Vogel (SPD) alluded to this poem: the murder of Buback, he said, "had received a certain approval even beyond the limits of the underworld." Vogel was, among others, thinking "of a writer who hastily got hold of the murdered in order to defame him in miserable verses. These events ... recall the onset of the Weimar Republic, when the murder of a Matthias Erzberger and a Walther Rathenau was enthusiastically applauded by the dazzled, or of the cynicism with which Adolf Hitler in 1932 affirmed his solidarity with the murderers of Potempa."[55] Read in this way, the poem would indeed represent an outright pamphlet; Fried, however, "amidst the most violent emotions" (mitten im heftigsten Affekt), as Schiller would put it,[56] preserved emotional freedom and removed the murder of the *Generalbundesanwalt* from the hot-tempered actual debate into a sublime sphere with a biblical tone and a rhythm reminiscent of Hölderlin. The phrases used in the second part of the poem ("This piece of flesh / was a man") served the critics of *Die Zeit* and the *Frankfurter Allgemeine Zeitung* as evidence for calling Fried inhuman and Nazis-like (Theo Sommer's article in *Die Zeit* was headlined "Wie im *Stürmer*") and for regarding him as a security risk (*Frankfurter Allgemeine*).[57] In contrast, Michael Zeller stressed that in the biblical use of "flesh" the "hope of an inviolable, supertemporal humanity becomes evident as it is expressed in the book of Psalms (78, 39): 'For he remembered that they were but flesh, a wind that passeth away, and cometh not again.' "[58] Fried himself referred to Shakespeare, to Mark Antony's lament for Caesar, "O, pardon me, thou bleeding piece of earth" (III:i:254).[59] At any rate, Fried transfers the political murder "from the abstraction of political notions to its existential dimension."[60]

55. Quoted from Joachim Wittkowski, *Lyrik in der Presse: Eine Untersuchung der Kritik an Wolf Biermann, Erich Fried und Ulla Hahn* (Würzburg: Königshausen & Neumann 1991) (Epistemata. Würzburger Wissenschaftliche Schriften. Reihe Literaturwiss. 67), 248.

56. Schiller, "Vom Erhabenen" . *Sämtliche Werke* (see note), 510.

57. Wittkowski, *Lyrik in der Presse* (see note), 140-41.

58. Zeller, *Gedichte haben Zeit* (see note), 180.

59. William Shakespeare, *The Riverside Shakespeare*, textual editor: G. Blakemore Evans, (Boston: Houghton Mifflin, 1974), 1120.

60. Zeller, *Gedichte haben Zeit* (see note), 180.

Buback, whose name is not mentioned in the poem, but only in the title, is transformed by rhetorical means into one sort of representative of mankind. The legal system of the Federal Republic is neither attacked, as most critics then put it, nor are current ethics suspended in favor of an advantage in power politics, as the Secretary of Justice mused, but a wrongful estimation of and judgment on an individual and the injustice practiced against him are confronted with the law in effect: "What he thought right / made men / shiver / What he thought right / brought the law / into disrepute." Apart from the question of whether Fried is factually right or not, the event, by calling the participants "the people", "he" or "a man", is existentialized through a rhetoric of the sublime. The topic of the poem thus also gains sublimity. In quite different ways Karl Heinz Bohrer, François Lyotard, or Theodor W. Adorno in his *Aesthetic Theory,* identified sublimity as the proper quality of modern art;[61] the utopian dimension of the sublime, however, has survived only in Adorno's arguments, which are closer to Schiller's and Kant's than to those of postmodernist thinkers.

The sublime relies on an experience of threat by a phenomenon that exceeds the limits of human experience and makes men shiver; murderer and murder cause a shudder in both Fried and the readers of the poem ("to his death // of which I am / terrified almost as much / as of his life") that fails to result in an experience of helplessness only because reason has knowledge of a "better world." Or, as Adorno puts it, quoting Kant: "with profound correctness Kant has defined the notion of the sublime as the resistance of the mind against superior force."[62] Only if reason resigns is the sublime experienced as powerlessness. Fried's poem concludes with a variation on Jesus's words about Judas: "It had been good for that man if he had not been born" (Matthew 26, 24): "Es wäre besser gewesen / so ein Mensch / wäre nicht so gestorben // Es wäre besser gewesen / ein Mensch hätte / nicht so gelebt." It is hardly possible to be more consistent in aesthetizing, i. e. alienating this terroristic murder and its ethic prerequisites from crude reality; both murder and murderers are actually *not* represented in this poem, as the horror resists representantion.

The passing of time seems to suggest that the sublime as a phenomenon resisting representation in literature after 1945 plays a role at least as important as the "beautiful". For Paul Crowther, in summarizing his reading of Lyotard, the object of the sublime in modern times also com-

---

61. Cf. Wolfgang Welsch, "Adornos Ästhetik: eine implizite Ästhetik des Erhabenen," in *Das Erhabene: Zwischen Grenzerfahrung und Größenwahn* ed. Christine Pries (Weinheim: VCH, Acta Humanoria 1989), 185-213.

62. Adorno, *Ästhetische Theorie. Gesammelte Schriften,* ed. Rolf Tiedemann, Gretel Adorno, Susan Buck-Morss and Klaus Schultz, vol. 1-20 (in 23) (Frankfurt: Suhrkamp, 1970-86), vol. 7, 296.

prises complex and obscure occurances; it is an experience of the "powers of rational comprehension" as a "source of profound satisfaction, in so far as through it we enjoy a felt transcendence of the limitations of embodiment."[63] Thus the sublime, as Crowther emphasizes, in an appropriate context, is able to "promote deeper political awareness."[64] According to this interpretation, the autonomy of poetry explicitly does not exclude truth and ethics, since it does not adhere to mere appearances, but maintains the independence of what is laid down in the work of art against the complex reality. The inheritance of the sublime, according to Adorno, is "the transformation of the works into something true by the means of their content." The condition of truth is, so Adorno elsewhere, the "necessity to let suffering speak."[65] Or, what Schiller called the "two basic principles of all tragic art": "The first: representation of suffering nature; the second: representation of the moral resistance *(Selbständigkeit)* to suffering."[66] Unlike Schiller, Adorno does not rely on affirmative ethics; moral demands, according to Adorno, result "from nothing else than the historical interest of mankind in a rational change of the 'damaged life' "[67], and this can be claimed for any function of modern literature. It is thus worth comparing here the demands for an aesthetic without truth and ethical substance with what Schiller wrote to the philologist Johann Wilhelm Süvern 195 years ago: "Beauty is meant for a happy generation, but an unhappy one must be moved in a sublime way."[68]

4. "A Special Kind of Questioning Language"

Fried's proper identification tag, however, is what he himself called "serious puns",[69] and what Alexander von Bormann, following Johann Holzner, has

63. Crowther, *Critical Aesthetics and Postmodernism* (Oxford: Clarendon Press 1993), 172.
64. Ibid., 175.
65. Adorno, *Negative Dialektik. Gesammelte Schriften* (see note), vol. 6, 7-412, here 29: "Das Bedürfnis, Leiden beredt werden zu lassen ist Bedingung aller Wahrheit.".
66. Schiller, "Über das Pathetische". *Sämtliche Werke* (see note) vol. 5, 512: "*erstlich:* Darstellung der leidenden Natur; *zweitens:* Darstellung der moralischen Selbständigkeit im Leiden."
67. Gerhard Schweppenhäuser, *Ethik nach Auschwitz: Adornos negative Moralphilosophie* (Hamburg: Argument-Verlag, 1993) (Argument-Sonderband. N. F. AS 213), 6: "einzig und allein aus dem historischen Interesse der Menschen an an einer rationalen Veränderung des 'beschädigten Lebens'."
68. Letter No. 215 of July 26, 1800. Schiller, *Werke: Nationalausgabe* (Weimar: Böhlau, 1961), vol. 30: Briefwechsel: Schillers Briefe 1.11.1798-31.12.1800, ed. Lieselotte Blumenthal, 177: "Die Schönheit ist für ein glückliches Geschlecht, aber ein unglückliches muß man erhaben zu rühren suchen."
69. Fried, *Ein Soldat und ein Mädchen: Roman. Gesammelte Werke* (see note) vol. 4, 5-211, here 41.

assiduously worked out as his concept of literalness.[70] Fried can very easily be incorporated into the tradition of a literature that deliberately plays with language, and with regard to the rhetorical structures one might well note his extreme fixation on literality, on the written word, with a quotation from Derrida: "The advent of writing is the advent of this play."[71] Bormann applied Derrida's semiotics to Fried's poems in claiming that his concept of literalness relies on the conviction that "there is no meaning beyond language, and consequently language cannot be understood as its binding."[72] Fortunately, the opposite is the case with Fried. For him, there is unquestionably a given meaning that can be expressed by the "proper words"; the core of meaning is accessible to everyone by "relying on the most simple, the common sense of reason Fried certainly borrowed from Anglo-Saxon pragmatism."[73] The serious puns are grounded on the common sense of language, and the ethical substance of everyday life thus gains an unmediated evidence against the deformed language of media and politics: "a piece of unalienated life is made visible."[74] Confronting in serious puns complex political situations with the ethical substance of everyday life brings about the correlative of the sublime, and both strategies secure "some free possiblities of acting in front of political rulers."[75]

The criticism of the misuse of language by serious (and untranslatable) puns, as in the poem "Verstandsaufnahme", suggests that language can be used in a "right" way:

Seht die Bemarktung
der menschlichen Arbeitskraft
die Bezahnung der Staatsorgane
in immer neuen Verreichen
seht die Verleidigung der Würde des Menschen
und fragt euch dann ob ihr das
verjahen wollt
oder beneint[76]

70. Bormann, "'Ein Dichter, den Worte zusammenfügen': Versöhnung von Rhetorik und Poesie bei Erich Fried," *Text und Kritik*, No. 91: "Erich Fried" (1986), 5-23., especially 12 and 17.

71. Jacques Derrida, *Of Grammatology*, (De la grammatologie, engl.), transl. Gayatri Chakravotry Spivak (Baltimore, London: Johns Hopkins University Press, 1976), 7.

72. Bormann, "'Ein Dichter, den Worte zusammenfügen'" (see note), 12.

73. Michael Zeller, "Im Zeichen des ewigen Juden," *Erich Fried: Gespräche und Kritiken*, ed. Rudolf Wolff (Bonn: Bouvier, 1986) (Sammlung Profile. 12), 138.

74. Peter Rühmkorf, *Die Jahre die Ihr kennt: Anfälle und Erinnerungen* (Reinbek: Rowohlt 1972) (Das neue Buch. 1), 213ff.: "ein Stück verstellten Daseins zur Kenntlichkeit zu entwickeln."

75. Zeller, *Gedichte haben Zeit* (see note), 190.

76. Fried, *Gesammelte Werke* (see note) vol. 2, 355-56, here 356; first published in Fried, *Die bunten Getüme: Gedichte* (Berlin: Wagenbach, 1977) (Quartheft. 90), 48-9, here 49.

Fried's linguistic concept and his poetic language are based upon the longing for the "good, yet little useful words":

Kommt	Come
ihr guten	you good
ihr wenig brauchbaren Worte	you hardly useful words
Ihr taugt zu keiner Losung	You are of no use for any slogan
ihr schillert in keinen Farben	you don't shine in various colors
zu denen man sich bekennt	with which one can identify
Ihr eignet euch für kein Kampflied	You are of no use for a battle-hymn
Ihr laßt euch auf keine	You cannot be written
Fahnen schreiben	on any banner
Auch nicht auf Fahnen	Not even on banners
gegen Fahnen	against the banners
von Feinden[77]	of enemies

Such words, of course, belong to an old utopian concept of language in which sign and signification are congruous. Modern critics of language of course deny any such correlation. But in adhering to Nietzsche's condemnation of the poet "climbing around on deceitful word-bridges, *that I am banished / from all truth! / Only a fool! Only a poet! ...*",[78] some critics are inclined to forget that this is not Nietzsche's last word on this topic; for Nietzsche, art, which is grounded in "life," is more powerful than knowledge.[79]

Language, according to Cassirer, "becomes one of the human spirit's basic implements, by which we progress from the world of mere sensation to the world of intuition and ideas."[80] This is why Fried considers doubts about language *(Sprachzweifel)* to be "political obscurantism."[81] In his cyclical poem "Zweifel an der Sprache" (Doubts about Language) Fried almost overtly takes up the poetic concept Rilke formulated in his *Die Aufzeichnungen des Malte Laurids Brigge* (The Sketchbooks of Malte Laurids Brigge): "He was a poet and hated vagueness; or perhaps he only was concerned about truth ..."[82]

77. Fried, *Gesammelte Werke* (see note) vol. 2, 513-14; first published in Fried, *Lebensschatten: Gedichte* (Berlin: Wagenbach, 1981) (Quartheft. 11), 78.

78. Nietzsche, *Sämtliche Werke* (see note) vol. 6, 377-380, 378 and 380: "herumsteigend auf lügnerischen Wortbrücken / [...] *dass ich verbannt sei von aller Wahrheit! Nur Narr! Nur Dichter!*" English translation: Nietzsche, *Dithyrambs of Dionysus*, transl. R. J. Hollingdale (Reckling Ridge, CT: Black Swan Books, 1984), 23 and 27.

79. Vgl. Peter Pütz, *Friedrich Nietzsche* (Stuttgart: Metzler, 1967) (Sammlung Metzler. 62), 31.

80. Cassirer, *The Philosophy of Symbolic Forms*, transl. Ralph Manheim, (New Haven and London: Yale University Press, 1955), vol. 1: *On Language*, 87-88.

81. Zeller, "Im Zeichen des ewigen Juden" (see note), 139.

82. Rilke, *Sämtliche Werke*, vol. 1-6, hrsg. vom Rilke-Archiv in Verbindung mit Ruth Sieber-Rilke. Besorgt durch Ernst Zinn (Frankfurt: Insel, 1955-1966), vol. 6, 863: "Er

Der Glaube der Dichter an die Sprache war lange schon
eine besondere Form des Zweifels an der Sprache:
Das Genaunehmen zeigt die Ungenauigkeit, um sie
zu verändern hin zur Genauigkeit oder
um zu erkennen wo ungenaue Sprache
der Ungenauigkeit der Erkenntnis entspricht[83]

The poet's belief in language has long been
a special kind of doubt about language:
Being precise about everything reveals the imprecision in order
to change it into precision or
to recognize where imprecise language
is equivalent to imprecise knowledge

Modern literature does not reconcile the conflict between word and
knowledge in aesthetic illusion, on the contrary, it is, according to
Adorno, a form of art that "aspires to a degree of truth, which embraces
the unsettledness of conflicts."[84]. Literary criticism like that of Paul de
Man, which "takes its starting point from the extreme ambivalence and
ends in aporia (i. e. in an indifference to value and truth)", [85] cannot do
justice to such texts. For Erich Fried, there is an equivalent to the lost
transcendence, the lost "metaphysical and religious assumptions."[86] In
one of his serious puns he deliberately puts the poet's task and religion
on the same level by playing on the notion of *Fügung*, meaning both
composition (of words) and providence

Fügungen	Providence/Composition
Es heißt	It is said
ein Dichter	a poet
ist einer	is one
der Worte	who composes
zusammenfügt	with words
Das stimmt nicht	That is not true
Ein Dichter	A poet
ist einer	is one
den Worte noch halbwegs	who is halfway
zusammenfügen	composed by words

---

war ein Dichter und haßte das Ungefähre; oder vielleicht war es ihm nur um die Wahrheit
zu tun."

83. Fried, "Zweifel an der Sprache". G*esammelte Werke* (see note) vol. 2, 239-49, here
. 247; first published in Fried, *Gegengift: 49 Gedichte und ein Zyklus* (Berlin: Wagenbach,
1974), 69-79, here 77.

84. Adorno, *Ästhetische Theorie. Sämtliche Schriften* (see note) vol. 7, 294: "Kunst, die
auf eine Wahrheitsgehalt drängt, in den das Ungeschlichtete der Widersprüche fällt."

85. Vgl. Peter V. Zima, *Literarische Ästhetik: Methoden und Modelle der Literaturwissenschaft* (Tübingen: Francke, 1991) (Uni-Taschenbücher. 1590), 355.

86. Habermas, *Moral Consciousness* (see note), 43.

wenn er Glück hat	if is lucky
Wenn er Unglück hat	If he is unlucky
reißen die Worte	the words
ihn auseinander[87]	tear him apart

Self-referential literature, pure literature with abstract signs that do nothing but refer to themselves, might be a comprehensible goal in a tension test of modernism and postmodernism; the belief, however, that words are mere signs is undermined by the ethical substance *(Sittlichkeit)* of life circumstances and their representation in language and culture. I think the central point in regard to the "system" of art is that language need not lose this everyday function within it, though language as an expression of actual *Sittlichkeit* and cultural memory is used in poetry highly reflexively and playfully, in the serious sense of the words.

One of Fried's poems that adapts both Hölderlin's tone and poetics can serve as a summary of the various aesthetic and ethical components discussed in this paper. Style, rhythm, and theme are sublime both in the rhetoric and in the meaning, as defined by Kant and Adorno; unlike Hölderlin, Fried no longer links earthly life with transcendence, but in this poem, "Hölderlin an Sinclair," in an almost Adornian sense pleads for an "undamaged life"; poetry, in this context, has a function that is neither pure art nor an expression of aesthetized morality, but goes beyond them in connecting life and poetry in an essential aesthetic *Sittlichkeit* (Friedrich Schlegel), as most of the incriminated authors of the FRG and the GDR did: Christa Wolf, Heinrich Böll, Günter Grass, Erich Fried, Martin Walser, Hans Magnus Enzensberger, Peter Weiss etc., who deliberately use "extra-literary themes" in their work.[88] The last of all, even in art, for Fried and others, is life. The close of Fried's poem reads:

Viel kann verstört sein,	Many things may be confused
Daß der suchende Blick es	So that the searching glance
Kaum noch erkennt.	Barely recognizes them again.
Nicht alle Vögel, die singen,	Not all birds that sing
Helfen dem Himmel. Doch wo	Give help to heaven. But where
Gesang fehlt, dort erblindet	Song fails, there blindness comes
Der arme Gefangene.	To the poor prisoner.
Das letzte aber ist Leben.	Yet the last of all is life.[89]

87. Fried, *Gesammelte Werke* (see note) vol. 2, 517; first published in *Lebensschatten* (see note), 83.

88. Greiner, "Die deutsche Gesinnungsästhetik. Noch einmal: Christa Wolf und der deutsche Literaturstreit. Eine Zwischenbilanz," *"Es geht nicht um Christa Wolf"*, ed. Anz (see note), 208-16, here 213.

89. Fried, *Gesammelte Werke* (see note) vol. 2, 328-29, here 329; first published in *Die bunten Getüme* (see note), 17; English translation: Fried, *100 Poems Without a Country*, transl. Stuart Hood (London: Calder, 1978), 79.

A REVIVAL OF CONSERVATIVE LITERATURE?

The "*Spiegel*-Symposium 1993" and Beyond

*Jay J. Rosellini**

I.

The present study is an exploration rather than a definitive presentation. Few Germanists have pondered the nature of conservative literature and/or literati since the 1960s. A look at a representative sampling of literary histories demonstrates that scholarship on this topic has been a rather peripheral phenomenon. In the Reclam volume *Deutsche Gegenwartsliteratur* (German Contemporary German Literature, 1981), one finds merely a section on Ernst Jünger in Manfred Durzak's article "The Rediscovery of the Loners."[1] The second edition of Thomas Koebner's *Tendenzen der deutschen Gegenwartsliteratur* (Tendencies of Contemporary German Literature 1984) contains nothing more than a sub-chapter by Frank Trommler entitled "Conservative Literary Criticism: Sieburg and Rychner."[2] In the tenth volume of Hanser's *Sozialgeschichte der deutschen Literatur* (Social History of German Literature, 1992) Ralf Schnell provides an insightful analysis of the works of writers like Carossa, Weinheber, Bergengruen, Wiechert, Reinhold Schneider, Hagel-

---

* All translations from German into English are my own.

1. Durzak, Manfred, "Die Wiederentdeckung der Einzelgänger. Zu einigen 'Vater-figuren' der deutschen Gegenwartsliteratur," *Deutsche Gegenwartsliteratur*, ed. Manfred Durzak (Stuttgart: Reclam, 1981) 374-403.

2. Trommler, Frank, "Auf dem Weg zu einer kleineren Literatur. Ästhetische Perioden und Probleme seit 1945." *Tendenzen der deutschen Gegenwartsliteratur*, 2nd rev. ed., ed. Thomas Koebner (Stuttgart: Kröner, 1984) 33-36.

stange, and Le Fort in his essay "Traditionalist Concepts," but he does not go beyond the late 1950s.[3] In volume 12 of the Hanser series, Keith Bullivant discusses "Literature and Politics," but limits himself to writers on the left.[4] In the final volume of the literary history produced by Germanists in the GDR, the authors refer to "restoration in literature" and "elitist-conservative authors,"[5] but here again such terms are applied only to the 1950s and writers like Benn and Jünger. The picture is the same in the monumental twelfth and final volume of the venerable "de Boor/ Newald," arguably the standard and even normative history of German literature: Instead of a chapter on conservative literature, there are scattered references to nature poetry, theocentric texts, and the "mythic literature" (*Mythenliteratur*) of the 1950s.[6] In general, one can state that most critics use the term "conservative literature" – if they use it at all – to designate a phenomenon which existed until the beginning of the student movement and was represented by authors with a clear religious orientation or by certain old reactionaries (*Ewiggestrige*).[7] This is due at least in part to the exclusion of the literature read by *most* people. It has been pointed out that the "actual political literature of the Federal Republic" consists of "trivial, not literary literature," i.e., "popular fiction," "novels serialized in magazines," or "war stories published as dime novels."[8] The

3. Ralf Schnell, "Traditionalistische Konzepte," *Literatur in der Bundesrepublik Deutschland bis 1967* (Munich & Vienna: Hanser, 1986), 214-29. (*Hansers Sozialgeschichte der deutschen Literatur vom 16. Jahrhundert bis zur Gegenwart*, ed. Rolf Grimminger, Vol. 10.) Ludwig Fischer's treatment of "Literarische Kultur im sozialen Gefüge" (142-63) is also relevant here.

4. Keith Bullivant, "Literatur und Politik, *Gegenwartsliteratur seit 1968*, ed. Klaus Briegleb and Sigrid Weigel (München: Hanser, 1992), 279-301. (*Hansers Sozialgeschichte der deutschen Literatur vom 16. Jahrhundert bis zur Gegenwart*, ed. Rolf Grimminger, Vol. 12.)

5. Hans Joachim Bernhard et al., *Literatur der BRD* (Berlin: Volk und Wissen, 1983), 127-28. (*Geschichte der deutschen Literatur von den Anfängen bis zur Gegenwart*, ed. Kurt Böttcher et al., Vol. 12.)

6. Wilfried Barner et al., *Geschichte der deutschen Literatur von 1945 bis zur Gegenwart*, ed. Wilfried Barner (Munich: C.H. Beck, 1994) 39-43, 188-90. (*Geschichte der deutschen Literatur von den Anfängen bis zur Gegenwart*, ed. Helmut de Boor and Richard Newald, Vol. 12.)

7. The exception to this rule is Keith Bullivant, who has occupied himself with the "Conservative Revolution" and literary elitism for some time. Cf. his essay "The Conservative Revolution" in *The Weimar Dilemma. Intellectuals in the Weimar Republic*, ed. Anthony Phelan (Dover, N.H.: Manchester UP, 1985), 47-70, the remarks on Handke and Strauß in his *Realism Today* (Leamington Spa/Hamburg/New York: Berg, 1987) and his recent study *The Future of German Literature* (Oxford/Providence: Berg, 1994). There are a number of parallels between his conclusions and mine, but they are the result of a certain intellectual affinity, rather than direct influence.

8. Jan Berg et al., *Sozialgeschichte der deutschen Literatur von 1918 bis zur Gegenwart* (Frankfurt.: Fischer, 1981), 639. Berg is quoting from the following: Wolfgang Langen-

following inquiry will attempt to come to terms with something quite different, namely a conservative literature that has purportedly arisen in Germany since 1989, a literature that is not a mere extension of past developments. Actually, the focus will be less on actual literature than on a certain mind-set and the language which accompanies it. It seems logical to focus on a collection of essays that have come to symbolize the recent intellectual sea change, namely the 1993 symposium initiated by the weekly magazine *Der Spiegel.*

This symposium consists of three essays, namely "Impending Tragedy" (Anschwellender Bocksgesang) by Botho Strauß, "Views of Civil War" (Ausblicke auf den Bürgerkrieg) by Hans Magnus Enzensberger, and "German Concerns" (Deutsche Sorgen) by Martin Walser. In the announcement "Concerning Intellectuals" at the beginning of issue no. 26, a kind of contextualizing afterword, one finds phrases like "outrageous utterances" and "a number of taboo violations by German intellectuals." Anticipating the key question, the *Spiegel* editors go on to ask it and provide an answer of sorts: "Has the *Spiegel* lost its leftist, left-liberal grounding too? As much or as little as the entire critical intelligentsia, which has been seeking new values and orientation since the abrupt end of the well-ordered bipolar world divided into East and West."[9] If there are in fact new values and a different orientation in the works here, they must be reflected in a new language, for it would not be possible to use the concepts of the New Left to circumscribe a neoconservative world view. Observers of the German scene are well aware that after the collapse of the Third Reich, attempts were made to understand nazism by scrutinizing the terminology of the system. (The best known studies were Klemperer's *LTI* and *From the Dictionary of the Barbarian* by Dolf Sternberger, et al. The East German volume *Language Change in the Third Reich* was never widely discussed in the West.)[10] In contrast to

bucher, "Politische Literatur – für die Millionen. Aspekte des Unterhaltungs- und Illustriertenromans in der Bundesrepublik," *Frankfurter Allgemeine Zeitung* [hereafter: *FAZ*], 14 February 1968.

9. "Hausmitteilung: Betr.: Intellektuelle," *Der Spiegel* 26 (1993), 3. The Strauß essay is found in No. 6 (202-207), Enzensberger's is in No. 25 (170-75), and Walser's concluding piece is in No. 26 (40-47). "Anschwellender Bocksgesang" is a "Polemik" listed under the rubric "Kultur," "Ausblicke auf den Bürgerkrieg" is categorized as "Zeitkritik," also under "Kultur," whereas "Deutsche Sorgen" is in the section "Deutschland" under the subheading "Intellektuelle." Page numbers of specific citations are provided in the text of this paper.

10. Victor Klemperer, *LTI* [*lingua tertii imperii*] (1946; Leipzig: Reclam, 1982). Dolf Sternberger, Gerhard Storz, and W.E. Süskind, *Aus dem Wörterbuch des Unmenschen* (1945; Hamburg: Claassen, 1957). Eugen Seidel and Ingeborg Seidel-Slotty, *Sprachwandel im Dritten Reich. Eine kritische Untersuchung faschistischer Einflüsse* (Halle/Saale: VEB

these analyses, the point here is not to examine an era in retrospect, but rather to search for evidence of a *new* era.

In order to analyze the language of the three essays, a list of terms commonly used in leftist and rightist discourse was compiled. (This list, which was revised several times, contains 175 items in its present form.) Typical terms used by the left include "emancipation," "exploitation," "imperialism," "liberation," "progress," "progressive," and "solidarity." On the opposite side, one finds "authority," "community," "elite," "evolutionary," "morality," "organic," "patriotic," "service," and others. The context in which these terms are used is naturally of great importance. Also included are several "neutral" terms common to almost all cultural and political discussions in Germany, such as "history", "ideology", and "spirit", The analysis will begin with Enzensberger, move on to Walser, and turn to Strauß, by far the most controversial figure, at the end.

There are basically two schools of thought regarding Hans Magnus Enzensberger's role as a writer and social commentator in postwar Germany. Some see him as the former *enfant terrible* of the stifling Adenauer years who became one of the driving forces behind the student movement of the 1960s, only to turn his back on it all, becoming ever more conservative or at least apolitical in the course of the 1970s and 1980s. One could express this in shorthand by referring to the titles of his various projects: from the *Kursbuch* and the project boldly termed "the political alphabetization of Germany"[11] to the slippery *TransAtlantik* and the bibliophile *Andere Bibliothek*.[12] Others argue that one can dis-

---

Verlag Sprache und Literatur, 1961). More recently, East German linguists published an analysis of the changes in the German language since 1989. Cf. *Wer spricht das wahre Deutsch? Erkundungen zur Sprache im vereinigten Deutschland*, ed. Ruth Reiher and Rüdiger Läzer (Berlin: Aufbau Taschenbuch Verlag, 1993). The preface begins with the following words: "It would be surprising if our language were not also affected by the political changes of the last few years" (7).

In the context of the debate about "political correctness," Klaus Bittermann and Gerhard Henschel have published a new lexicon: *Das Wörterbuch des Gutmenschen. Zur Kritik der moralisch korrekten Schaumsprache* (Berlin: Edition TIAMAT, 1994). It is noteworthy that the editors reprint the entry "Anliegen" from the *Wörterbuch des Unmenschen*, implying that "politically correct" speech is as totalitarian as the verbal violence of the Nazis. There must be an audience for such views, since a second volume of the lexicon appeared in 1995.

In a recent commentary on the policies of the EC, the *Süddeutsche Zeitung* made ironic reference to Sternberger's work: " Appearance, lifestyle, corporate identity – those are not merely terms out of *From the Dictionary of the Barbarian*, but, even worse, blueprints for the dehumanization of the planet." Cf. "Streiflicht", *Süddeutsche Zeitung* 18-19 March 1995.

11. Hans Magnus Enzensberger, "Gemeinplätze, die Neueste Literatur betreffend," *Kursbuch* 15, 1968, 197.

12. Cf. Rolf Warnecke, "Kurswechselparade eines Intellektuellen. Konsequent inkonsequent: Hans Magnus Enzensberger," *text und kritik* 113, January 1992, *Vom gegenwärtigen Zustand der deutschen Literatur*, 97-105.

cern a basic continuity from the 1950s to the 1990s. This has been characterized as "the freedom of care-free, independent reflection",[13] or a "humanistic basic conviction in thinking and writing."[14] What can we glean from the essay "Views on Civil War"?

Most of the German readers of this essay, now part of the 1993 book *Prospects of Civil War* (Aussichten auf den Bürgerkrieg),[15] probably remembered another rather famous *Spiegel* essay by the same author, namely the 1991 piece equating Saddam Hussein with Hitler.[16] Enzensberger spoke of the doomsday program of each of these "enemies of humanity": "His death wish is his motive, his mode of rule is destruction" (26). Ideology is irrelevant to the author's "anthropological" analysis. If the fanatical leader can find followers who wish to die themselves, anything is possible. According to Enzensberger, this is what happened in Germany in the 1930s, and this constellation was duplicated in Iraq in the 1980s.[17] Normal political maneuvering was thus useless, making war an inevitability. This conclusion transformed Enzensberger into one of the despicable warmongers *(Bellizisten)* in the eyes of the German left.

The essay on civil war takes up many of the same themes, placing more emphasis on the global situation. The "New World Order" is one characterized primarily by civil wars in every corner of the planet, according to Enzensberger. In contrast to the Cold War era, he goes on to assert, none of the participants in these conflicts is motivated by ideals, ideology, or a Weltanschauung of any kind. In fact, they have absolutely no convictions at all. One even reads that they are "autistic" and incapable of distinguishing between destruction and self-destruction (171). The actual goal is none other than "collective self-mutilation" (172). In such a climate, none of the political thinkers – from Aristotle to Max

13. Hermann Korte, "Hans Magnus Enzensberger" *Kritisches Lexikon zur deutschsprachigen Gegenwartsliteratur*, 1978ff., 39. Nachlieferung 1992, 20.

14. Holger-Heinrich Preuße, *Der politische Literat Hans Magnus Enzensberger. Politische und gesellschaftliche Aspekte seiner Literatur und Publizistik* (Berne: Peter Lang, 1989), 191.

15. H.M. Enzensberger, *Aussichten auf den Bürgerkrieg* (Frankfurt: Suhrkamp, 1993).

16. H.M. Enzensberger, "Hitlers Wiedergänger," *Der Spiegel* 6, 1991, 26-28. André Glucksmann, one of the so-called "new philosophers" in France, praised the essay on Saddam but castigated Enzensberger for his piece on the global civil war as an excuse for passivity in the face of barbarity. Cf. A. G., "Ein neuer Vogel Strauß," *Der Spiegel* 37, 1993, 247-49.

17. In actuality, Enzensberger meant to say that the Germans should refrain from demonizing Saddam and his followers as some kind of foreign, pre-modern barbarians, since they themselves had engaged in the same behavior not long ago. This line of reasoning can be traced to traditional leftist internationalism and anti-imperialism, although the conclusion does not seem to fit such a mode of thinking.

Weber – have anything to tell us. Only Hobbes' *bellum omnium contra omnes* remains an accurate, if depressing, description of the situation.

Of particular interest is Enzensberger's assessment of the contemporary German scene in the context of his scenario. He refuses to call the perpetrators of violence against foreigners "right-wing radicals" or "neo-Nazis": "He knows nothing about National Socialism. History does not interest him. The swastika and Hitler salute are mere props. His clothing, music and video culture are thoroughly American. "Germanness" is a slogan devoid of meaning that only serves to cover up the empty spaces in his brain" (172). This does not, however, imply that he fails to take these people seriously. On the contrary: He calls for action (without going into specifics) to eliminate the anti-social violence from German society. If the Germans were to refrain from doing so, he says, they would lose every right to criticize conditions in other countries: "It does not befit the Germans to act like guarantors of peace and world champions of human rights as long as gangs of German thugs and arsonists are spreading fear and terror day and night" (175). This is hardly the voice of a conservative. If anything, it is an example of leftist melancholy stemming from the grudging admission that the universalist morality of the Enlightenment is not realizable on any grand scale. It is not stated triumphantly, but rather in a tone of deep sadness. Enzensberger approvingly cites Hannah Arendt's theory of totalitarianism, but hastens to add that it does not apply to our world. His cultural pessimism is not coupled with a call to return to traditional values, and there is absolutely nothing in the language of the essay to indicate a turn to the right. Since 1993, Enzensberger has expressed his great respect for Denis Diderot, the quintessential representative of the Enlightenment,[18] and in a recent interview, he praised the student movement of the 1960s for finally making West Germany "suitable for habitation."[19]

Martin Walser, who is two years older than Enzensberger, has been dissecting the old Federal Republic since the 1950s, and until the mid-1980s he was also viewed as a founding member of the left-liberal literary phalanx. Of late, he has complained of isolation and the loss of old friends. This is directly attributable to his changed attitude *vis-à-vis* Ger-

18. Hans Magnus Enzensberger, *Diderots Schatten* (Frankfurt: Suhrkamp, 1994). In the afterword to this collection, he writes of Diderot: "He was responsible for everything and got involved in everything. ... He didn't throw himself into the adventure of helping others out of an ideological sense of duty or because of party discipline, but rather out of a naive curiosity" (382f.).

19. "'Ich will nicht der Lappen sein, mit dem man die Welt putzt.' " André Müller spricht mit Hans Magnus Enzensberger," *Die Zeit* 4, 1995. In his essay "Im Fremden das Eigene hassen?", Enzensberger refers to the Aryan as "a ridiculous construct" and speaks of Germany's "especially fragile national identity." Cf. H.M.E. in *Der Spiegel* 34, 1992, 176.

man history and national identity. The general public first became aware of the change in 1986, when *Die Welt* published an interview with the writer (29 September). One could venture to say that it was less the content of the interview than the fact that it appeared in the flagship paper of media czar Axel Springer that caused an uproar. Beyond this, a full-page advertisement hyping the interview appeared in *Der Spiegel* (40, 1986) with a photo of Walser and the following quote in bold type: "I will not become accustomed to the division of Germany." One was not a little surprised to hear such pronouncements from the author of the anti-fascist plays *The Rabbit Race* (Eiche und Angora) and *Der schwarze Schwan* (The Black Swan), who had been politicized by the Vietnam War, felt affinity with the German Communist Party (DKP) for a time (cf. the controversial work *Gallistl's Illness*), and even signed an open letter to Erich Honecker "With socialist greetings."[20]

The first literary manifestation of Walser's preoccupation with the German nation was the 1987 novella *Dorle and Wolf* (No Man's Land), whose main character makes the following oft-quoted observation at the Bonn train station: "Halved people were hustling back and forth. The other halves were running back and forth in Leipzig."[21] In actuality, Walser had been ruminating about the division of Germany for quite some time, but this had somehow gone unnoticed. In his provocative speech "Speaking about Germany," given in November 1988 as part of the series "Speaking about our Country," he made a point of quoting from remarks which he had made in Bergen-Enkheim in 1977: "The existence of these two countries is the product of a catastrophe whose causes can be known. I find it unbearable to let German history – as badly as it went in recent times – end as a product of catastrophe. I refuse to participate in the liquidation of history. Within me, another Germany still has a chance."[22] Walser was not only criticized by Günter

20. Martin Walser, "Treten Sie zurück, Erich Honecker!", *Der Spiegel* 1974, 136. In this letter, Walser is reacting to the Guillaume affair and Willy Brandt's resignation. He is upset that the rapprochement between the two German states has suffered a setback. In a way, he is calling for a kind of socialist nationalism, so this is clearly a foreshadowing of later developments in his thinking.

21. Martin Walser, *Dorle und Wolf* (Frankfurt: Suhrkamp, 1987), 54.

In his review of this book, Martin Lüdke wrote: "Walser confronts a problem that we – almost without exception – have repressed … Today, no one loses sleep over the division of Germany." Cf. M.L., "Nichts Halbes, nichts Ganzes. Martin Walsers deutsch-deutsche Novelle", *Die Zeit* 13, 1987. In Peter Schneider's 1982 novel *The Wall Jumper* (Der Mauerspringer) the division of Berlin and Germany is really little more than a curiosity.

22. Martin Walser, "Über Deutschland reden. Ein Bericht," *Über Deutschland reden* (Frankfurt: Suhrkamp, 1988), 88-89. It is interesting that Walser praises Enzensberger for pondering the German question in his "Katechismus zur deutschen Frage," which appeared in *Kursbuch* 4. Enzensberger's fellow intellectuals are criticized sharply: "If leftist

Grass and others for relying on a very vague "historical feeling" rather than rational analysis,[23] but also for accepting CSU politician Theo Waigel's invitation to discuss his speech with Waigel's Bavarian party comrades at Franz Josef Strauß' old stomping ground Wildbad Kreuth.[24] All this had happened before he published the essay "German Concerns" in *Der Spiegel*. Can one discover an even more pronounced turn toward conservative and patriotic positions in this essay?

This text, like so many of Walser's fictional and non-fictional writings, is an attempt at therapy, including self-therapy. It came about as a reaction to his appearance in Lea Rosh's talk show in February 1989, in the course of which the author was verbally assaulted by Günter Gaus and Klaus Wagenbach, who called his "Speaking about Germany" superficial and no better than "barroom bluster" (*Stammtischreden*, 40). The next day, Walser barricaded himself in a Paris hotel room and wondered whether he was still a leftist, since he had just been attacked "in the name of such glorious positions as internationalism, rationality, and enlightenment" (40). He had hoped, he writes, that his call for reunification would not affect his location on the political spectrum *(Links-Rechts-Skala),* since his attitude toward the various contradictions and problems in German society had not changed (47). This turned out to be an illusion, and his ostracism led to a scathing critique of the German left: "Left – now I see that as an assortment of credos put together according to changing fashions that I cannot go along with. [It is] a chic and scurrilous fundamentalism" (47). Having said this, he explains why he considers it to be so important to come to terms with German nationalism. It turns out that in his opinion, the success of right-wing extremists is

---

and rightist intellectuals are in agreement about anything at the moment, it is probably in the view that the division [of Germany] is acceptable." (92) The inclusion of intellectuals on the right is worthy of note in the face of the quite different neoconservative program of the 1990s.

23. "Viel Gefühl, wenig Bewußtsein. Der Schriftsteller Günter Graß über eine mögliche Wiedervereinigung Deutschlands," *Der Spiegel* 47, 1989, 80: "I have these feelings too, but that does not lead me to yield to mawkishness." In the same interview, Grass describes several surprising flip-flops in Walser's world view: "When I met him, he was an enlightened conservative from Lake Constance with a certain cautious leaning toward the SPD which developed via the student movement into a brief flirt with the DKP. Now he's chatting with [CSU leader Theo] Waigel – I don't like all these inexplicable turnabouts." (ibid.) It is of course Grass himself who has remained steadfast in his support of the *Kulturnation* Germany, as opposed to the geographically and politically unified version. Walser also used the term "feeling for history" (*Geschichtsgefühl*) in his article "Zum Stand der deutschen Dinge," which was published in the *FAZ* on 12 December 1989.

24. Walser defended himself in the *tageszeitung* of 16 January 1989. Excerpts from his text were reprinted in *Die Zeit* 4, 1989. He claimed there that he had maintained his independence: "I see no possibility of being exploited by anyone as an author or intellectual."

directly attributable both to the exclusion of nationalism from societal discourse since 1945 ("for the best of reasons," he hastens to add), and the refusal to engage in dialogue with those who cannot tolerate this exclusion.[25] Instead of the demonization of skinheads and their ilk, Walser calls for a kind of national conversation about German history and identity. This is not, however, because he himself is a nationalist: "If someone has nothing to be proud of but his nationality, he is truly in dire straits [especially] as a German ... The nation – that is no one's major concern. And it hasn't been for a long while. And it will never be again" (41-42). Such utterances bear little resemblance to conservative or nationalist rhetoric. Walser may not call himself a leftist anymore, but he still sounds like one more often than not. For example, he still views National Socialism as the worst catastrophe in German history (no trace of Ernst Nolte here), and he castigates the West Germans for profiting from the labor of the *Gastarbeiter*, only to turn against them in times of economic decline. Words like "community," "morality," or "national pride" are absent from his essay, and his critique of the Enlightenment Project stems – as does Enzensberger's – from disappointment rather than ideological opposition (47). As a final note, one could point out that Walser has been a vocal supporter of exiled Bangladeshi author Tamila Nasreen, who is anything but a darling of the right.[26]

Walser's 1990 essay "A Writer's Morning" reads like a practice run for "German Concerns." In it, he refers to two writers whose works provide him with great consolation. The two are Peter Handke and Botho Strauß, who are portrayed as transcending the superficial "opinionated style" (*Meinungsstil*) which Walser abhors. As an example of poetic profundity, Walser quotes from the 1985 Strauß poem, *This Memory of One Who Was a Guest for Only One Day:* "Knew no Germany all my life / Only two foreign states who kept me from / Ever being the German in the name of the people. / So much history, only to end like this?"[27]

25. Some years ago, Erich Fried – hardly a conservative nationalist! – was vilified by Henryk M. Broder for daring to speak with skinheads.
26. Cf. Walser's letter "Lieber Herr Kinkel," *taz*, 16 July, 1994. In this endeavor, Walser found himself in the company of Salman Rushdie and Elfriede Jelinek, among others. He inveighed against religious terror and "orders to kill issued by fanatical monotheists," adding that "Europe has put religious calamities (*Religionskrankheiten*) behind her." Walser's support for Nasreen is exactly the kind of activity that A. Glucksmann had in mind when he criticized Enzensberger for his inactivity and cynicism (cf. footnote 16).
27. Martin Walser, "Vormittag eines Schriftstellers. Über Deutschland reden – und die Folgen: Warum einer keine Lust mehr hat, am Streit der Meinungen teilzunehmen," *Die Zeit* 51, 1990. Reprinted in M.L., *Vormittag eines Schriftstellers* (Frankfurt: Suhrkamp, 1994), 9-26. Walser is quoting from Botho Strauß, *Diese Erinnerung an einen, der nur*

This is more than a random citation. It is meant to illustrate the fact that most of the thoughts and many of the images in "Impending Tragedy" can be found in other works by the same author, such as the 1985 poem, the prose volumes *Pairs, Passersby* (1981), *Fragments of Indistinctness* (1989), *No Beginning* (1992), and *Living, Dawning, Lying* (1994), as well as in the plays *Choral Finale* (1991) and *Equilibrium* (1993).[28] What has made the "Bocksgesang" perhaps the most controversial essay written by a German author since the 1950s (Wolf Biermann's "Agitation for War / Agitation for Peace" ("Kriegshetze Friedenshetze"), Enzensberger's "Hitler Reincarnate," and Heinrich Böll's "Safe-Conduct for Ulrike Meinhof" also come to mind)[29] is that Strauß made a conscious choice not to utilize fictional characters or the institution of the theater to transmit his assessment of the contemporary malaise in both Germany and the Western world in general. Up until 1993, only a small segment of the population was aware of the direction of his thinking, and this thinking of course took on added significance after the fall of the Berlin Wall. In addition, he was surrounded by a rather mysterious aura, given that he had kept himself out of the public eye as much as possible and refused to participate in the "democratic public sphere" as defined by the visual media. He was vaguely associated with the left, but most people could not point to any concrete actions in this regard. (The anecdote that one sometimes hears about Strauß collecting for the Viet Cong at the Berlin *Schaubühne* in the early 1970s might well be apocryphal.)

The relatively brief text entitled "Impending Tragedy" has been dwarfed by the astounding number of critical responses to it.[30] These

---

einen Tag zu Gast war (Munich, Vienna: Hanser, 1985), 48. Here is the original German: "Kein Deutschland gekannt zeit meines Lebens. / Zwei fremde Staaten nur, die mir verboten, / je im Namen des Volkes der Deutsche zu sein. / Soviel Geschichte, um so zu enden?"

28. I have discovered numerous parallels in the following editions: *Paare, Passanten* (Munich, Vienna: Hanser, 5th edition, 1982); *Fragmente der Undeutlichkeit* (Munich, Vienna: Hanser, 1989); *Beginnlosigkeit. Reflexionen über Fleck und Linie* (Munich, Vienna: Hanser, 1992); *Wohnen Dämmern Lügen* (Munich, Vienna: Hanser, 1994); *Schlußchor* in *Theaterstücke II* (Munich, Vienna: Hanser, 1991), and *Das Gleichgewicht* (Munich, Vienna: Hanser, 1993). These works demonstrate that the development of Strauß' ideas has been a gradual one, not a sudden eruption.

29. One might also include Alice Schwarzer's afterword to the legendary volume *Frauen gegen den § 218* (Frankfurt: Suhrkamp, 1971), although Schwarzer is a journalist rather than an imaginative writer.

30. Those who wish to delve into this debate should begin with the surveys of the year in German literature published by Reclam, i.e.: *Deutsche Literatur 1993. Jahresrückblick* and *Deutsche Literatur 1994. Jahresrückblick*, ed. Franz Josef Görtz et al. (Stuttgart: Reclam, 1994 and 1995, respectively). Another useful collection is *Das Werk von Botho Strauß und die 'Bocksgesang'-Debatte*, a special edition of *Weimarer Beiträge* (40.2, 1993)

range from a few expressions of solidarity to the vilification of the alleged closet fascist Strauß. Such sentiments have more to do with the German context – both historical and political – than with the text itself. The two words which best characterize this object of controversy are "contradictory" and "vague."[31] It is difficult to imagine how anyone could use this rambling tract, written in highly opaque language accessible only to the educated elite, as a manifesto of any kind, although it was used, or rather, misused in just this way by the editors of the recent volume *Die selbstbewußte Nation* (The Self-Confident Nation). [32] Although the author mounts a broad attack against the German left (the *68er*), even to the extent of tracing the term itself back to "that which is in error" *(das Fehlgehende)* and dubbing it "a sign for the jinxed and wrong" (203-204), one also reads that "in politics, everything and its opposite can be united in one person's head" (205). There is also no clear distinction made between "leftist" and "liberal." When Strauß speaks of the hypocrisy of public morality, which has led to "the ridiculing of eros, the ridiculing of the soldier, the ridiculing of the church, tradition, and authority" (203), does he mean that the left determines this morality in Germany? Are the public television stations under the sway of the anti-fascist street fighters or at least the (mildly) anti-capitalist wing of the SPD? Is the tabloid *Bildzeitung* agitating against Bishop Dyba and his anti-abortion crusade? Will future historians consider Christian Demo-

---

edited by Sigrid Berka. Much attention was also given to two articles in the *FAZ*, i.e.: Gerhard Stadelmaier, "Zittern und sagen. Szene Deutschland: Woran ist Botho Strauß schuld? (I)," 11 April 1994, and Gustav Seibt, "Was die Rechten lasen oder Woran ist Botho Strauß schuld? (II)," 16 April 1994.

31. In a response to the original version of this study, Ingeborg Hoesterey correctly emphasized that "Impending Tragedy" is above all a postmodern text, i.e. something by definition both contradictory and vague. It should be pointed out, however, that the kind of playfulness and evasiveness that is generally acceptable in the cultural sphere is not appropriate in the realm of political discourse, and this is the arena which Strauß has entered with his "Bocksgesang." Peter Handke has entered this arena more than once, but he is no more capable of accepting criticism of his opinions than Strauß. In this regard the two authors are, regrettably, very similar. The following assessment of Handke's career would not have had much relevance *vis-à-vis* the pre-1993 Strauß, but it does now: "Handke has always had two faces: the brooder and observer engrossed in books and landscapes, and the rebel and beserk madman (*Amokläufer*)." Cf. Anon., "Dichters Winterreise", *Der Spiegel* 6, 193.

32. *Die selbstbewußte Nation. "Anschwellender Bocksgesang" und weitere Beiträge zu einer deutschen Debatte*, ed. Heimo Schwilk and Ulrich Schacht (Frankfurt, Berlin: Ullstein, 1994; 3rd. ed. 1995). Page references will be found in the body of the paper. This volume contains the expanded version of Strauß' essay, which was originally published in the conservative journal *Der Pfahl*. It is important to note that the word *selbstbewußt* means both self-aware and self-confident. The book title is thus, in fact, an untranslatable double entendre.

crat Helmut Kohl, who has been Federal Chancellor since 1982, a man of the left in light of his radical politics? Is Strauß perhaps thinking of the Greens? No, the ecology movement is *praised* for having made us aware of the concept of limits (205). On closer inspection, it appears that not just the left, but the entire system of the Federal Republic is under attack here, and it is ironic that Strauß, who considers himself to be a "national" writer,[33] uses the term "Mainstream" to describe this system. He sees a titanic battle brewing "between the forces of tradition and those bent on continually clearing away, throwing out, and obliterating" (203). It was Henry Ford who stated that history is bunk, and Ford was a leading representative of the capitalist system. One recalls that the Marx of the *Communist Manifesto* was also extremely impressed by the ability of capitalism to bring about change, i.e. "clear away, throw out, and obliterate." It is thus some breed of traditionalist versus the sages of Dearborn *and* Trier.

Strauß observes that the system has vanquished both "totalitarianism" and "theocracy" (202), but he sees an Achilles heel, namely its inability to satisfy non-economic needs. And what will we do if our prosperity is threatened by "legions of the dispossessed and displaced?" (203). The tragic dimension of history has not disappeared, we are told, and our modern egoistic paganism is in dire need of re-christianization if we are to maintain our empathy toward these masses. This is because "forty years of a civilized way of life have not changed the soul of the people at all."[34] But is not this so-called "soul of the people" also a component of the German tradition? Amazingly, Strauß has no qualms about asserting the following about the immigration/asylum debate in Germany: "[A] hard, bare, dramatic dichotomy: It is absolutely despicable to raise one's hand against foreigners - it is despicable to naively let in hordes of people who cannot be housed and fed."[35] (This passage was not included in the *Spiegel* version of the essay.) Is it possible that a writer acclaimed for his sophisticated, sensitive use of language did not consider the various connotations of the word "hordes"?[36] The use of a hyphen between the two parts of this assertion is also not a mere stylis-

33. Cf. Volker Hage, "Schreiben ist eine Séance. Der Künstler als nicht mehr ganz junger Mann: Botho Strauß – ein Portrait," *Die Zeit* 4, 1987.
34. Botho Strauß, "Anschwellender Bocksgesang," *Die selbstbewußte Nation*, 34.
35. Ibid.
36. To be fair, this is still rather mild in contrast to the following statement by Frank Castorf: "[E]ven today, I sometimes wish for storms of steel, or that the huns would overwhelm us, or that the Amazon jungle would take over here, I mean, an apocalypse or something like that." Quoted in Stephan Lebert, "Der Fall Frank Castorf: Verwirrende Rollenspiele eines deutschen Intellektuellen," *Süddeutsche Zeitung*, 20 February 1995. This may have been mere posturing, however. At this time, Castorf was presenting his

tic quirk. To equate a government policy – which has of course changed in the meantime – with atavistic violence on the streets is either politically naive, dangerous, or both.

Rather than continuing in this vein, one should turn to the alternative to the reigning system proposed by Strauß. This is where the word "vague" must be applied. He defines being on the right as experiencing "the predominance of memory" as a revolt against "absolute rule of the present, which strives to deprive the individual of all vestiges of the unenlightened past, historical evolution, and mythical time" (204).[37] In other words, the memory he is advocating extends back from the beginning of human civilization to the Enlightenment. How do we return there? Should we restore the monarchy (Strauß *is* fascinated by the "play of kingship" [205]) or even attempt to free our community from hate by reintroducing the ritual of stoning a scapegoat, as described by the French anthropologist René Girard?[38] No, this is not conceivable for Strauß, who allies himself with the power of entropy: "No matter what one does, be it murdering, praying, making revolution or electing parliaments, at some point every form crumbles, the vessels break, and time comes to an end."[39] In the meantime, a self-selecting cultural elite has the duty to save the treasures of our culture for an era when they will once again be appreciated. This model is reminiscent of the conclusion of Ray Bradbury's *Fahrenheit 451*, where small groups of people walk about memorizing the classics. It is a quaint vision, but hardly the program for a conservative revolution. If one applies the criteria elucidated by Wolfgang Benz, Strauß is anything but a right-wing extremist.[40] He is, however, a current manifestation of the otherworldly bard *(Dichter)* so characteristic of German culture. His very existence runs counter to the claim that the past is being eradicated. Some aspects have demon-

---

version of Brecht's *Puntila* in Hamburg, which may have been cathartic, but hardly apocalyptic. Cf. "Lauter Knechte," *Der Spiegel* 3, 1996, 156.

37. One wonders how Strauß can speak of "historical evolution" *(geschichtliches Gewordensein)* and at the same time call past history "the long immutable time" *(die lange Zeit, die unbewegte)* (204).

38. For a brief summary of Girard's ideas, cf. David McCracken, "René Noel Girard," *Encyclopedia of Contemporary Literary Theory*, ed. Irena R. Makaryk (Toronto, Buffalo, London: U. of Toronto Press, 1993), 338-40.

39. Botho Strauß, "Anschwellender Bocksgesang" (cf. footnote 34), 20.

40. The only criterion that does apply is "elitist, impatient consciousness of mission" *(elitär-unduldsames Sendungsbewußtsein)* and the defamation of those who disagree." Benz' criteria are quoted in the following: Dieter Schmidt, "Rechtsextreme und nationalistische Publizistik – ein Netzwerk," *Börsenblatt des deutschen Buchhandels* 48, 17 June 1994, 19. The original source is *Rechtsextremismus in der Bundesrepublik*, ed. Wolfgang Benz (Frankfurt: Fischer, 1989).

strated an uncanny ability to survive the relentless onslaught of the modern world. Above and beyond otherworldliness, he also embodies the German tradition of what one might call "attack discourse." When he finally answered his critics – including Ignatz Bubis, the peripatetic spokesman for Germany's growing Jewish population – in April 1994, he dismissed anyone who could associate him even remotely with anti-Semitism or neo-Nazi atrocities as "either an idiot, a barbarian, or a political slanderer."[41]

Despite their disparate viewpoints, Enzensberger, Walser, and Strauß share a core belief which is of no little significance. All of them condemn National Socialism in the strongest terms, and none of them believes that a revival of the Third Reich is even remotely conceivable. Although one would hope that this prognosis proves accurate, hope is not enough. There is still room for critical analysis in the tradition of the Enlightenment, an activity that Strauß would like to consign to the dustbin of history.[42] In this post-1989 era, such an analysis would be fruitful not only with regard to Strauß, but also vis-à-vis certain other writers, journalists, and academics. The second part of this study should be seen as a brief foray into this largely unexplored territory.

41. Botho Strauß, "Der eigentliche Skandal," *Der Spiegel* 16, 1994, 168. This brief text contains a prime example of Strauß' political naiveté. "Here [on the right, JR], the categorical differentiation is still not as common as on the left, where *no one* [my emphasis, JR] would accuse a writer who advocates democratic socialism of agitating for the return of the Stalinist blood-baths." Ibid., 169.

It should be emphasized that Enzensberger has a very different attitude toward Strauß than Walser does. The following quote from the 1995 interview (cf. footnote 19) illustrates this: "God, he [i.e., Strauß, JR] is a very talented man, but his preoccupations are not mine. I find it indecent to portray oneself as a tragic figure. It is difficult to speak correctly of the tragic, since that can lead all too easily to self-stylization, self-heroization, and kitsch. I don't like any of these poses. … [A]ll this stuff from the 20's that he is constantly referring to, Ludwig Klages, Rudolf Borchardt, all of these leftover, faded motifs … I don't know why he keeps hanging on to these things. A gifted person has to recognize that those are no longer relevant themes."

42. Along this line, Susan Sontag recently defended Enlightenment values in the face of cultural relativism. The occasion was a PEN press conference in support of Chinese democracy activist Wei Jingsheng. Cf. S.S., "On Wei Jingsheng," *The New York Review of Books*, 15 February, 1996, 42. The accompanying open letter protesting Wei's imprisonment was signed by Günter Grass and Peter Schneider, two German writers who have been speaking out on political issues for many years. This jibes with my comments in footnote 52. It is significant that an Austrian philosopher has praised Sontag for her human rights activism while criticizing Peter Handke and other Austrian writers for not accepting the idea of human rights. He calls Handke's stance a "mixture of naiveté and pigheadedness" (Mischung aus Ahnungslosigkeit und Verbohrtheit)." Cf. Wolfgang Müller-Funk, "Perspektivische Blindheit. Österreichs Intellektuelle und die Tragödie am Balkan," *Der Standard*, 10/11 February 1996. This dictum is, in my view, also applicable to Strauß.

At *Der Spiegel,* things have returned to "normal." Since 1993 the magazine has published an essay on Bosnia in which Enzensberger's passivity is sharply criticized,[43] Rudolf Augstein has taken on Ernst Nolte,[44] and pre-1989 political terminology is alive and well.[45] The 1993 "symposium" has proved to be little more than a blip on the screen at the renowned and reviled news magazine.

II.

Anyone who wishes to ponder the prospects of a revival of conservative literature in reunified Germany must begin with the above-mentioned volume *Die selbstbewußte Nation.* The contributors to this collection seek to re-evaluate the past, but their project is not primarily an exercise in intellectual history. They strive above all to formulate a political agenda for reunified Germany. This distinguishes them from other observers who have begun to take a second look at the "Conservative Revolution" of the Weimar era, with an eye to providing it with a measure of intellectual, if not political, legitimation *ex post facto.* In contrast to a figure like Armin Mohler (born in 1920), for whom the encounter with the past had an experiential component,[46] younger scholars such as Rolf Peter Sieferle (1949) or Michael Rupprecht (1965) believe that an objective, distanced reassessment is now possible. Sieferle asserts that it is only now, after the collapse of the radical left, that the Conservative Revolution can be dissected "as a purely historical phenomenon which

43. Günter Franzen, "Bosnien und die Deutschen," *Der Spiegel* 5, 1994, 168-70.

44. "Ein historisches Recht Hitlers? Der Faschismus-Interpret Ernst Nolte über den Nationalsozialismus, Auschwitz und die Neue Rechte," *Der Spiege* 40, 1994, 83-103. At one point, Augstein says the following: "Lately, you have even been speaking of the 'greatness and tragedy' of National Socialism, conceding it a 'historical right,' as if the development had been unavoidable – probably to retrospectively lend significance to what was senseless. That is nothing but cynical historical metaphysics which abstracts from the suffering of the victims" (94).

45. One recent example: No. 23, 1995, contains an article about educational reform. The following passage can be found in that article: "Conservative teachers want to abolish the system of elective courses on the upper level. Progressive pedagogues, on the other hand, are calling for more interdisciplinary courses" (72).

46. Cf. his *Die konservative Revolution in Deutschland 1918-1932* (Stuttgart: Friedrich Vorwerk, 1950) and the revised and expanded version *Die konservative Revolution in Deutschland 1918-1932. Ein Handbuch* (Darmstadt: Wissenschaftliche Buchgesellschaft, 1972). Mohler's aim is to refute the claim that National Socialism was the realization of the visions of the conservative revolutionaries. Although he does not dispute that many of these people were – at least initially – naive about the nature of the Third Reich, he characterizes their efforts as "that movement for spiritual renewal that attempts to clear away the debris left by the 19th century and create a new order of life" (1950, 8.).

should be primarily comprehended, not opposed," although he does conclude that both it and National Socialism were "designs for an alternative modernity ... that fortunately failed."[47] Rupprecht emphasizes that it is necessary to counter the positions of the extreme right – and left – without demonizing them, an act of differentiation that Germany's intellectuals have generally not been capable of in this century.[48] (A great many responses to Strauß' "Bocksgesang" mirror this lamentable state of affairs, one could add.) His plea for a free exchange of ideas unfettered by well-intentioned, but often wrong-headed political correctness is far removed from the thrust of *Die selbstbewußte Nation*, whose editors and essayists strive (with some exceptions) to replace one kind of political correctness with quite another.

The dedication – "To the patriots of July 20, 1944 and June 17, 1953" – is telling in itself.[49] It creates the image of a project directed primarily against totalitarianism per se, implying an equal rejection of Hitler and Stalin and a current political stance somewhere in the center. This is not the case, however. It is true that co-editor Ulrich Schacht (an East German who was imprisoned in the GDR in the 1970s and allowed to leave for the West in 1976) rejects the terror of class or race and rails against "National Socialism, communism, and ignorantism" (57-58), but he also attacks the "block warden *(Blockwart)* system of the West German PC society and its PC commissars" (60). Instead of committing national suicide by shouldering guilt until the end of time, the Germans should, he asserts, realize that Auschwitz was "not unique, but rather a human possibility" (66). Such statements continue the "historians'

47. Rolf Peter Sieferle, *Die Konservative Revolution. Fünf biographische Skizzen* (Frankfurt: Fischer, 1995), 21 and 221.

48. Michael Rupprecht, *Der literarische Bürgerkrieg. Zur Politik der Unpolitischen in Deutschland* (Frankfurt: Josef Knecht, 1995), 29. Rupprecht's book "borrows" part of its title from another work of a very different sort. Cf. Gordon Craig, *The Politics of the Unpolitical. German Writers and the Problem of Power, 1770-1831* (New York and Oxford: Oxford UP, 1995). The title of the original German edition is *Die Poltik der Unpolitischen. Deutsche Schriftsteller und die Macht 1770-1831* (Munich: C.H. Beck, 1993). Both Craig and Rupprecht are of course thinking of Thomas Mann's *Reflections of an Non-Political Man (Betrachtungen eines Unpolitischen).*

49. Of related interest are the two political manifestos issued by co-editor Heimo Schwilk and others. The first criticizes the portrayal of the collapse of Nazism as a "liberation" of the German people, whereas the second protests against the elimination of June 17 as a national holiday and claims that it is pathological for the Federal Republic to allow soldiers to be called "murderers" and to build memorials to deserters. Cf. "8. Mai 1945 – Gegen das Vergessen." *FAZ*, 7 April 1995 and "17. Juni 1953 – Gegen das Vergessen," *FAZ*, 10 June 1995. See also the counter-manifesto "Wider das Vergessen, denn wie sollte man vergessen," *FAZ*, 6 May 1995 and the "second installment" of the original manifesto, "8. Mai 1945 – Gegen das Vergessen," *FAZ*, 5 May 1995.

debate" of the 1980s, and it is thus not surprising that Ernst Nolte's essay contains the oft-heard dictum that the NSDAP was "primarily a militant anti-Communist party," and that there were "objective reasons" for that, i.e., the growing influence of the KPD in the 1920s (152). After assuring the reader that the purported "nationalism" of the "moderate right" is actually nothing more than the attempt to defend "national consciousness" (160), Nolte emphasizes that the true enemy and possible destroyer of the human race is "liberism" *(Liberismus)*, a degenerate form of liberalism which will eliminate the nation states and might well cause a "gigantic shift of population" leading to the apocalypse (161). This "liberism," the consumerist and hedonistic character of reunited, post-Cold-War Germany, has, one reads, brought about the "disappearance of community spirit" and liberated the individual from all ties to "the family, the church, the ethics of one's social rank *(Standesethos)* and the state" (156). Such views are in close proximity with Strauß' "Bocksgesang" article and they actually seem rather tame in comparison to others found in the same volume.

Peter Meier-Bergfeld's paean to Austria, which bears an uncanny resemblance to the campaign speeches of right-wing populist Jörg Haider, culminates in the hope that this small country could lead the way to "fortress Europe" (220). The Austrians, who supposedly ignore the maxims of the Enlightenment, are still capable of distinguishing between natives and foreigners, we are told. (This is attributable to the fact that they are not plagued by "national self-hatred" like the Germans [212]). Felix Stern's polemic against feminism and his warning that this "last of the great totalitarian utopias" would be more inhumane than all of its predecessors (306) is compromised by unintentionally humorous passages. One example: He longs for the old days, when the "little flirt" in the office was taken care of by a box on the ears *(Ohrfeige)* rather than bureaucratic rules (297). He assures us that love in the office can not only injure, but also inspire *(beflügeln)*. Such sophomoric meanderings are at least relatively harmless compared to Gerd Bergfleth's thoughts on the essence of the homeland *(Heimat)*.

Despite references to Carl Schmitt, Heidegger, Klages, and others, this is not an philosophical treatise. It is a broadside against the "ideologies of destruction" produced by the modern era, i.e., "capitalism, communism, National Socialism, and liberalism" (121). Bergfleth agrees with the postulate in Nietzsche's *Genealogy of Morals* that the entire development of the Western world, beginning with Plato, has led to the devaluation of man (113). The last remaining hope for humankind, the "future realm of freedom which is the homeland," is not to be found in the nature of society, but rather in the "natural state" (110). To reach this paradise, we must execute a "turnabout in thinking" *(Denkkehre)* which will take us away from the "superficiality of the Enlightenment" to the "primordial knowledge of myth" (120). This is all vaguely disturbing, but passages in which the incapability of the South to understand the "tragedy of the earth" is contrasted with the "Nordically dark, tragic elemental force" (117) are truly alarming and nothing less than a rehashing of "blood and soil." Bergfleth's call for a return to the "anti-modern tradition of German thought" is in itself enough to discredit the entire volume (122).

Given that there are a number of quite conventional pieces in *Die selbstbewußte Nation,* one wonders what the guiding principle behind the collection might have been.[50] Rainer Zitelmann's call for an alliance of democrats from right and left to defend "pluralistic democracy" is not earth-shaking (165). His anti-utopian project of a democratic conservatism has little in common with Bergfleth's convoluted conjurations. Jochen Thies's call for the rebuilding of a national elite based on ability and achievement rather than class background is worthy of discussion, as are Rüdiger Safranski's observations concerning the fragility of democracy and the necessity of defending civilization against barbarism, even if the outcome is not a foregone conclusion. In light of the strange bedfellows who have been bound together in this weighty tome, would it be possible to imagine the book as a source of inspiration for a new generation of conservative writers in post-1989 Germany?

There are at least two reasons why this would be difficult to imagine. First of all, literature remains on the absolute periphery of most of the contributions, which taken together add up to almost five hundred pages. For example, the following authors are mentioned only once: E. Canetti, M. Frisch, K. Hamsun, H. Heine, H. v. Hofmannsthal,[51] G.E. Lessing, G.C. Lichtenberg, R. Musil, Novalis, F. Schiller, and R. Schneider. Aside from Botho Strauß, whose "Bocksgesang" is the source

50. It is difficult not to look back to the early 1930s, when National Socialism was supported by people with divergent viewpoints. It remains to be seen whether a "Night of the Long Knives," even a purely symbolic one, will befall the group of contributors to *Die selbstbewußte Nation.* This is not said to slander these individuals; it is simply impossible to ignore the historical parallel, since this is a German undertaking.

51. This is not what one would expect, since Hofmannsthal's essay "Literature as the Spiritual Sphere of the Nation" (Schrifttum als geistiger Raum der Nation, 1927) is a key text of the Conservative Revolution. In contrast to this omission, Gerd Bergfleth idolizes romantic writers like Eichendorff, Kerner, and Tieck for helping to reconstruct the "house of the homeland" *(Heimathaus)* (106). In praising *these* writers, he unfortunately compares them to "late modernity," where the culture is rootless and hyper-intellectual (*intellektualistisch*). This of course echoes the way in which Nazi cultural functionaries spoke of Jewish writers.

of the motto at the beginning of each section, it is Ernst Jünger who is by far the dominant figure. And it is not Jünger in the role of prose writer and model for future generations of authors, but rather the "poet-philosopher," (28) who is given this title – together with Heidegger – by Strauß. Secondly, if a literature derived mainly from Nietzsche and Heidegger were actually created, one might well ask who the addressees of such a literature might be in today's Germany. Consider the following statement by co-editor Heimo Schwilk in his epilogue entitled "Mindless Pyromaniacs:"

> They [the generation of 1989, JR] are once again discovering freedom of thought, which includes a knowledge of Critical Theory, Bloch's utopianism, Benjamin's spiritual materialism, Hannah Arendt's analysis of totalitarianism, Heidegger's existential ontology, Carl Schmitt's theory of the state, and Ernst Jünger's esthetics of the miraculous. As necessary as a polarization is in the political sphere, it is nonsense in the esthetic sphere. There are no leftist or rightist metaphors, only good ones and bad ones. (468)

It could be argued that only one group of contemporary Germans would be capable of synthesizing this vast body of knowledge, namely those former leftists from the generation of 1968 who have taken a right turn, embracing the tradition which they previously condemned. This group is the last remnant of a humanistically educated middle class *(Bildungsbürgertum)* that has been on the wane for decades.[52]

---

52. It is thus not surprising to this observer that the controversy surrounding Peter Handke's recent call for "Justice for Serbia" is being monopolized by intellectuals of Handke's generation. The *68ers* are not only products of a different upbringing and education, they are also much more willing to make public pronouncements about controversial issues than their successors. Cf. Peter Handke, "Gerechtigkeit für Serbien," *Süddeutsche Zeitung*, 5 and 13 January 1996. (The two parts were published in book form by Suhrkamp in February 1995. Then new title is *Eine winterliche Reise zu den Flüssen Donau, Save, Morawa und Drina oder Gerechtigkeit für Serbien.)* Cf. Peter Schneider, "Der Ritt über den Balkan," *Der Spiegel* 3, 1996, 163-165; Michael Thumann, "Das andere Serbien," and Andreas Kilb, "Das Neunte Land," *Die Zeit* 4, 1996; Michael Scharang, "Erfahrung schrecklicher Fremdheit," *Der Standard*, 24 January 1996; Peter Vujica, "Ein Elfenbeinturm im Kreuzfeuer," *Der Standard*, 3/4 February 1996. A documentation of the debate can be found in the *Süddeutsche Zeitung*, 27 January, 1996. This contains an excerpt from the *Corriere della Sera* (6 January 1996) in which none other than Enzensberger's nemesis André Glucksmann (cf. footnote 16) refers to Handke as "a mono-maniacal terrorist." In an interview about the controversy, Handke said something that could have been a statement by Strauß about his "Bocksgesang:" "Again and again, people speak of the hatred in my article about Serbia, a hatred which I supposedly felt. Of course rage and anger are part of it, but they are converted into a language game." Cf. "'Ich bin nicht hingegangen, um mitzuhassen.' Peter Handke antwortet seinen Kritikern. Ein ZEIT-Gespräch mit Willi Winkler." *Die Zeit* 6, 1996.

The change in curriculum in the *Gymnasium* (away from the transmission of classical texts) and the incredible expansion and concomitant underfunding of the universities, not to speak of the proliferation, even domination of the visual media, militate against the preservation of a cultural elite inclined to grapple with the textual conundrums produced by a Benn, a Jünger, or even a Strauß. Any new conservatism with real staying power would in all likelihood not be anchored in the realm of literature or even centered around bookish culture of any kind.[53]

53. In his book about Jünger, Marcus Bullock addresses this phenomenon: "without the influence of a conscious fraction capable of critical thinking, the forces of a rightist extremism become still more inclined to indulge in outrageous delusions and come yet more exclusively to feed on and draw strength from the most irrational tendencies of the collective domain." He goes on to say: "It appears to me that the disappearance of this fraction is inevitable with the growing capacity of technology to disseminate political images and imaginings without reference to the traditional institutions of cultural legitimacy." Cf. M.B., *The Violent Eye. Ernst Jünger's Visions and Revisions on the European Right* (Detroit: Wayne State UP, 1992), 10. I would tend to agree with the first statement and question the second, since there has never been a dearth of intellectuals trained in critical thinking willing to offer their services to the powers-that-be. (There is a fine line between representing the status quo and defending it against threats – be they real or imagined.) The interpretative coterie will probably not vanish, but transform itself in order to survive.

After finishing this essay, I received a copy of the Winter 1996 issue of the *German Quarterly*, which contains an insightful article entitled "Syberberg's Germany." The author, Stephen Brockmann, who is also a contributor to this volume, speaks of an ideological affinity between "the two conservative aesthetes" Hans Jürgen Syberberg and Botho Strauß (59). Although there are indeed similarities between the two figures, one cannot ignore significant differences. Strauß is not an anti-Semite, and he is not obsessed with the notion of a purely Germanic culture. He is more concerned with the hermetic texts of an international cultural elite, wherever it may be found (cf. his references to T.S. Eliot, Ezra Pound, Robinson Jeffers, or Nicolás Gómez Dávila) than with canonizing everything of German origin. *Au fond,* he wants to make it possible again for German writers to be critical of or at least skeptical about the Enlightenment Project and its repercussions without being accused of fascist tendencies. Unlike Syberberg, who spent the first decade of his life in the Third Reich, he is also not fascinated by Hitler.

RE/FUSING PAST AND PRESENT

Cinematic Reunification under the Sign of Nationalism and Racism: Helke Misselwitz's *Herzsprung*

Nora M. Alter

(For A.X.A)

Racism is constantly emerging out of nationalism, not only towards the exterior but towards the interior … It is racism which continues to effect the imaginary 'fusion' of past and present in which the collective perception of human history unfolds. (Balibar, "Racism and Nationalism" 45 and 53)

I

The classification and periodization of postwar German literary production within and/or between East and West Germany has been marked from its inception by several tensions and fissures demanding or resisting fusion and/or refusal. Many of these revolve around the relationship between past and present, a relationship sometimes more or less critically and anxiously affirmed, sometimes denied out of hand for various reasons. At the same time, the question of precisely which past and which present are at stake is itself part of the problem. Is it an exclusively German past, for example? In such questions racism and nationalism almost inevitably coalesce or collide, but do so especially in post-reunification Germany and Europe: reunified, that is, under late-capitalist economic and cultural hegemony. "Nation," Raymond Williams remarked, derives from the Latin *nationem:* breed or race, "originally with a primary sense of a racial group rather than a politically organized grouping" (213). Today we are the uneasy witnesses of the return of the etymologically repressed around the globe. The theoretical framework for the following is being developed by French philosopher Étienne Balibar, in dialogue with the American economic historian Immanuel Wallerstein, to the effect that the articulation of racism and nationalism constitutes a structure deeper than any imagined continuity or discontinuity within cultural history, which is in fact determined or conditioned by that structure, and I ask how this hypothesis might bear on our understanding of film.

Noting that historically racism and nationalism have always been on the most intimate of terms, the one as the necessary "supplement" (Jacques Derrida) or "excess" (Georges Bataille) of the other (Balibar, *Masses* 203), and then applying this thesis to the current crisis situation, particularly in the UK and in Europe, Balibar argues that "it does not follow from the fact that racism is becoming more *visible,* that it has arisen out of nothing, or almost nothing" ("Racism and Crisis" 218). He continues: "What would clearly be true for other societies, such as that of the US for example, is in fact also true for our own: racism is anchored in material structures (including psychical and sociopolitical structures) of very long standing, which are an integral part of what is called national identity. Though it experiences fluctuations, though the tendency comes and goes, it never disappears from the social scene, or at least it remains waiting in the wings" (218-19). It remains to know how these structures might be figured – more or less critically – in the audio-visual mass media, including film. I will argue that one film may be particularly useful for this purpose. But first we are forewarned by Paul Willemen about a constitutive paradox of film history. On the one hand "in film studies, the issue of specificity is primarily a national one: the boundaries of cultural specificity in cinema are established by governmental actions implemented through institutions such as censorship and its legislative framework, industrial and financial measures on the economic level, the gearing of training institutions toward employment in national media structures, systems of licensing governed by aspects of corporate law, and so on"; but on the other hand: "The issue of national cinema" – which qua medium, to a far greater extent than literature, also exists in especially complex, dialectical relation to transnational economies and other forces – "is ... primarily a question of address rather than a matter of the filmmakers' citizenship or even the production finance's country of origin" (25 and 28). What, then, is cinema's (one film's or all films') specific address to us in this volume?

In the general terms of our debate, there is the argument that the nationally divided Germany produced two ultimately separate canons of literature and its interpretation. Alternatively, however, in the theory advanced in the seventies by leading cultural critics and producers, it was precisely, if not even exclusively, in the realm of literary production that Germany was *not* subject to socio-economic and political bifurcation. Instead Germany ostensibly was unified, no matter how tenuously, at least as a *Kulturnation*. With Germany's political and economic unification – or rather reunification as nation – this debate has been reopened, the situation once again reassessed. The debate now is rather more nuanced and complex, however, in part for merely quantitative, empirical reasons. That is, in the face of the growing Turkish-German, Afro-German, and other "minority" cultural scenes, the question is no longer really one literature or two? but how many? (To be sure, this question had been posed much earlier with regard to Austrian and Swiss literature, not to mention Tacitus.) More specifically, in the German variant of the perennial, global problem of the dialectic between nationalism and racism, there is the question of how anti-Semitism relates to other forms of discrimination in Germany – old or new. Each xenophobic phrase and act in Germany is shadowed by the spectre of National Socialist anti-Semitism and the Final Solution. Some Germans understandably complain that purportedly identical racist phrases and acts in other countries (from the UK and France to the USA, ex-Yugoslavia, and the former Soviet bloc) are not automatically filtered through this mnemonic grid and thus do not receive similar global attention in the media. Like it or not, however, "Germany" and "the Holocaust" remain virtually inseparable terms.

Whatever the resolution of such debates will or should be, there is some degree of self-legitimation in them, so we participants ought to distinguish as clearly as possible our claims about how German literary history "really was" or "is" from our own perceived need periodically to create problems and rubrics to revitalize a discipline that, like many disciplines, often comes dangerously close to having little other *raison d'être* except to create work for ourselves. In other words, the writing and rewriting of literary history are no more free from ideological determination than its purported texts and contexts of study. It is also interesting to note, in relation to this, that much of the focus of our current debates is on written literary cultural production, novels, poetry, essays, etc. Drama, because of its constitutive tension between text and performance, is a somewhat special, mediatory case. Nor are the fine arts often addressed either. In both Germanies, popular music taste tended to follow the global trend toward English-language production more than toward any indigenous one. And the reception of Federal German

Republic television in some parts of the former German Democratic Republic (GDR) complicates the dialectic between intra- and inter-mural mass cultures even further. In any event, the question of film – still hegemonic among visual media – has been symptomatically ignored in too many current discussions of literary categorization and periodization. But if film is our debate's audiovisual "other," this does not mean we should assume that merely by focusing on film we are necessarily expanding the terms of our debate. This would be as mistaken as assuming that merely by focusing on the irreducibly racist component of nationalism we are necessarily being "progressive." "By insisting on the discreteness and the separateness of the 'other' cultures," Willemen cautions, "the host culture conspires with the conservative upholders of an imagined 'ethnicity' to draw lines around those 'other' cultural practices, ghettoising them" (23). Which ought not, however, foreclose the possibility that a radically different "other" *might* exist.

The full explanation why cinema and the cinematic – my main concerns here – have not been given equal attention compared to their literary counterparts is clearly overdetermined, and in any case too complex to be treated on this occasion except speculatively and en passant. This comparative neglect may be inherent in the elusive nature of the audiovisual medium and the shaky institutional status of film studies as a discipline, but certainly stands in ironic contrast to its power as a particularly effective and popular tool of mass persuasion and propaganda, both overt and covert. On one side of the ideological divide, Lenin had held cinema to be the most powerful of all the media in disseminating the October Revolution; on the other side, Goebbels was to promote the same view for radically different ends. After the war, West Germany was occupied not only by the U.S. military but by a concomitant cultural presence – the often remarked colonization of the German subconscious (as Wim Wenders has said) as manifested primarily in jukeboxes and Hollywood movies.[1] Film production and distribution are different from their literary equivalents insofar as they entail greater technological and logistical problems, and are a fully collaborative enterprise normally demanding far more extensive funding and greater financial risk. Obviously, in the market and commodity economy of the West, commercial success has been a more determinant, driving engine of cinema than it was in the East. But this is hardly reason to refuse to engage the latter and its legacy.

Very early on (May 1946) the GDR created DEFA (Deutsche Film Aktiengesellschaft), the State-operated and -financed film production

---

1. "The Yankees have even colonized our subconscious" is the phrase from Wenders's *Kings of the Road* (1976).

and distribution system. Whereas the American occupation forces stated frankly that they would be totally uninterested in German-made, -directed, or -written films "for at least 20 years," as one U.S. official famously put it (Mückenberger and Jordan 22), the Soviets (partly because their analysis of the roots of national socialism was very different from that of the Americans) were immediately supportive of a new German cinema, and remarkably open to artistic experimentation and freedom, at least initially.[2] The majority of all major types of East German film production came from DEFA, influenced by the great tradition of Soviet-style filmmaking and criticism. Whereas in the West the cinematic paradigm was the even greater power of Hollywood, the GDR attempted to work more or less directly against the hegemony of the capitalist culture industry, specifically its U.S. and the related Weimar, then Nazi variant: UFA *(Universum-Film Aktiengesellschaft).* The result was two — ostensibly — radically different and opposed types of filmmaking: encompassing modes of production and consumption as well as narrative, camera, and editing style in the two major genres, feature film and documentary.[3]

2. In addition to Mückenberger and Jordan, on film in the GDR, see Heimann. For general accounts of cultural politics in the Soviet Occupation Zone (SBZ) and later GDR, see Dietrich, Pike, and Bathrick. A pivot event in the postwar film history of the GDR occurred on 22 November 1945 at the Hotel Adlon, in a meeting that brought together the communist-lead Filmarchiv group along with Soviets, members of the KPD, and several "bourgeois" filmmakers, including some who had worked in Nazi Germany. On contrasting developments in the Western zones of occupation, see the anthology *Zwischen Gestern und Morgen.* I am indebted to Jaimey Fisher for discussion of these issues.

3. Although I cannot speak authoritatively of all or even most DEFA products, my impression is that, in fact, its documentaries departed rather more radically than did the feature films stylistically (as well as in content) from the Western paradigm, whereas GDR feature films differed less in cinematographic style than in content and overt ideology (at least with regard to, say, industrial and working-class narratives and settings). For example, the leading East German team known as H&S (Heynowski and Scheumann) were very overtly ideologically aggressive in their documentaries, in comparison with either French *cinema verité* or American direct cinema, the dominant trends in the West at the time. Heimann argues that there was little or no *thematic* split in films between the occupation zones until around 1948. And the lack of a radical *cinematographic* split, in many cases at least, arguably endured much longer, if there ever was one. Silberman follows German film historians in noting that, during the period of most extensive Stalinization in the GDR, Socialist Realism obviously dominated film production and criticism, and thus often "bogged down in unproductive arguments such as how many weaknesses a protagonist might possess and still be considered a positive hero"; but in the 1960s there came a partial decentralization of "the administrative control of feature film productions," which resulted in "relatively autonomous, self-managed production groups within the DEFA studios"; and, with the erection of the Berlin Wall in 1961, the climate was deemed "stable enough internally to tolerate the kind of experimentation that New Wave Polish cinema or Soviet directors had implemented successfully after 1956" (147).

In addition to the supposed incompatibility of the two "national" types of cinematic apparatus (though some important overlaps and notable exceptions do exist), there was the partly successful attempt of West German New German Cinema to crack the world (capitalist) market. As has often been pointed out, however, the popularity of New German Cinema was in effect a creation of New York City audiences and critics, before being cultivated and codified into a coherent (in part self-legitimating) genre by both American and West German scholarship.[4] Thus, what has become the best known "German" genre and/or period of filmmaking (whose by no means homogeneous practitioners include Wenders, Fassbinder, Herzog, Kluge, von Trotta, and Syberberg) was in good measure an American capitalist phenomenon, in spite of the movement's general critique of capitalism and of Hollywood in particular.[5] With regard to the question before us, it is unfortunate that almost no comparable effort, recognition, and critical scrutiny have occurred in the case of East German cinema, the audience for which remained largely within the former GDR and Soviet bloc. The critical and scholarly balance is similarly lopsided and isolated with the one in film production: in spite of growing interest, GDR cinema remains largely terra incognita. And this is part of the reason why I will focus on a film by a former East German filmmaker. (It is necessary to add that *all* film history remains widely disregarded in many discussions in the academy about "culture." As recently as 1996 – the centennial of the medium – philosopher Stanley Cavell remarked that "film has barely begun, with certain revelatory exceptions, to inspire a degree and continuity of critical or philosophical response worthy of itself. It seems to me a cause of wonder that universities at large remain unpuzzled by this lag" [xi]). In terms of distribution, after reunification just as before, East German films are exceptionally difficult to obtain, making scholarly work on them or their use in the class-

4. One might even argue that this moment of cross-cultural exchange went back to film's very first incarnation. Silent film, as Schlüppmann has been showing, was a fundamentally *international* medium at the point of both production and reception, including ostensibly "national" cinemas; henceforth all cinema history has moved in a more or less visible and audible dialectic process from local to global styles and markets. While Schlüppmann's *Unheimlichkeit des Blicks* (1990) focuses especially on women's issues, her more recent work is on the earliest cinema more generally.

5. West German New German Cinema – arguably the *only* German cultural product with a legitimate claim to play a significant role in the global cultural market – has been nurtured and cultivated at home and abroad by scholarly books, journals, conferences, university courses, and so forth. This includes the efforts of individuals, but also of institutions such as the German Academic Exchange Service (DAAD) and the Goethe Institute, both of which work closely with West German production companies to distribute these films to the widest possible world audience. In fact, it is now easier to obtain New German Cinema films and videos in the United States and in France than in Germany.

room prohibitively difficult, indeed well nigh impossible.[6] All this is to say that cinema and the cinematic – and *a fortiori* that of the former GDR – are still not full-fledged members either of the German *Kultur-nation* or of debates about its very existence, and likely will not be for some time. Rather than provide a survey of post-war or post-reunification films (which would presuppose what is by no means certain: namely, that we are able to "read" each film thus systematized), I want to take a different tack, Which is to provide an interpretive model based largely on a single film that I argue brings together significant themes and structures informing both the period of film history and the critical debate here at issue, and does so in the context of the nationalist-racist nexus.

II

Helke Misselwitz's 1992 feature film *Herzsprung* is a co-production between the revamped DEFA and the western German channel ZDF, thus straddling the 1989 divide by way of financial backing as well as in other ways.[7] The first German – followed mainly by French – films about the fall of the Wall were documentary or quasi-documentary media events, globally transmitted with remarkably stereotypical redundancy (see Alter, Geisler, and *Mauer-Show*). *Herzsprung* is one of a growing number of feature films on post-reunification, and the first major example made by a former East German filmmaker. It is Misselwitz's second major film. The first was *Winter Adé* (1988), a documentary recording the lives of East German women. Made on the eve of reunification, it is a remarkable film, pointing to the social inequities and disparities between men and women in the GDR, and arguing that radical gender equality was attained only nominally.

Herzsprung opens in a post-reunification female work space reminiscent of those depicted in *Winter Adé*, and to DEFA industrial images

6. These factors play an important role, of course, in the creation and canonization of any body of cultural production and study. In sharp contrast to the treatment of former East German films is the recent availability of the huge number of Third Reich feature films (which were typically not overtly propagandistic, following Goebbels's memorable dictum that strong nations don't need propaganda), resulting in an steadily growing number of articles and books on the topic, conferences, and circulating film series both in Germany and the United States. It is to be hoped that the situation with regard to GDR production, film criticism, and theory will change through the current efforts of Barton Byg and others to establish a center in North America for the study of DEFA.

7. On specific and general problems regarding the survival and direction of DEFA after reunification, see the ongoing dialogue since the 1990s in the the former East German publication *Film und Fernsehen*, especially "Quo vadis Babelsberg," Radevagen, *Das zweite Leben*, and *Kinemathek*. I am indebted to Eric Rentschler for these references.

and narratives generally – this time a goose processing factory in the actual former East German town of Herzsprung (literally, heartbreak or fissure in the heart).[8] As they work, the women sing popular trans-German melodies, among them "Heimat süsse Heimat," with what we might call the "n/ostalgic" refrain "when will we ever see you again?"[9] The referent is ambiguous: the shifter "you" could refer as much as to the former East German *Heimat* as to any more generic one. As she is preparing to leave her shift for the day, the lead female protagonist, Johanna (in her late-twenties or early thirties and who may allude, at once appreciatively and ironically, to Brecht's 1932 didactic play *Die Heilige Johanna der Schlachthöfe* [St. Joan of the Stockyards])is told by the supervisor that she is being laid off due to the closure of the factory kindergarten where she has been working. (In the GDR most factories had social services and day care centers for the employees.) With the selling off of these businesses to Western buyers through the establishment of Treuhand, these services were deemed unprofitable and were widely abolished. Concomitantly, the number of employees was dramatically reduced in a radical downsizing that left large portions of the population unemployed and even unemployable. Another reference to the often draconian economic restructuring by Treuhand, memorably brought on stage by Rolf Hochhuth in his 1992/93 docudrama *Wessis in Weimar: Szenen aus einem besetzten Land* (Westerners in Weimar: Scenes from an Occupied Country)[10] will occur later in the film, when a new West German owner of a former East German chocolate factory tries to seduce Johanna with French champagne and chocolates, assuming that her new economic plight makes her an easy sexual target. But Johanna resists this potential and actual, literal and figurative, "rape by the West", keeping her gender, if not also class, integrity intact by emptying a cold glass of bubbly onto the crotch of the New Order of bosses. Thus does Misselwitz allegorize economic tensions as gender relations, with the dominant male obviously standing for the capitalist West and the victim/female for the formerly socialist East. To be sure, this use of the female as social, historical, and political victim or scapegoat has long been a popular, if

8. At the end of the film, Misselwitz provides a suitably ambiguous caveat in her credits to the effect that, although the town of Herzsprung actually exists, we ought not necessarily expect to find there what we see in the film.

9. "Ostalgie" was a popular term circulating in the years following unification, referring to a nostalgia for the life in the former East Germany and even East Bloc generally.

10. *Wessis in Weimar* was first performed in Berlin by the (East) Berliner Ensemble – a performance, directed by Einar Schleef, that greatly shortened the play, added gratuitous sex, and was quickly denounced by Hochhuth, who threatened to issue a restraining order to have the play shut down. A second performance, in February 1993, in Hamburg directed by Yves Jansens, however, met more with his approval.

highly problematic filmic trope, not least throughout New German Cinema. Yet Johanna is not the only victim for Misselwitz, who further complicates the problematic of national identity in explicit terms of race. And it is this remarkably continuous problematic, I argue, that complicates, if not obviates, any clear periodization or classification of "German" film history "beyond 1945" or "beyond 1989."

On her way home after her dismissal, Johanna encounters a group of Russian troops standing next to their truck near a wood; the music track we hear turns out to be diegetic, produced by an accordion played by a young civilian (though he may also have been in the army once) who swaps his bicycle for an army greatcoat. Johanna offers to give him a ride to town with her two children in her red car (one of many significant flashes of color that will flare up in the predominantly grey and brown Eastern German landscape). When she asks him where he would like to go, his reply is "where I am not from – farther and farther away." In response to one child's direct question about who he is, he calls himself "the wind." He has or is not given a proper name in the film. Only in the final credits is he retroactively named as "der Fremde" (the foreign man, or stranger). And we should recall throughout the movie Gilman's having demonstrated that in Germany "Terms such as *Neger*, with the implication of 'loner' ... reflect the borrowing of preformed concepts of blackness from an American racist model of the black" (xii). It is equally important, I think, that in the film this young person's skin color – black – may be registered by the audience non-diegetically, but is registered diegetically by other protagonists in the film only much later, after he returns from an unexplained and unmotivated absence from Herzsprung. In other terms, the first racist "in" the film is not in the film at all – it may be us.

In the scene at the edge of the forest and in the abstract nature of the young man's reply to the question of his identity, he becomes an overdetermined, polysemous figure. Reminiscent of an *actant* in fairy tale or other narratives, "he" changes according to narrative situations, but nevertheless retains a certain rigid structural function in the narrative.[11] The

11. Jameson usefully paraphrases Greimas's theory of the *actant* for film criticism as follows: "It is in order to distinguish between the surface content of the enunciation-spectacle (which may involve philosophical concepts or abstract entities just as much as the characters of ordinary narration) and this deeper underlying structure that Greimas evolves the term *actant*, which can be articulated either as a function (as the possibility of a certain type of performance) or as a qualification (involving the conferral of a certain number of attributes). Such a distinction permits us at once to reorganize our reading of a given text and to recognize more fundamental mechanisms at work beneath the surface. So, for instance, it may turn out that a character or actor in a given narrative in reality serves as a cover for two separate and relatively independent *actants*; or that two actors,

Stranger is overcoded: a stereotypical wanderer (a racially displaced Wandering Jew?) or some other quintessentially homeless or cosmopolitan person (gypsy? communist?); a latter-day Pied Piper (a possibility reinforced later in the film); a picaresque antihero (Grimmelhausen's Simplicissimus, Kosinski's painted bird, or Grass's tin drummer?); a runaway slave (Twain's Jim?); and, not least in the German context, a (male) "guest worker" propelled by the flow of transnational capital. And we may note with Paul Gilroy that,"It is often forgotten that the term 'diaspora' comes into the vocabulary of black studies and the practice of pan-Africanist politics from Jewish thought" (205), and is thus part and parcel of the deep interconnection between all forms of more or less systemic racism and nationalism and what Gilroy terms the resulting "double consciousness" they produce or maintain. This particular "stranger" speaks fluent German, apparently his mother tongue. The possibility that he is "Afro-German" (or, alternatively, "Afro-American," "African," or "Negro") is explicitly noted by Johanna later in the film in conversation with her father, but she concludes that above all (visually, we should add, not audibly according to her standards) he is "simply black." Thus, while he may be a radically shifting signifier, the shift is always anchored by the sheer visible fact of having a black body, which is, lamentably, a near-universal referent for the outsider, though one often brutally delimited by racial particularism. So too, he is a sign with a multitude of possible referents, and we are left to fill in many blanks, but not quite all.

Another way of viewing The Stranger, then, is not (only) as an *actant* but (also) as Johanna herself does: namely, for her he is a sexually desirable, black, male body. As such, he might seem to be a positive version of what Bill Nichols (referring to the savage beating of Rodney King by the "ordinary fascism" of the LAPD) has called "that excess beyond the frame" (19). Alternatively put, The Stranger would be what (developing an argument by Michael Rogin) Ella Shohat and Robert Stam call "the 'surplus symbolic value' of oppressed people; the way Blacks, for example, can be made to stand for something beside themselves" (183 and 187), indeed *are always required*, whether by coercion or consent, to stand for something other than what they might otherwise possibly be. In contrast with George A. Romaro's cult classic *Night of the Living Dead*

---

independent personalities and separate characters in the story-line, amount to little more than alternating articulations of an *actant* structurally identical in both contexts" (Jameson 124-25; and Greimas 173-85). In *Herzsprung*, for example, one might view The Stranger as covering several national and racial *actants* and view, say, Johanna's suicided husband as having the same actantial function as that of the skinheads who murder her, with respect to the fact that both are unemployed and that this leads both to her harm and to its structural explanation as advanced by the film, and so on.

(1969), where the black protagonist's race is never acknowledged by others in the film (unless perhaps at the very end the moment he is killed), the black male body in *Herzsprung* is identified as such at first only by the viewer (as in Romero's zombie film), and further (in Misselwitz's case), by other protagonists eventually. The consequences of this performative recognition are lethal, but, as we will see presently, not so much for The Stranger as for his lover, Johanna, who is murdered at the film's dismal end. With her dies more than one individual. For she, along with certain other young working women in the film, are arguably the *only* strong points of explicit verbal and physical resistance offered to fascist resurgence by Misselwitz in this film. In this regard at least Misselwitz seems to have continued the tradition of one stage in the failed and counterproductive East German and Soviet analysis of fascism and national socialism, namely, that true resistance would come from the working class, to which Misselwitz has merely added the gender supplement: the female working class. The Stranger (along with the CEO of the chocolate factory) becomes a virtual exception to Misselwitz's film rule that all men are unemployed, while all women work, or at least try. Needless to say, this way of forging a German *Kulturnation* (i.e., neo-Stalinist workerism fused to Western feminist essentialism) would certainly not provide a very savory answer to the deeper questions at hand. Were Misselwitz's film easily reducible to this solution, it would be a far less interesting and important film than it is.[12]

Clearly, Johanna's victimhood as class and gendered "other" appears displaced by the insertion into the diegesis of a visually and racially more striking "other," at least in the German context. So how might this "other", this blackness, then function fully as a signifier in *Herzsprung*? But before attempting to answer this question, we would do well to recall in passing Roland Barthes's seminal semiotic analysis of the photograph of the black French soldier on the cover of *Paris Match* in which Barthes showed that, whereas visual images are always already infused with ideologically *coded* messages, their actual effects remain unstable, unpredictable, and cannot be ideologically *fixed* once and for all (116-21).

---

12. Although I cannot deal adequately with Misselwitz's complex soundtrack here, I should at least note that it can be interpreted as an attempt to produce another kind of "German" *Kulturnation*. The music track, for example, is part nondiegetic (e.g., *Aïda*) and part diegetic. The latter is particularly interesting in the several dance hall scenes in the town of Herzsprung. Here or elsewhere in the film, we hear a fusion of various types of musical styles, ranging from variations of German, African, and Russian folk music (there are Russian officers as well as young German people in the dance hall) to neo-punk of both German and international inspiration. In other terms, Misselwitz's critically expansive notion of a *Kulturnation* is effectively expressed as much aurally as visually.

After his initial encounter with Johanna, The Stranger disappears for a time from Herzsprung, as we learn more about her everyday life. She lives with her Polish-German father, whose wife died giving birth to Johanna. (As the film progresses it is certainly possible to read an incestuous relationship here, though I prefer here to stress other aspects.)[13] Johanna is estranged from her husband, who, in his despair at being laid off, drinks heavily, beats her, and then commits suicide at the co-operative dairy farm where he had worked before privatization. (He shoots first the herd of cows in a barn, then himself in the pool of their blood.) Johanna finds part time work in the beauty salon of her girl friend (who later splits for the hedonistic – not to say orientalist – pleasures of Greece), and later is refused work as a cook at the local nunnery because of her relationship to The Stranger. (Interestingly, in light of the role played by churches in the *Wende*, in Misselwitz's film, neither the Protestant nor Catholic Church offers resistance to the racist upsurge in the town.)

The Stranger's reappearance in Herzsprung is marked in a striking way, neatly filming, as it were, philosopher Balibar's theory, expressed in my epigram, that "racism is constantly emerging out of nationalism" and that "It is racism which continues to effect the imaginary 'fusion' of past and present in which the collective perception of human history unfolds." First, we see Johanna's old father staring despondently at the graffiti on a plaque commemorating the dead at Sachsenhausen: "Foreigners belong in concentration camps." This palimpsest text, desecrating the memory of past crimes with the present call for their repetition, is isomorphically matched in the narrative, camera work, and editing by cinematographic palimpsest that overlaps two races, generations, and modes of "otherness," which are all simultaneously fused, re-fused, confused, and refused. Suddenly redeposited in town by local bus, The Stranger is immediately shown looking at the same graffiti and directing an enigmatic question to Johanna's father: "Communist?" The father's reply is equally laconic: "Not all were communists." This can also be read several ways, including as a restoration of the communists to the long list of victims of the Nazi Holocaust from which, in the West, the communists are commonly omitted. But I take it as significant that the more common referent, at least in the West, "Jew", is absent not only in this sequence, where one might first or most expect it, but also throughout the film. Why? Johanna's father immediately adds to his mysterious answer to the question "Communist?" just: "No," presumably meaning that *he* is not one, either. Or is it *no longer*? Instead he says simply: "I am

13. Stephanie Ortega has given several public papers on the incestuous aspect of *Herzsprung*; I am also grateful to her for providing me a copy of the film.

something like you." But that "something" too, is left inarticulated: indeed, is the key absent signifier of the film, insofar as it articulates the post-reunification national question to the problem of race, both literally and figuratively. But then the notion that Jews *are* blacks is an old German fairy tale.[14]

Johanna's father and The Stranger now enter the local pub and start drinking schnapps and beer chasers and smoking cigars in unexpected camaraderie and manly *Gemütlichkeit*. The old man, yet another laid-off "farmer on a collective farm," expresses his old impossible, but properly communistic dream to travel the entire world, including, he says, Africa. His most fervent desire was to have been washed up on a desert island accompanied by a Girl Friday (whereupon The Stranger laughs, in an act of male bonding). Thus Johanna's father brings a tacit colonial plane of reference almost to the surface, and further links (via Marx's seminal critique of the "Robinsonade" of classical bourgeois economists) his discourse (and, allegorically, that of his generation and nation) with recent and current German history. We later learn that Johanna's father was indeed incarcerated in a concentration camp, perhaps for being a communist, perhaps for being (also) a Pole, though this, too, is left palpably unspecified in the diegesis. At any rate, this interpersonal connection between the two persecuted "others" (i.e., communists and/or Poles and/or blacks; once again, Jews are not mentioned) serves to articulate an audiovisual link rooted in some form of imperialist aggression and/or colonialism, with the black as a visual referent registering the long history of exploitation, domination, murder, and genocide. It should be recalled that the German National Socialist theory and practice of racial stereotyping and genocide began not with reference to the Jewish people but, in South West Africa at the turn of the last century, which brought to a crisis point a long tradition of German racism regarding Subsaharan Africa.[15]

14. As Gilman has shown, in both Hitler's *Mein Kampf* and Rosenberg's *Der Mythos des 20. Jahrhunderts*, "the presence of the 'Blacks' in Germany is linked with or paralleled to the central stereotype of German racism, the Jew. This interconnection marked the projection of the image of the other onto the reality of the "Jewish Question" in twentieth-century Germany. Indeed one of the qualities ascribed by Anti-Semites to the Jews (as well as to the Gypsies) was their 'blackness,' a quality of the world of the stereotype rather than of reality" (xiv).

15. On turn of the century genocide, see Swan. It was led and studied, respectively, by Heinrich Göring (Hermann Göring's father), who was "Reich Commissar for South West Africa," and by Eugen Fischer, later the Nazi's leading "racial hygienist" and head of the Kaiser Wilhelm Institut in Berlin. On the long history of German stereotypes about Subsaharan Africa, dating back at least to the middle ages, see *Négritude et Germanité*. For a discussion of eighteenth-century German racism and racial stereotyping with regard to blacks, see Harris-Schenz. And for various aspects of German-black relations, organized around the phenomenon "blackness without blacks," see Gilman.

If The Stranger is to be read, at least in part, not only as an Afro-German but also as an *East* German Afro-German, he can also be read as the legacy of the GDR presence in Subsaharan Africa: fighting racism, capitalism, and apartheid in Angola. Be this as it may (and it is *not* clear that *any* fixed historical referent is ultimately at stake in this film), by also figuring The Stranger as a former East German, perhaps, and the father as a former communist, perhaps, one possible argument by association is that the model of colonialism can be applied to the exploitation of defeated East Germany, defeated not by West Germany, *nota bene*, but by the collapse of "socialism in one country" and by transnational capitalism *en marche*, with West Germany equally a victim someday. Whatever stand one takes on the issue, the argument that East Germany can be considered as a kind of colony to the West is hardly controversial. (Recall Hochhuth's subtitle, "scenes from an occupied land.") But a specifically *racial* colony? Now, that's a much more controversial premise. And, if that is indeed the point (intended or unintentional) of *Herzsprung*, it requires nuanced interpretation, especially as it might bear on our own debate about the German *Kulturnation*.

However, a further level of signification emerges in this early part of Misselwitz's film. The nascent fraternal relationship between The Stranger and Johanna's father breaks down immediately when the old man realizes that the former has come to see "a woman with blonde hair, a red car, and two children." The fear of miscegenation, it appears, cancels all previous bets and potential historical blocs. Blackness becomes *particularly* "visible" at this moment, it appears, at least diegetically. (It is in the next sequence when Johanna runs down the list of possible racial "identities" – including "Afro-German" and "Afro-American", before deciding that The Stranger is ultimately "black.")[16] Nevertheless, The Stranger decides to stay and is asked by some locals if he is looking for a job. They are opening an American-style diner on the autobahn link between the former East and West. Upon his affirmative answer to this, his first possibility of work, a local responds: "Good, now we know what we'll call it." Incredibly, that name is "Onkel Toms Hütte" – Uncle Tom's Cabin. Actually, the allusion in the name is not only literary, but analogous: namely (as a German might know), to the former American military occupation colony in the Nazi-built suburbs of West Berlin, as well as (clearer to a North American audience) to the image of black slavery in the American South.[17] Thus another conceptual link is forged –

16. This difficulty in accepting or acknowledging a name for racial "identity" is hardly uncommon among Germans with African ancestry (see, e.g., the interview "Es gibt keinen selbstverständlichen Namen für uns" in *Farbe bekennen* 159-61).

17. Actually, images of Uncle Tom's Cabin were available in Germany, by at least the late nineteenth-century, including in the form of collectible "advertising cards" for

via a work place, if only in the service industry – between on the one hand a vast geopolitical past and foreign backwardness, underdevelopment, economic depression, and above all, slavery and racism, and on the other, part ironically, of course, but not only that, a contemporary Germany that is uncannily closer to all "homes."

Roaming Herzsprung are three jobless, ferociously male-bonded youths. We watch their interspliced evolution from bored kids, and Johanna's former classmates, into explicitly racist skinheads (Johanna and her hairdresser friend do the honors) who are ultimately responsible for terrorizing The Stranger, in a miniature, allegorical reincarnation of American Klu Klux Klan or German *Freikorps* strongarm tactics. This will eventually lead to the inadvertent murder/sacrifice of Johanna. But first, the punks harass The Stranger in an increasing crescendo of explicitly racist incidents: beginning with verbal taunts, they then simulate a lynching with a black baby doll, or tar baby, at Uncle Tom's Cabin. Finally, they incinerate the diner, after having tied the bound and gagged Stranger to a tree where he mutely watches the eerie conflagration on New Year's Eve. They wile away the time by throwing knives at The Stranger, as if at the side show of a circus or carnival. Their intent is not to kill him, or so they say, but it is one of these knives that unintentionally kills Johanna as she attempts to intercede, having barely escaped the diner with her own life. (The skinheads didn't know she was inside.) While the actions of these youths are obviously depicted in and by Misselwitz's film as heinous, their actions and racism are also depicted as being, at least in part, structurally (i.e., economically) motivated, much as was the suicide of Johanna's husband after beating her. In other words, her beating at the hands of one solitary unemployed man foreshadows her death at the collective hands of others. Predictably, the skinheads claim that "foreigners" are taking away their jobs, by which they do not mean the West German CEOs sent by the Treuhand, needless to say. For the tacit compact between German big business and the vanguard of nazism is a spectre that continues to haunt the world. Too, although Johanna is very vocal in rejecting the skinheads' racism directed against both her own lover and "others" in general (it was they who desecrated the Sachsenhausen plaque), she flirts with one of them. So they are not figured as entirely heinous after all, but at most reveal the banality of evil.

Leibig's Beef Extract. Gilman explains: "In the card illustrating *Uncle Tom's Cabin*, the German public was presented with a visual image of the Black which bore little resemblance to any contemporary reality. Rather it reflected the German adaptation of an external tradition of seeing the Black. The American literary image of the Black was altered by the German tradition to fit the idea of the Black in this world without Blacks" (frontisepiece).

So perhaps Misselwitz is attempting what may be the impossible: namely, to forge an *ideological-cum-cinematographical* link between the film and political theory of the GDR (an economic, not to say econo-mistic, explanation of racism and nazism) on the one hand; and a psy-chological portrait, a reduction of history and economic structures to a love story (Hollywood) on the other. Is this the term, then, by which Germany is properly figured as a *Kulturnation* cinematically? Whatever answer *Herzsprung* might ultimately give to this question, and perhaps this is the positive aspect of its DEFA Marxist legacy of structural analy-sis, this one film resists better than most what Raymond Bellour has dubbed "the Hollywood matrix", that is, "the machine for the produc-tion of the couple" (see Bellour; also Zizek 241), the relentless, nearly mechanical tendency of the dominant style of feature filmmaking to reduce complex historical events to love stories.

Now, in *Herzsprung* the string of referents drawing East Germany and the American South together in alliance remains overdetermined in its implications. It obviously displaces, and/or maps onto, the former East Germany the racist South – a highly clichéd albeit true image – effectively establishing a suitably complex cross-temporal, geopolitical, and geo-aes-thetic referent. But does this articulation then whitewash the specificity or peculiarity of past and present acts of German aggression against so-called foreigners (not least Jews and communists once and Turks, Arabs, or Asians today), by placing them in a broader and more properly universal problematic of racism? To put it bluntly, is this a kind of revisionist filmic history? And are all East Germans – including racist skinheads – the nig-gers of Germany, all internal differences aside? It is striking – by its prox-imity but ultimate absence – that neo-nazism as such never figures in the Herzsprung depicted in *Herzsprung*. Anti-Semitism is simply not men-tioned, explicitly or implicitly. Paradoxically, I'd say that it is so obviously not mentioned that it is mentioned all the time *ex negativo*. The skinheads do not sport swastikas, for example, and the reference to the murdered of Sachsenhausen, as we have seen, was immediately and obviously diverted away from Jews to communists. Before lamenting this displacement as revisionist (even labelling it as displacement), I'd like to illuminate it (which is not to explain it away or affirm it) by another central thesis of Balibar's in his argument about the mutual imbrication of nationalism and racism, past and present. But I want to do so as the first phase of a two step process: the first will offer a relatively benevolent reading of the artic-ulation of nationalism and racism in *Herzsprung*; the second will be more critical. To anticipate my overall point: the film would be less exemplary for our purposes here if we could easily resolve this apparent antinomy between negative and positive interpretations of it.

III

Balibar notes that, at the end of our century, we possess three or four basic paradigms of racism: "Nazi anti-Semitism," "the segregation of Blacks in the USA (perceived as a long sequel to slavery)," and "the 'imperialist' racism of colonial conquest, wars and domination" – with South African apartheid combining elements of all three ("Racism and Nationalism" 38 and 40). And one question now might be: How many paradigms does *Herzsprung* attempt to fuse or refuse? At the same time, however, Balibar warns that current racism should not be reduced to *any* historical paradigm, and hence explained away: "the figures of Nazi anti-Semitism and colonial anti-racism or indeed slavery cannot simply be evoked as models against which to measure the purity and seriousness of such and such a 'racist upsurge' nor even as periods or events which mark out the place of racism in history, but they must be considered as ever active formations, part conscious and part unconscious, which contribute to structuring behaviour and movements emerging out of present conditions" (40).

I would suggest that the most benevolent ideological reading of Misselwitz's *Herzsprung* would follow Balibar, expanding his thesis to include the case of Germany and its post reunification films:

> the identification of racism with anti-Semitism – and particularly with Nazism – functions as an alibi: it enables the racist character of the "xenophobia" directed against immigrants to be denied. Conversely, however, the (apparently quite gratuitous) association of anti-Semitism with anti-immigrant racism in the discourse of the xenophobic movements that are currently developing in Europe is not the expression of a generic anti-humanism, of a permanent structure of exclusion of the "Other" in all its manifestations, nor the simple passive effect of a conservative political tradition (whether it be called nationalist or fascist). Much more specifically, and much more "perversely," it organizes racist thought by giving it its conscious and unconscious models: the character of the Nazi extermination, which is strictly unimaginable, thus comes to be lodged within the contemporary complex as the metaphorical expression of the desire for extermination which also haunts anti-Turkish or anti-Arab racism. ("Racism and Nationalism" 45)

And, it appears evident, haunts anti-black culture and actions generally.[18]

18. More specifically, though it is unclear to me whether Misselwitz is buying into this problem or critiquing it, her film seems inscribed by European, but most especially German, anxieties about the racial migrancies that are likely to increase with European integration: enabling, say, "black" British or French citizens of all classes to circulate more frequently, in and out of jobs, throughout the EEC. This German anxiety is by no means new, either, reflecting as it does a very old problem in its cultural, social, and intellectual

But let me now suggest a more critical reading of the film. I return to the conversation between Johanna and her father after he learns that The Stranger has come to Herzsprung in pursuit of his daughter. He informs her that "a Negro's come for you" *(für dich ist ein Neger angekommen)*. She quickly retorts that *Neger* is pejorative (especially in its resonance with "nigger"), and that one might prefer instead "African," "Afro-American," or "Afro-German," though she herself uncritically retains the skin color designation "black." Thus a German variant of the American politically correct seems to emerge. But does the PC-vocabulary (ever) run any deeper than lip service? In other words, is a radically, thought-through multi-cultural stance sustained either by a protagonist or by Misselwitz's film itself?

As might be expected, following the nearly universal paradigm of racism directed against the colonized other, The Stranger is simultaneously exoticized and eroticized. Johanna is immediately and viscerally attracted to him when she – and we – first see him, playing the accordion for the Russian troups. The later shower scene is reminiscent of Fassbinder's *Ali, Fear Eats the Soul* (1974), in which the older German woman, Emmi, stares transfixed when her much younger Moroccan lover, Ali, showers.[19] In *Herzsprung* The Stranger's naked body becomes, almost exclusively, the object of Johanna's female gaze, which is also momentarily our own point of view. Misselwitz's shower scene is one of several significant times when the viewer is interpellated as Johanna, The Stranger eroticized by the camera as Johanna's gaze. Still fully clothed, she joins him in the shower (being half pulled in, willingly), and this elicits his remark that "whites shower with their clothes on" – spoofing the common progression of all stereotyping, all ideology, from the singular observation to the universal claim. Upon the removal of her clothes, the camera tracks down the length of their bodies pressed together in simu-

---

history. One of the most recent German collective memories was of the occupation, particularly by integrated French forces (the U.S. army was not racially integrated until the Korean conflict, though similar if not greater fears were projected onto segregated U.S. divisions). In the case of the French, "At their peak Blacks numbered about 10,000 out of a force of about 200,000. The 'Black' troops which occupied Frankfurt turned out to be Moroccan and Algerian Tirailleurs. Other 'Black' troops were from Indochina (indeed the Indochinese formed the majority of French colonial troops in Germany)" (Gilman xiii). The fabricated legend of the "Black Horror" (which had been inculcated deliberately by the Nazis in their *Götterdämmerungstimmung* propaganda campaigns to get the Germans to fight to the last man and woman) was not only German, however. It also infected high government officials in the United States and Great Britain (Gilman xiii-xiv). That the first act of The Stranger in *Herzsprung* is to trade his bike for an army overcoat, which he wears throughout much of the remainder of the film, would presumably trigger these anxieties, as well: yet another link between "1945" and "1989."

19. For a discussion of racism and gender in *Ali, Fear Eats the Soul*, see Mennel.

lated sex, visually stressing white flesh against black. Johanna washes him, saying playfully "I can't get the black off" – leaving open whether she might *want* it off or not. Be this as it may, the eroticization of his body, and its power of seduction over her, is thus implicitly and explicitly linked to the wholly contingent fact of skin hue. Indeed, The Stranger's main character trait – beyond his extreme, saint-like passivity and pacifism – appears to be heightened sexual prowess. It is by no means limited to Johanna, although, as he puts it when she discovers him with the waitress in the diner: "My body belongs to me, my heart belongs to you." At any rate, we see absolutely no character development in The Stranger. Moreover, aside from a few minimal – albeit always fluent and pithy – comments or even philosophemes, he is otherwise in several senses mute and muted. His space in the film is both visual, as occupied by his sheer physical presence, and aural, in the music soundtrack which accompanies him or which he produces himself (he also appears to be a great dancer!). But, again like Ali in *Fear Eats the Soul,* he is not given a full discursive space in which to speak his mind or interact socially. The painful, hurtful (and undoubtedly unintentional) cliché of the sexually active black "other" is also played out when Johanna (wearing her dead mother's wedding dress) discovers him embracing the other waitress: she is similarly black, but has no other part or voice in the film.

In an instructive comparison, West German filmmaker Dorris Dörrie's 1995 film, *Nobody Loves Me,* features a gay Afro-German male, born and raised in the GDR. He dies, we may infer, of AIDs. In Dörrie's film, the exoticism is overtly figured and thematized when he tries to disguise his East German origins, performing extravagant rituals as an African mystic masked in "foreign" clothes, often in drag. Like The Stranger in *Herzsprung,* this person becomes an object of fascination for another very white European woman, though in this instance sexual alliance is eschewed. In the case of both films (one East, one West), Afro-Germans are signifying monkeys of an especially stereotypical kind: they dance, perform, play music, are sexually promiscuous, and, in *Herzsprung,* the mere presence of such a figure leads to the murder/sacrifice of the no less stereotypical Good White Girl. Their function is not sufficiently dissimilar from that of blacks in early (and not only early) Hollywood films who, in the words of Shohat and Stam, "appeared … as images in spectacles whose social thrust is primarily shaped by others: " 'Black souls as White man's artifacts'(Fanon)" (187). *Qua* stereotypes, they become dangerously close to being mere foils. Unable to represent themselves (let alone to fight back), they at best passively complicate the increasingly common representation of the population of postunification Germany as being homogenized, or sufficiently so.

In this regard, Johanna's quasi-enlightened plea for multiculturalism rings somewhat false, or seems at least motivated primarily by sexual desire. Instead of reflecting genuine diversity, the Afro-German trope is still being constructed and exploited by German cultural workers and intellectuals in an attempt to redeem or resuscitate a dying "dead white man's" discourse – even if in some cases it is women filmmakers who are performing the CPR. And, perhaps also not fortuitously, both *Nobody Loves Me* and *Herzsprung* are marked by the death of former East German protagonists who are basically innocent. If we also take them allegorically as standing for the former East German State *tout court* and/or the alleged death of communism, then we can ask what will be born in the resulting ashes. Is there anything to be salvaged out of what is being deemed a wholly failed experiment? It would seem that the legacy of communism, according to Misselwitz and Dörrie at least, would be an ostensibly multicultural or transsexual German society, yes, but one whose diversity can be easily exploited, and the representation of which remains sadly fixated in some of the oldest, most stereotypical and lethal racism. In that case, Andreas Huyssen may be right in his ominous prediction that a new *Nullpunktthese* is fast emerging in post-reunification Germany, one that "will be constructed differently from that of 1945, but will similarly be based on denial of the past and serve to legitimize the new state and the desired and anticipated new culture. And it will be similarly false" (52).

Thus, in any event, does reunification provide Germans with a vehicle to try to prove that theirs is a multicultural society? In other words, the presence of Afro-Germans is exploited to add a new dimension to the almost inherently monochrome, arguably still distressingly *Blut und Boden* orientation of far too many Germans. Multi-culturalism and diversity appears to be the overarching trend in the phenomenon of postmodern migrancy and most other major "first world" countries (especially the UK, France, the United States, and significant areas of the former East Bloc) bear witness to the rich intellectual and cultural traditions of racial interaction – no matter how suppressed, harassed, punished, maimed, murdered, coopted, or exploited many of the races in question have commonly been. By comparison, the history, scope, and intensity of interracial interaction is relatively lacking in Germany. This is not the least poisonous legacy of the institutionally and popularly legitimated racism of the Third Reich. Germany – and German cultural production and scholarship – has a long way to catch up; and even progressive women cultural workers are hardly exempt from this rule, particularly in the matter of "racial stereotypes regarding the sexual sensibilities of blacks" (Adelson 235).[20] Finally,

20. In addition, see Lennox.

however, we also should take to heart Rey Chow's passionate attack against the academic and cultural exploitation of positions of "otherness" and "alterity": "sexist and racist reaffirmations of sexual and racial diversities that are made merely in the name of righteousness ... create new 'solidarities' whose ideological premises remain unquestioned. These new solidarities are often informed by a *strategic* attitude which repeats what they seek to overthrow. The weight of old ideologies being reinforced over and over again is immense" (17).

IV

For its part, however, *Herzsprung* itself does not end on this or any other definitive note. Furthermore, I think this apparent undecidability or antinomy may be fully appropriate to the complexity of the debate before us, even hopeful, in its own dark, negative dialectical manner. As Misselwitz's often very active camera circles around the burning Uncle Tom's Cabin on a New Year's Eve somewhere on the bleak stretch of autobahn between former East and former West Germany, now united under the hegemony of the latter, we are not the exclusive witnesses to the pathetic destroyed diner and murdered woman in her dead mother's wedding dress. That is, we are not the only witnesses in the film and hence, following an ancient convention in the visual arts called "the surrogate viewer", there is the possibility of an alternative to our mode of vision. Surrogate viewers are at once wholly identical to, and yet wholly different from, not only the film protagonists with which we have been more or less successfully identified, but also ourselves. The conflagration that fuses – but also, if you prefer, refuses or confuses – past and present, U.S. and German racism is also witnessed by the nameless, remarkably passive Stranger, mutely tied to his tree of virtual crucifixion. But he is not alone, even in the film. He is embraced by a truly strange figure – whom I have intentionally not mentioned until now – who has been appearing periodically throughout the film, especially when explicitly racist events are about to occur or have just occurred. Unlike The Stranger and *a fortiori* all other protagonists, she never once speaks. Named only *post festum* in the final credit sequence as "Die Verrückte" (the mad or, literally, dis-placed woman), this figure, white-skinned and/or white-masked, cuts at least two ways historically and allegorically: into the deep past of the Greek chorus (updated by Brecht's epic theatre as an alienation effect) but also into present film history around the time of German reunification. So it is that she becomes in effect what I'd call the "magical realist" fusion of DEFA social realism and

Hollywood, UFA or ZDF illusionism. In a sense, one might say that The Stranger and The Mad Woman are *identical* as *actants*, for in this film as elsewhere in the long history of anti-black racism, particularly in Germany, there has forever been, and there remains, a profound "nexus between blackness and madness" (Gilman 1-18). In this one filmic artifact at least, we see the problem of the continuity or discontinuity of the German *Kulturnation* in some of its radical complexity. The fact that we viewers are momentarily figured – simultaneously – as one mute, male, black stranger and one mute, white mad woman, both of whom precisely may, or may not, also happen to be German – should caution us about thinking that we can easily know who "we" are, and what our attitude really is or should be towards the enormously complicated issue of cultural periodization and classification in and around German reunification and European integration – not to mention the increasing global integration, and concomitant polarities of race, nation, and class, that are unconditionally demanded by late capitalism. Thus there remains, then, a deeply re/fused fissure in Germany: "the heart of Europe," *das Herz Europas*. In *Herzsprung* the main surviving witnesses to this re/fused fissure are mute. Mute, that is, if the piercing scream heard over the final credit sequence, superimposed over the burning skeleton of that ambiguous diner, cannot be identified and rectified.

Select Bibliography

Adelson, Leslie A. "Racism and Feminist Aesthetics: The Provocation of Anne Duden's *Opening of the Mouth.*" *Signs* 13:2 (Winter 1988):234-52.

Alter, Nora M. "German Reunification as 'Musical Comedy': Marcel Ophüls' *November Days.*" *Unelective Affinities: Interdisciplinary Cultural Studies of German Reunification*. Eds. Ruth Starkman et al. Bloomington and Indianapolis: University of Indiana Press, forthcoming.

Balibar, Étienne. *Masses, Classes, Studies on Politics and Philosophy Before and After Marx.* Trans. James Swenson. New York and London: Routledge, 1994.

_____. "Racism and Crisis" [1985]. Balibar and Wallerstein 217-27.

_____. "Racism and Nationalism" [1987/88]. Balibar and Wallerstein 37-67.

Balibar, Étienne and Wallerstein, Immanuel. *Race, Nation, Class: Ambiguous Identities* [1988]. Trans. Chris Turner. London and New York: Verso, 1991.

Barthes, Roland. *Mythologies.* Trans. Annette Lavers. New York: Hill and Wang, 1983.

Bathrick, David. *The Powers of Speech: The Politics of Culture in the GDR.* Lincoln: University of Nebraska Press, 1995.

Bellour, Raymond. "Psychosis, Neurosis, Perversion." *A Hitchcock Reader.* Eds. Marshall Deutelbaum and Leland Poague. Ames: Iowa State University Press, 1986, 311-31.

Cavell, Stanley. Introduction to *Beyond Document: Essays on Nonfiction Film.* Ed. Charles Warren. Hanover and London: Wesleyan University Press, 1996, xi-xxviii.

Chow, Rey. *Writing Diaspora: Tactics of Intervention in Contemporary Cultural Studies.* Bloomington and Indianapolis: Indiana University Press, 1993.

Dietrich, Gerd. *Politik und Kultur in der SBZ, 1945-1949.* Berne: Peter Lang, 1993.

Farbe bekennen: Afro-deutsche Frauen auf den Spuren ihrer Geschichte. Eds. Katharina Oguntoye, May Opitz, Dagmar Schultz. Berlin: Orlanda Frauenverlag, 1986.

Fehrenbach, Heide. *Cinema in Democratizing Germany: Reconstructing National Identity after Hitler.* Chapel Hill: University of North Carolina Press, 1995.

Geisler, Michael E. "Mehrfach gebrochene Mauerschau: 1989-1990 in den US-Medien." *Mauer-Show* 257-75.

Gilman, Sander L. *On Blackness without Blacks: Essays on the Image of the Black in Germany.* Boston: G. K. Hall, 1982.

Gilroy, Paul. *The Black Atlantic: Modernity and Double Consciousness.* Cambridge: Harvard University Press, 1993.

Greimas, A. J. *Sématique structurale.* Paris: Larousse, 1966.

Harris-Schenz, Beverly, *Black Images in Eighteenth-Century German Literature.* Stuttgart: Akademischer Verlag Hans-Dieter Heinz, 1981

Heimann, Thomas. *DEFA, Künstler, und SED-Kulturpolitik.* Berlin: Vistas, 1994.

Hochhuth, Rolf. *Wessis in Weimar: Szenen aus einem besetzten Land; mit einem Anhang: Das Stück in der Diskussion* [1992/93]. Munich: DTV, 1994.

Huyssen, Andreas. *Twilight Memories: Marking Time in a Culture of Amnesia.* Routledge: London and New York, 1995.

Jameson, Fredric. *The Prison-House of Language: A Critical Account of Structuralism and Russian Formalism.* Princeton: Princeton University Press, 1972.

Kinematek 82 (December 1993). Special issue: " DEFA NOVA - nach wie vor?"

Kreimeier, Klaus. *Kino und Filmindustrie in der BRD: Ideologie und Klassenwirklichkeit nach 1945.* Kronberg: Scriptor, 1973.

Lennox, Sara. "Divided Feminism: Women, Racism, and German National Identity." *German Studies Review* 28:3 (October 1995): 481-503.

Mauer-Show: Das Ende der DDR, die deutsche Einheit und die Medien. Eds. Rainer Bohn, Knut Hickethier, Eggo Müller. Berlin: Sigma, 1992.

Mückenberger, Christina and Jordan, Günther. *"Sie sehen selbst, Sie hören selbst": Die DEFA von ihren Anfängen bis 1949.* Marburg: Hizeroth, 1994.

Négritude et Germanité: L'Afrique noire dans la littérature d'expression allemande. Dakar: Les Nouvelles Éditions Africaines, 1983.

Nichols, Bill. *Blurred Boundaries: Questions of Meaning in Contemporary Culture.* Bloomington and Indianapolis: Indiana University Press, 1994.

Pike, David. *The Politics of the Culture of Soviet-Occupied Germany, 1945-49.* Stanford: Stanford University Press, 1992.

"Quo vadis Babelsberg: Wie geht es weiter mit Babelsberg? Fragen zur DEFA, zur Filmförderung, zum Filmstock. Gespräch mit Wilhelm Neufeldt." *Film und Fernsehen* 4 (1992):10-13.

Radevagen, Thomas Til. "Die Defa zwischen dem Verschwinden der DDR und einem möglichen neuen Anfang." *Mauer-Show* 189-200.

Schlüpmann, Heide. *Unheimlichkeit des Blicks: Das Drama des frühen deutschen Kinos.* Stroemfeld: Roter Stern, 1990.

Shohat, Ella and Starn, Robert. *Unthinking Eurocentrism: Multiculturalism and the Media.* London and New York: Routledge, 1994.

Silberman, Marc. *German Cinema: Texts in Context.* Detroit: Wayne State University Press, 1995.

Swan, Jon. "The Final Solution in South West Africa." *The Quarterly Journal of Military History* 3:4 (Summer 1991) 37-53.

Willemen, Paul. "The National." *Fields of Vision: Essays in Film Studies, Visual Anthropology, and Photography.* Eds. Leslie Devereaux and Roger Hillman. Berkeley, Los Angeles, London: University of California Press, 1995, 21-34.

Williams, Raymond. *Keywords: A Vocabulary of Culture and Society,* revised edition. New York: Oxford University Press, 1983.

Zizek, Slavoj. "'In His Gaze My Ruin Is Writ Large.'" *Everything You Always Wanted to Know about Lacan (But Were Afraid to Ask Hitchcock.* Ed. Slavoj Zizek. London and New York: Verso, 1992, 211-272.

Das zweite Leben der Filmstadt Babelsberg: DEFA-Spielfilme, 1946-1992. Ed. Ralf Schenk. Berlin: Henschel, 1994.

Zwischen Gestern und Morgen: Westdeutsche Nachkriegsfilme, 1945-1962. Ed. Deutsches Filmmuseum. Frankfurt: Deutsches Filmmuseum, 1989.

WHAT SHOULD REMAIN?

Exploring the Literary Contributions to
Postwar German History

Frank Trommler

From Story to History

What should remain? The appraisal of German literature between 1945 and 1990 implied by this question has been suggested by the editor of this volume. The question is both banal and challenging. The Germanist dismisses, of course, the banality and goes for the challenge. In his own variation on Christa Wolf's title *What Remains*, Keith Bullivant placed the final chapter of his study, *The Future of German Literature*, under the heading "What *Will* Remain?"[1] This makes the challenge even stronger than asking, "What *Should* Remain?" Having followed the development of German literature since the 1960s Bullivant, as an extremely well-informed critic, was able to clear the forest without cutting down the best trees. I yield to his well-informed judgement on writers and their achievements any time.

In comparison, my own credentials for following up on the question are rather limited, consisting mainly of some articles that I contributed to a first scholarly appraisal of postwar writing in West and East Ger-

---

1. Keith Bullivant, *The Future of German Literature* (Oxford/Providence: Berg, 1994), 161-84.

many in the early 1970s, putting a then unusual emphasis on the *and*.[2] Since then I have written, aside from an update of my study in 1982, which was published in 1984,[3] some essays on specific topics in the works of Martin Walser, Tankred Dorst, and Peter Weiss. Why no broader assessments? I know the answer when I go back to the earlier articles around 1970. At that time, applying the tools of *Germanistik* to contemporary literature had some innovative consequences. Eberhard Lämmert, Karl Otto Conrady, Jost Hermand, and younger Germanists had begun to address the awkward silence regarding the discipline's accommodation to National Socialism.[4] The new "historical turn" helped dismantle the concept of Point Zero or Zero Hour 1945 *(Nullpunkt or Stunde Null)* upon which a certain mythology of achievements was based. It also helped structure postwar literary developments as a story.[5] Ten years later the story had become history, leaving little room for extending or modifying it *vis-à-vis* the intellectual currents of the 1970s and 1980s.

In 1982 the title, "Auf dem Wege zu einer kleineren Literatur," corresponded with the prevailing assessment of the declining role of writers in public life. In contrast, emphasizing the concept of one German literature instead of two or four went against the dominant perception of literary scholars.[6] My argument was that after 1945, literature had resurrected itself by shaping identities in the four different societies of the Federal Republic, the German Democratic Republic, Austria, and Switzerland, with Swiss authors well-ensconced in an uninterrupted tradition of free literature and theater. By the early 1980s, authors had given up their representational allegiances in favor of ecological, feminist, regional, and other commitments which transcended political borders, including those between West and East.

---

2. Frank Trommler, "Der 'Nullpunkt 1945' und seine Verbindlichkeit für die Literaturgeschichte," in *Basis: Jahrbuch für deutsche Gegenwartsliteratur* 1 (1970), 9-25; "Der zögernde Nachwuchs: Entwicklungsprobleme der Nachkriegsliteratur in Ost und West," in *Tendenzen der deutschen Literatur seit 1945,* Thomas Koebner, ed. (Stuttgart: Kröner, 1971), 1-116; "Realismus in der Prosa," ibid., 179-275.

3. Trommler, "Auf dem Wege zu einer kleineren Literatur: Ästhetische Perioden und Probleme seit 1945," in *Tendenzen der deutschen Gegenwartsliteratur*, Thomas Koebner, ed. (Stuttgart: Kröner, 1984), 1-106.

4. *Germanistik - eine deutsche Wissenschaft*, Eberhard Lämmert, Walther Killy, Karl Otto Conrady, Peter von Polenz, eds. (Frankfurt: Suhrkamp, 1967); Jost Hermand, *Synthetisches Interpretieren: Zur Methodik der Literaturwissenschaft* (Munich: Nymphenburger, 1968).

5. *Revisiting Zero Hour 1945: The Emergence of Postwar German Culture*, Stephen Brockmann and Frank Trommler, eds. (Washington: American Institute for Contemporary German Studies, 1996).

6. "Gibt es vier (oder fünf) deutsche Literaturen? Nein, aber es gab sie eine Zeitlang." Trommler, "Auf dem Wege...", 29.

Another ten years later the painful literary debates surrounding the unification of the two German states have made me rethink this assessment. The commercial and institutional unification of German literature was not accompanied by the expected post-Cold War spirit that would bring together West and East in new intellectual ventures. Instead, writers retreated into the language of exclusion that had been considered, until the fall of the Wall, the very impediment to an inspiring German literary life. Having received attention as a medium for shaping identities after the war and National Socialism, literature again helped stabilize a particularistic identity. Writers served once more as symbols for the particularities of postwar existence; they and their works helped clarify the historicity of the events that one had lived through. This recognition of its commercial potential led to the publication of collections and book series[7] that expand on the wave of nostalgia that had received resounding commercial endorsements in the 1980s.[8]

Since predictions on the state of literature are still more ingenious when they concern the past and not the future, I will follow up with some observations on postwar developments that should counteract the trend to fill the blanks that the unification process left in the emotional life of the participants. In preparation for a future literary history, I will consider the rarely studied interaction with the German classical tradition that was the precondition for the growth of a postwar public culture; the poetics of identity creation for which Group 47 set the parameter; and the literary response to the Nazi extermination of Jews. Among the many issues which I have to omit are literary developments in East Germany, where individual writers such as Heiner Müller, Christa Wolf, Stefan Heym, Franz Fühmann, and Christoph Hein have long enjoyed particular attention. A fair appraisal would need more than fleeting remarks on their relation to the present *Ostalgie*. Despite post-Wall perspectives, both critics and defenders of their literature have rarely used arguments that have not been around for some time. A new critical language is necessary, one that points beyond the redundancy of most current discourses. Until such language is found it is necessary to assert that the works of these writers should be

7. See the collection, *Die deutsche Literatur 1945-1960*, 4 vols., Heinz Ludwig Arnold, ed. (Munich: Deutscher Taschenbuch Verlag, 1995); also the series, *Die DDR-Bibliothek,* to be published in forty volumes by Faber & Faber, Leipzig (Irmtraud Gutschke, "Nostalgie? Nein, Zukunftsarbeit! Etwas Besonderes auf dem deutschen Buchmarkt: Der Verlag Faber & Faber stellte 'Die DDR-Bibliothek' vor," *Neues Deutschland* 50, No 226, 27 September 1995, 9).

8. See *Gestylte Geschichte: Vom alltäglichen Umgang mit Geschichtsbildern*, Rainer Gries, Volker Hagen, Dirk Schindelbeck, eds. (Münster: Westfälisches Dampfboot, 1989).

counted among the most important entries in any future German literary history of our period.

Weimar and the Path to Public Culture

In his book, *Is Literary History Possible?*, David Perkins states: "The possible plots of narrative literary history can be reduced to three: rise, decline, and rise and decline."[9] One might hesitate to apply such reductionist terminology to a complicated issue of our discipline, yet in the case of postwar literature the practice of emplotting the developments as "rise" – and increasingly as "rise and decline" – has been clearly established. What writers began to formulate in their search for recognition in the 1950s and 1960s, most prominently in the promotion of Group 47, became the *Erfolgsgeschichte* of a new chapter of literature. It found different articulations in Austria, Switzerland, the German Democratic Republic, and the Federal Republic; its most broadly recognized expression was contained in the citation of the Nobel Prize Committee when Heinrich Böll received the prize for literature in 1972: "It is not the smallest German miracle that after such years of destitution a new generation of writers, thinkers and researchers was ready so soon to shoulder their country's and their own essential task in the spiritual life of our time."[10] The "story" of the German economic miracle had obviously made enough of an impression on the Swedish Academy to serve as a reference for its comments on literature. In addition to recognizing Böll's achievements as a realist novelist, it emphasized the fact that he was selected as a representative of a whole group of postwar German writers.

Perkin's distinction between rise, decline, and rise and decline could similarly be used for the preceding period, in which the fate of German literature and culture was determined by National Socialism. In fact, twentieth-century German history as a whole has been mostly represented as a story of a decline for which the devastation of 1945 is seen as a powerful closure. The plots of decline and rise usually have been kept separate. Historians tend to rely on established patterns and literary historians are not different. Until recently, the end of World War II and the defeat of Nazi Germany have been viewed either as the devastating closure of a national history gone awry or as the point zero of the spectacular take-off of a phoenix. Upon the collapse of the postwar

9. David Perkins, *Is Literary History Possible?* (Baltimore: Johns Hopkins University Press, 1992), 39.

10. Bernard Weinraub, "Heinrich Böll Wins Nobel for Literature," *The New York Times*, 20 October 1972, A 6, Col. 4.

order in Europe in 1989/91 the visions of earlier decades have returned, draining rhetorical energies from the reference to 1945. More and more historical narratives bridge this caesura, but a common pattern has not yet been found.

Within literary history the interface of destruction and negativity on the one hand, and the aesthetic continuities since the 1930s in the work of such authors as Günter Eich, Hans Werner Richter, Wolfgang Koeppen on the other, was rarely addressed. While Adorno's negative aesthetic, an emotionally-charged theoretical response to fascism, first received attention by writers in the mid-1950s, a more comprehensive understanding did not originate until a decade later. What had ended in 1945? If something had begun, was it new? For a long time, asking these questions in the realm of literature led to rather uninspired answers that were constantly sidetracted by the reference to *Kunst und Kultur* as the only achievements that would prevail even when German politics and the state were in shambles. The question "What Should Remain?" was fully in the purview of this period, when arts and culture not only functioned as a forum for an otherwise little tolerated political discourse but also invoked a window to the past, a door to a collective identity. Art, literature, and culture *should* remain, was the answer, usually connected either with some reference to Goethe or other classical authors.

To recall this predicament for a history of postwar writing runs against the prevailing trend that privileges all questions pertaining to newness, innovation, and the ability of German writers to jump on the train of modernism. This train, set in motion also by Germans and Austrians, apparently had been gaining speed on other countries while under Hitler Germany cut itself off from the civilized world. And yet, while the modernism paradigm helps define the rise of postwar literature, its legitimacy rests at least as much with our own perception as with the actual developments after the end of the war. Unlike the other postwar period after 1918, the promotion of aesthetic innovation was the rare exception rather than the guiding force. In order to understand the particular nature of innovation in these years, other more weighty factors have to be reconsidered.

After World War I, when the German monarchy collapsed and Emperor Wilhelm II had to leave the country, the founders of the first German republic invoked the spirit of classical Weimar in order to provide a point of reference for the shattered national identity. "Weimar" assumed a political role that went beyond the humanistic agenda that had originated in Goethe and Schiller's life and work. After World War II, when Germans had lost the right to rule themselves, the invocation of a democratic marriage of politics and culture gave way to the understanding that culture henceforth had to function *in lieu* of politics. Considering the much greater loss of national identity in 1945, the role of classical writers and humanists in what can hardly be called the public sphere was much stronger at this time than after World War I. Once used as a mere *Ersatz* for the historical aura of the *Kaisertum*, the conjuring up of "Weimar" and classical humanism now assumed a crucial function in intellectual and moral reorientation. From Friedrich Meinecke's call for "Goethe-Gemeinden" (Goethe communities) in *Die deutsche Katastrophe* (The German Catastrophe) to the agenda of Dolf Sternberger's much acclaimed journal *Die Wandlung* and Johannes R. Becher's East-Berlin-based organization *Deutscher Kulturbund*, the narratives of German identity were based on this foundation.

Of course, many contemporaries asked what kind of new beginning the reference to the spirit of Weimar represented after it had been tainted by the spirit of Buchenwald, the concentration camp right outside Goethe's town.[11] Did this reference not function as an alibi for intellectual elites who, by asserting this tradition as sane and positive, avoided analysis of its use under National Socialism, as well as their own entanglement in Nazi thinking? How painful the emulation of classical traditions was for those who had devoted much of their life to preserving their humanistic spirit can be ascertained in the speech that the Germanist Richard Alewyn gave at Cologne University after his return from American exile in the "Goethe Year" 1949. Alewyn cautioned his academic audience that the 1949 celebration of Goethe could not just be a resumption of the 1932 commemoration of Goethe's death: "Is it not appropriate and fair to ask, for once, how we can afford to celebrate Goethe? Whether is behooves us at all. Whether Goethe has anything to do with us. Can we really reach across the abyss that has opened between us and the past? Didn't we destroy the last bridges on which we used to go back and forth? And isn't Goethe's house, as an irrevocable sign of this fact, in shambles?"[12]

And yet, at this time Goethe was already being claimed by the two new German states. For the communist regime in East Germany – where Weimar is situated – Goethe's goodwill toward its operation was never much in doubt. In fact, the incantation of the classical heritage

---

11. A good survey in: *Beschädigtes Erbe: Beiträge zur Klassikerrezeption in finsterer Zeit,* eds. Horst Clausen and Norbert Oellers (Bonn: Bouvier, 1984).

12. See Klaus Garber, "Weimar und Buchenwald: Richard Alewyns Kölner Goethe-Rede aus dem Jahr 1949," in *"Wir tragen den Zettelkasten mit den Steckbriefen unserer Freunde:" Acta-Band zum Symposium "Beiträge Jüdischer Autoren zur deutschen Literatur seit 1945" (Universität Osnabrück, 2. – 5. 6. 1991),* eds. Jens Stüben and Winfried Woesler (Darmstadt: Häusser, 1994), 329-43.

became one of the two pillars of its claim to legitimacy, the other being Marx and Engels and the history of the German workers' movement. West Germans were allowed to express more skepticism, and Adenauer's connection was clearly with the "other" Weimar, the first German republic, which he and others evoked, though in a negative sense: Bonn is not Weimar, as the famous slogan went in the 1950s. Goethe was not neglected. He was put into service for external affairs: German culture abroad is still presented as Goethe's culture in more than a hundred and fifty Goethe Institutes. Any comprehensive study of the reconstruction of German culture as a viable, marketable culture (with an emphasis on high culture) in the postwar world must look to the enormous investment in the legacy of Goethe and German classicism.

This is not exactly new terrain for the literary historian. Earlier accounts of the postwar period took the turn to the classical tradition into consideration. What *is* new, or rather should be discussed anew, is the reinvigorated presence of classical works, especially in the theaters. Looking at the first attempts to create a public sphere by way of artistic presentation, one is struck by the intensity with which the literary word was listened to, whereby foreign plays alternated with classical dramas. The desire for an uplifting collective experience of literature that could be understood *in lieu* of politics placed theaters, well supported by the occupation forces, in the center of postwar cultural life. Despite the import of foreign plays, the *Staatstheater* style, developed under Göring's theater regime, again reigned over Schiller, Goethe, Lessing, Kleist, Shakespeare. It contributed to the perception of a two-tier culture: one in search of a representative public consensus for which the theater provided the highest expression, and another one in search of a subject-based expression of contemporaneity that conveyed, mostly in poetry and prose, a sense of resistance against the prevailing social consensus. The novels and stories of Wolfgang Koeppen, Arno Schmidt, Heinrich Böll, Hans Erich Nossack, Alfred Andersch, Wolfdietrich Schnurre, and later Martin Walser and Siegfried Lenz, project this sense, as do the poems of Ingeborg Bachmann, Günter Eich, and Hans Magnus Enzensberger.

How isolated these writers were can be ascertained by a closer inspection of newspapers and journals of the 1950s. Though they cherished their access to broadcasting stations and their literary programs, they were deeply suspicious about engaging in the public spectacle with which theaters seem to sell out to the philistines night after night, and even in matinees. Their distancing themselves from the theater, which dominated the agenda of public culture in cities and regions, extended to classical plays such as *Nathan der Weise,* as well as to other efforts to address the topic of Jews and Germans, especially the staging of *The*

Diary of Anne Frank, which in the mid-1950s became an obligatory part of discussions in schools. When the Swiss writer Max Frisch, in his play *Andorra* (1961), succeeded in portraying anti-Semitism as an aspect of current thinking, his German colleagues responded with both relief and suspicion to his symbolism. It is most telling, then, that the break-through of a postwar dramatist did not occur until an outsider, Rolf Hochhuth, created an international sensation with exactly those forms that had dominated representative public culture in German-speaking countries. In the style of Schiller, Hochhuth addressed in *Der Stellvertreter* (The Representative, 1962) the persecution of Jews and the lack of interference on the part of the Catholic church. Insisting on the moral responsibility of the individual, Hochhuth rehabilitated theater as a forum against the moral negligence and forgetfulness of his contemporaries. The more arguments critics amassed against Schillerian heroes in the service of *Vergangenheitsbewältigung*, the more it became obvious that the well-sheltered aesthetic of literary resistance – with the exception of the radio play – had been insufficient to prepare the institutions of German public culture for the confrontation with National Socialism.

Frustrated by his own unsuccessful attempts at dramatizing the involvement of contemporaries in the Nazi crimes, novelist Martin Walser was able to articulate the changing attitude toward the literary heritage in 1964. Instead of stressing the timeless qualities of classical works, Walser asserted, one should present them as history and *in* their history. In this way they would help achieve realism by approaching another part of history: the Nazi period as the pre-history of the present, not as a timeless evil.[13] Walser's crucial witness for a historicizing approach to the classics was Brecht, who orchestrated his plays in a constant dialogue with the established masters, exhibiting their use and value *(Gebrauchswert)* for current issues, and making them useful for a new breed of theater practitioners.

Overlooking the impressive recovery of the theater as a public catalyst for new inquiries into the consciousness of a society torn between the legacy of the Nazi state and the revolutionary energies of a new generation that took place between the 1960s and 1980s, one cannot ignore the crucial role of classical plays and heroes in this endeavor. Beginning with Peter Stein's re-interpretation of Goethe's *Torquato Tasso* at the Bremen theater in 1969 and Peter Weiss's play *Hölderlin*, the encounter with "the classics," with due emphasis on the "anti-classics" Hölderlin, Kleist, and Büchner, generated an explosive dialogue between past and

13. Martin Walser, "Imitation oder Realismus," in Walser, *Erfahrungen und Leseerfahrungen* (Frankfurt: Suhrkamp, 1965), 66-93.

present. Using the elevated status of classical plays and heroes for their own public grandstanding, directors, playwrights, and critics modeled the current conflicts on a higher level, creating a historical mirror effect that hit a chord with an audience that, by the end of the 1960s, had grown tired of the internalizing aesthetics of the postwar years. Playing canonical works against the grain not only saved the classics but also the players, as Brecht had maintained. At that time, one should add, it also helped at the box office, considering the public's booming interest in all kinds of controversial happenings and performances.

It is my thesis that this step into the three-dimensionality of theatrical mediations between past and present, tradition and innovation, provides more of a clue to the reconstitution of individual and collective identity after 1968 than the production of literary texts in this period. When the writers of Group 47, at their meeting in 1967, the last, as it turned out, were confronted by students who shouted condescendingly "Writers! Writers!", it was not just an encounter with the call for political action, but an indication of the changing aesthetic temper of the new generation. Searching for the most appropriate expression of the spirit of resistance and utopia led inevitably to some kind of *Inszenierung*, a *mis-en-scène* of life, self, and community that needed different aesthetic ingredients. In this context, the discourse about the new subjectivity as an antidote to the political action ideology in the 1970s has to be seen *vis-à-vis* the theatrical practices of staging the individual as a product and a response to history. It is hardly surprising that classical heroes from the works of Kleist (Prinz Friedrich von Homburg, Marquise von O., Penthesilea), Goethe (Tasso, Werther, Iphigenie, even Faust), Sophocles (Antigone), Shakespeare, Schiller, and others became the focus of an amazing cult of the young protagonist in search of himself or herself, a cult that also carried over into the concurrent films of the New German Cinema. One of the most momentous episodes in the explosive dialogue between classical and modern sensibilities occurred in East Germany in 1972, when Ulrich Plenzdorf challenged two official doctrines with his Werther in jeans, *Die neuen Leiden des jungen W.*: the doctrine of the affirmative role and character of the socialist individual and the dogma of the exemplary status of the classical heritage.

Brecht's notion of reading and performing the classics against the grain was practiced differently in East and West, yet stimulated similar intellectual energies. Its use for exploring the self by dismantling and refurbishing established heroes, both male and female, helped shape a discourse on self and identity that differed strongly from the delegitimation of subjectivity that characterized concurrent French poststructuralist theories. In Germany, it seems, the intellectual discourse on self and identity at this time owed more to Hölderlin, Kleist, and Büchner than to Foucault or Lacan. The fact that poststructuralism did not quite make it into the center of the German debate on the precarious state of the self had much to do with this exciting theatrical discourse about the representation of the individual. This might be lost on those who have been accustomed to draw evidence exclusively from texts and have been disappointed in their search for appropriate master texts. Some have found consolation in Christa Wolf's preoccupation with reconstructing female identities, most poignantly in her answer to Homer's classical texts, *Kassandra* (1983).

Searching for Identity: The Alliance of Work and Author

In 1962 Karl August Horst, an astute and influential literary critic, published a short "Epigraph auf eine Epoche" (Epigraph for an Epoch), in which he connected postwar writers with earlier developments. As in other articles, Horst looked beyond the immediate appeal of autobiographically based prose about war and postwar experiences, and exposed the characteristics of a representational structure in which the literary work, in order to overcome the levelling effect of its narrative, needs the "real" author as part of its literary appearance. "Didn't one notice," Horst asked, "that with increasing objectivity the writer and the artist in general step forward from their anonymity, because they become indispensable as partners of their model (*weil sie als Partner ihres Modells unentbehrlich werden*)?" It has become common practice for critics to present less the work than the author, Horst continued:

> One should take note of how much more frequently names of authors than titles of books are being mentioned in newspapers and journals, here and abroad. Or how comparably strong the effect of a pose has become that a writer assumes in front of the stage of his work in public. Could this not lead, in the course of time, to the result that, as a supplement to the anonymity of literature, a *spectaculum* of literati will install itself in the proscenium – whereby the partnership of advocacy (for the whole of literature) and current testimony once again would find expression?[14]

The remarkable public presence of Group 47, with meetings, readings, interviews, prizes, polemics, adversarial maneuvers, and publication strategies, is a case in point, although Horst delineated a general development in the twentieth century. Indeed, similar insights had already accompanied the rise of Expressionism, summed up by Franz Blei who

14. Karl August Horst, "Epitaph auf eine Epoche," *Merkur* 16 (1962) , 1168.

in 1918 argued that the exhibitionism of writers had moved in front of their work: "While formerly there was a work and no visible person, today there is a person in the spotlight and instead of a work books that at best represent sketches, drafts, attempts."[15] Wolfgang Borchert, who had been inspired by Expressionism, became the model for the representational alliance of work and author after 1945. No other writer achieved a similar stature as the quintessential writer-soldier returning from war to an empty world of ruins. While German theaters were busy rehearsing classical and newly imported plays, Borchert's morality play – written as a radio play – *Draußen vor der Tür* (The Man Outside, 1947) became the signature piece of the period that was written and rewritten by every new reader, every new school class, well into the 1950s, although literary critics were agreed on what Borchert had demonstrated: that Expressionism could not be revived.

What connected Borchert and the writers of Group 47 was not the style – though some prose pieces show similar characteristics – but the determination of the author to inject himself into the workings of the literary texts, and remain visible as part of the textual message. Heinrich Böll harvested where Borchert had sowed the seed. One of Marcel Reich-Ranicki's more generous statements about Böll's achievements is focused on the fact that Böll created the figure of the German common soldier *(Landser),* "who suffered in the war, who was no Nazi and did not want to have anything to do with the Nazis, who, however, did not participate in any resistance, who was honorable and who cannot be accused of evil, even barbarism. Millions of German readers have identified with him, also those, by the way, who did not behave so honorably in the war. Thus, millions of readers did not identify with resistance fighters but rather with the - in the last analysis - innocent, suffering soldier Böll."[16]

Böll's contribution to the recovery of German literature, for which the Swedish Academy found such high praise, can be seen more clearly in the context of the representational alliance of author and work that Horst recognized as a general condition of modern literature. (Not unaware of the "other," seemingly contradictory condition of the increasing anonymousness of the author, Horst indeed wrote an epitaph of an epoch – the epoch of existentialist resistance against the anonymity of the individual in war and persecution, something that has to be held up against the poststructuralist generalizations of the disappearance of the author as the author of the work.) Böll was, of course, only one of

---

15. Franz Blei, "Fragmente zur Literatur," *Summa* 3 (1918), 134.

16. Marcel Reich-Ranicki, *Der doppelte Boden: Ein Gespräch mit Peter von Matt* (Zurich: Amman 1992), 204.

those writers who created the figure of the stoically suffering young male as the quintessential witness of the misery of the century, and one might give him credit for making clear that he did not want this male figure to reincarnate Ernst Jünger's martial masculinity, an assumed pose of wisdom through soldierly nihilism, which others, Alfred Andersch for instance, liked to combine with Sartre's existentialism. In fact, Böll was probably even more successful in his later creation of exemplary woman figures such as Katharina Blum or Leni (in *Gruppenbild mit Dame*), who were characterized by their equally large capacity for suffering and resistance. But this occurred much later when female protagonists began to attract broader attention. For the first two decades after the war, Johanna Moosdorf's assessment speaks for itself: "It was just impossible to depict a woman who takes action, a woman protagonist. One had to take a male person. The male protagonists in *Nachtigallen schlagen im Schnee* (Nightingales Fight in the Snow) and also, later, in *Flucht nach Afrika (Flight to Africa)*, they basically represent me. I identified with them. In both books the women are passive and the men active not because I thought they are that way, but rather because it would not have been accepted otherwise. I projected my own active parts onto the man."[17]

Many years and a feminist movement later, one cannot let the opportunity pass to shine the spotlight on the annual exhibition of zealous, though subdued, young males that installed itself, under the tight rules of commander-in-chief Hans Werner Richter, in the proscenium of West Germany's undeveloped intellectual arena. While male bonding has always been one of the most powerful generators of literature and science, it has rarely been institutionalized with such sophisticated internalization of a common purpose, as in this case of the establishment of a German postwar literature by a group of determined loners. The fact that some female writers, among them Ilse Aichinger, Ingeborg Bachmann, Ingrid Bachér, Barbara König, Gabriele Wohmann, Renate Rasp, and Helga Novak, read at the meetings of Group 47, can be held against such a characterization, but not until the late 1950s and 1960s when most of them appeared upon Richter's invitation.[18] The original spirit of

17. Quoted from an interview with Johanna Moosdorf in 1885. In: Regula Venske, "Schriftstellerin gegen das Vergessen: Johanna Moosdorf," in *Frauenliteratur ohne Tradition? Neun Autorinnenporträts*, Inge Stephan, Regula Venske, Sigrid Weigel eds. (Frankfurt: Fischer Taschenbuch Verlag, 1987), 201. See also Sigrid Weigel, *Bilder des kulturellen Gedächtnisses: Beiträge zur Gegenwartsliteratur* (Dülmen-Hiddingsel: tende, 1994), esp. 135-62 ("Es ist immer Krieg"—Zum anderen Kriegsbegriff in der literarischen Kritik von Frauen").

18. See Irmela von der Lühe, "Schriftstellerinnen in der Gruppe 47," in *Dichter und Richter: Die Gruppe 47 und die deutsche Nachkriegsliteratur*, Jürgen Schutte et al., eds. (Ausstellung der Akademie der Künste, 28. Oktober bis 7. Dezember 1988) (Berlin: Akademie der Künste, 1988), 94-102.

the *équipe* that Richter put at the core of the group[19] reflected both a male and a military nation with a common goal.[20] It had nothing to do with Stefan George's esoteric and homoerotic circle, but rather with groups whose anti-establishment poetics originated in the brigade mentality of World War I as, for instance, in the case of Martin Raschke's group *Die Kolonne* in the early 1930s.

Calling participation in this ritualistic competition therapeutic for another lost generation might, in fact, illuminate the difference in the generational therapy attributed to authors like Ernest Hemingway and Erich Maria Remarque, whose stars rose after World War I with neither support groups nor group support. Similar in having re-created a male identity in a metaphorical relationship to a postwar society, the writers of Group 47 seem to have produced less gripping works, but definitely acted more as a catalyst for a critical stance *vis-à-vis* the prevailing politics of burying the past. This is where their true contribution to the recovery of German culture lies: in forging a memory link with the Nazi past which, though individual, aimed at a general attitude of historical awareness.[21] Though rarely engaging in the specifics of the Nazi system, these writers drew from this link a strong motivation to make up in opposition and resistance what had been missed under Hitler's reign. Their poetics of a belated resistance *(nachgeholte Resistance)*[22] reflected the path of existentialist self-extrication that French and Italian intellectuals had laid out after the entanglement with fascist or Vichy collaboration. While keeping their distance from the truly gripping political debates of the 1950s on Germany's new ties to the West which took place between the parties in the Bundestag, writers advanced, under the rubric of bringing back literature, a moral accounting for the legacy of National Socialism in everyday life.

Limited as this contribution was, it compares favorably with the failure of the universities and the academic disciplines, of history, sociology, psychology, political science, and *Germanistik,* to reconstitute their scholarly legitimacy by addressing their accommodation with National Socialism and deliver pertinent information to the public about "What happened." For most of their academic representatives, reconstituting

19. Hans Werner Richter, "Fünfzehn Jahre," in *Almanach der Gruppe 47, 1947-1962,* ed. Richter (Reinbek bei Hamburg: Rowohlt, 1962), 13.

20. On the military association of this anti-militaristic group see Roland H. Wiegenstein, "Die Gruppe 47 und ihre Kritiker, " in *Dichter und Richter* (note 18), 103-9.

21. Jochen Vogt, *"Erinnerung ist unsere Aufgabe:" Über Literatur, Moral und Politik 1945-1990* (Opladen: Westdeutscher Verlag, 1991).

22. Frank Trommler, "Die nachgeholte Resistance: Politik und Gruppenethos im historischen Zusammenhang," in *Die Gruppe 47 in der Geschichte der Bundesrepublik,* Justus Fetscher, Eberhard Lämmert, Jürgen Schutte, eds. (Würzburg: Königshausen, 1991), 9-22.

the discipline meant rearranging the institutional setting with the least disturbance of existing structures and personnel.[23] It took the German-ists until the mid-1960s and the historians until the mid-1980s to address and overcome the failure to address the legacy of National Socialism. In order to account for the differences between writers and academics, one needs to credit the already-described organization of lit-erary activities, which had its roots in the rituals of Group 47, with cre-ating a more independent, yet coherent, spirit of criticism than was possible under the restored traditions and hierarchies of academe. At the same time, the fact that such coherence could originate at all so soon after the devastations of war was contingent upon that peculiar bonding among males who tried hard to establish an identity against the prevail-ing forces. As long as the audience felt that these writers were indispens-able as partners in their aesthetic model, their authority as a literary opposition grew; as soon as a more encompassing and democratic pub-lic sphere unfolded, this balance collapsed. The widening public sphere of the 1960s meant both the end of the coherence of mind and purpose and a new and troubling engagement with two truly public phenomena, politics and theater.

It hardly needs to be pointed out that acknowledging the moral con-tribution of these writers cannot be separated from recognizing the frailty of their literary composition. The fact that a considerable number of these writers have been publishing well into the 1980s and even 1990s distorts rather than clarifies the special nature of their achievements, as much as their topics, techniques, and biographies differed from each other. In most cases the indispensability of the author as a partner of his literary work, which Horst delineated, manifests itself in ways that have more in common with literary endeavors of French and other foreign authors of the immediate postwar period than with those of later Ger-man writers. Sartre's concept of literature as an act of freedom or, rather, liberation, lies at the heart of these endeavors. The wavering between opportunism and resistance characteristic of the moral horizon of a whole generation of participants in the war retained its fascination well into the 1950s and shaped the ambition for a self-liberation through lit-erature. As they recede back into the history of the "older" generation

23. A short survey of several disciplines in East and West Germany in *Wissenschaft im geteilten Deutschland: Restauration oder Neubeginn nach 1945?*, Walter H. Pehle and Peter Sillem, eds. (Frankfurt: Fischer Taschenbuch Verlag, 1992). See also the "Bio-Bibli-ographische Dokumentationsserie zeitgeschichtlicher Texte," *Deutschlands Erneuerung 1945-1950: Geistesgeschichte in Deutschland nach Hitler,* edited by Christoph Cobet and published as catalogues of the Antiquariat Cobet, Frankfurt, Holzhausenstr. 56 (Nr. 29 ff., 1984 ff.).

since the late 1960s, the chances are slim that many of the works will be remembered in the twenty-first century. Siegfried Lenz has pleaded for an understanding of the works as a peculiar kind of historiography,[24] and it seems that his novels and those of Horst Bienek, Uwe Johnson, Heinrich Böll, Martin Walser, and some other writers, will survive under this label. Taking Horst's analysis a step further, it might not be surprising if the authors, always present as partners of their works, will attract at least as much if not more interest than their books for their experience and belated attempts to master the moral ambiguities of a post-Nazi society. In the case of Gottfried Benn, public interest in his poetry, a matter of identification with a shrewdly melancholic voice, vanished, while the poet still drew attention as a guru of the double life *(Doppelleben)* of artists and intellectuals of the war period. Nonetheless, what appeared to be mastery in the 1950s lost its credibility a decade later.

Addressing the Holocaust

The most problematic area for which the question "What Should Remain?" might inspire a rethinking of existing assessments is that of the writings with which German authors tried to account for the persecution and murder of Jews under National Socialism. This area is particularly problematic for the literary historian because its definition itself has undergone changes that reflect a profound transformation both of the terms of the discourse and the structure of the public sphere between 1945 and 1990.[25] Once the term "Holocaust" had come into use in Israel in the 1960s and was increasingly accepted in the United States in the 1970s, and subsequently, most effectively with the American TV series *Holocaust* in 1979, also in German-speaking countries, it became a decisive factor in shaping a new attitude toward the genocide that had been committed by Germans and Austrians. What had been a growing debate about the Germans and *The Destruction of the European Jewry*, as Raul Hilberg called his seminal study in 1961, to which literary writers had increasingly contributed, became a debate about the Holocaust, i.e. an historical event that, according to the totalizing term, appears to project a metahistorical

24. Siegfried Lenz, "Geschichte erzählen – Geschichten erzählen," in Lenz, *Über das Gedächtnis: Reden und Aufsätze* (Hamburg: Hoffmann und Campe, 1992), 20-34.

25. Susan E. Cernyak-Spatz, *German Holocaust Literature* (New York: Peter Lang, 1985), 9-12; Dagmar C.G. Lorenz, *Verfolgung bis zum Massenmord: Holocaust-Diskurse in deutscher Sprache aus der Sicht der Verfolgten* (New York: Peter Lang, 1992); Lawrence L. Langer, *The Holocaust and the Literary Imagination* (New Haven and London: Yale University Press, 1975).

telos, the telos of the unmitigated reign of evil that destroys the original connotation of sacrifice. Connecting literature with this term substantially changes the parameters of the debate from the concerns of its earlier phase.

It seems appropriate to emphasize that the discourse on literature and the Holocaust is in itself tied to a later phase of confronting the historical event, and that this discourse – or the lack thereof – cannot be projected back into the first years after the Nazi death mills had fallen silent. It would demonstrate little understanding of the impact of such world-shattering events – for which the numbing effects of World War I have often been seen as characteristic - if one tried to look for a full-fledged conception of the cataclysm that everyone had experienced in different ways.[26] Even in Israel, the state that had been formed as a result of the attempt to annihilate the Jewish people, the construction of a new society was accompanied by a post-catastrophic numbness toward the facts of the persecution. Although they became aware of the reemergence of perpetrators of the genocide, many Israelis did not engage in a comprehensive rational assessment of the historical facts until – and after – the Eichmann Trial in 1961. Living with the experience itself, the older generation did not necessarily possess the language to convey it to the younger generation which, in turn, questioned the reaction of their parents toward the persecution. Under Ben Gurion, most of Israel's contacts with Adenauer's Federal Republic concerned the political solution to the questions of restitution and compensation, culminating in the treaty of 1952. The language used in these negotiations tended to be legalistic and bureaucratic.

There can be little doubt that in this period Germans generally avoided confronting the involvement in the Nazi crimes.[27] However, a differentiated picture of the attempts to engage various segments of society in a moral reckoning has not emerged yet. Aside from general regrets about "What happened" and revulsion to the violence of *Kristallnacht*, the escalation from discrimination against Jews to their deportation and extermination was usually remembered as an anonymous process in the "stereotype of the disappearance of the Jews."[28] The ratification of the 1952 treaty, for which Adenauer forged a razor-thin bipartisan majority in the Bundestag, was accompanied by new anti-Jewish resentments in the population. Since the payment of compensation meant acknowl-

26. One might compare the distinct phases in addressing the Vichy Syndrome in France after World War II: Henry Rousso, *The Vichy Syndrome: History and Memory in France since 1944* (Cambridge: Harvard University Press, 1991).

27. Frank Stern, *The Whitewashing of the Yellow Badge: Antisemitism and Philosemitism in Postwar Germany* (Oxford: Pergamon Press, 1992).

28. Ibid, 237.

edging collective responsibility or guilt for Nazi crimes, Theodor Heuss, the first president of the Federal Republic and, aside from the Social Democratic leaders Kurt Schumacher and Ernst Reuter, the foremost advocate of a public recognition of such responsibility, insisted on the need to develop catagories for the comprehension of and public accounting for the crimes. Heuss's notion of collective shame, though, was too weak to serve as basis for a new language; his plea for a new approach at the dedication of the memorial at the former concentration camp Bergen-Belsen on 30 November 1952, which followed a passionate speech of Nahum Goldmann, the President of the World Jewish Congress, found only limited resonance in the German public.[29] The topic shaped official politics, especially toward Israel and the United States, but not the political discourse. This discourse was dominated by the need to confront the legacy of the war and the division of Germany. At the same time, there were many sincere attempts to address the persecution of Jews on the part of journalists, teachers, actors and theater directors, artists, television executives, film makers, church leaders, writers, and politically active citizens. Writers were by no means the most probing voices in this venture. Their ambition to gain a widely respected place in the public's mind often ran counter, at least in the 1950s, to the thorough exploration of this topic. And yet, the voices of younger writers seem to have had a more lasting impact since they have articulated, *vis-à-vis* the growing presence of first-hand accounts of the persecution of Jews, a learning curve that others, especially in the younger generation, could embrace. The question remains as to what extent they succeeded in addressing the topic as part of their literary agenda.

As so often, there is a short and a long answer to this question. The short answer: German-speaking writers, set on the restitution of identity as the core of their writing, did not rise to this challenge, some exceptions – usually Jewish writers such as Ilse Aichinger, Paul Celan, Nelly Sachs, Peter Weiss[30] – notwithstanding. What they were able to articulate, though, was a moral plea to address and overcome the numbness by getting rid of the Nazi perpetrators and accomplices in higher public positions. While the crimes seemed still present behind the black wall of numbness and *Verdrängung*, the writers devoted most of their energies to a long-lasting debate about the question whether these events should be

29. See Jeffrey Herf, "Divided Memory, Multiple Restaurations: West German Political Reflection on the Nazi Past, 1945-1953," in *Revisiting Zero Hour 1945* (Note 5), 89-102; also Herf's forthcoming book, *Divided Memory: The Nazi Past in the Two Germanies* (Cambridge: Harvard University Press).

30. For the situation in East Germany see Paul O'Doherty, "German-Jewish Writers and Themes in GDR Fiction," in *German Life and Letters* 49 (1996), 271-81.

aesthetically represented at all. Their arguments pointed to the *limits* of representation, i.e. to the inadequacy and even moral dubiousness of aestheticizing the sufferings of the victims, the reality of the concentration camps, the gassing in Auschwitz. It was not until the trials of the early sixties (Eichmann Trial in 1961, Auschwitz Trials in 1963-1965) changed this approach, when the lack – and avoidance – of a pertinent language was filled by the language of documentation of the concrete events which seemed to shield against most pitfalls of the literary articulation. In the late 1970s it became clear that the documentary approach, exemplified by Peter Weiss's Auschwitz play, *Die Ermittlung* (The Investigation, 1965), had not succeeded in stirring up much public self-questioning; at this time a new public concern took its clue both from the emotional involvement with the victims, intensified by the TV series, and the international discussion of Germany's responsibility for the Holocaust, now an encompassing, almost authoritative notion. The topic inserted itself into the life and identity of the individual without literary mediation.

The long answer – only outlined here – would have to go deeply into an area of postwar history that has receded into the background, although it is the single most important reason for the psychic numbness that permeated individuals and families, as well as society at large and its continued workaholism: the experience of war as an excruciating confrontation with bombs, violence, and *Massentod* (mass death).[31] Only a thorough knowledge of the internalization of *Massentod* – a psychological repression that led to an uncanny emotional torpor in the older and a silent accommodation in the younger generation – can provide criteria for an evaluation of the effect that writers had on the thinking and feeling of Germans. Poised to constitute a semblance of postwar identity, writers were able to engage readers in a catalytic reliving of the traumatic war experience, but hardly able to break out of the emotional cocoon and forge identities with Jewish people whose emotional existence had been excluded from any communality.

In this context, the long answer would have to reflect the fact that postwar authors, eager to reinstitute literature, completely avoided the terrain on which the majority of the German population reasserted its moral existence as survivors of the self-inflicted mass destruction: the working world. Typically, in most studies of the psychological and spiritual fabric of postwar German society this area has been left blank. Yet

31. A first critical attempt to address this side of the experience of mass death in Michael Geyer, "Das Stigma der Gewalt und das Problem der nationalen Identität, " in *Von der Aufgabe der Freiheit: Politische Verantwortung und bürgerliche Gesellschaft im 19. und 20. Jahrhundert. Festschrift für Hans Mommsen zum 5. November 1995*, Christian Jansen, Lutz Niethammer, Bernd Weisbrod, eds. (Berlin: Akademie Verlag, 1995), 673-98.

it is the world of work, socially and privately controlled work, in which Germans (and Austrians) recovered a sense of themselves that was not without constant, though not always conscious, response to recent events. Despite its public distancing from the Nazi period and the emotional shutdown *vis-à-vis* war and mass death, this identity drew its energies from a sense of working through the experience through work. The individual, having been a victim of or having participated in the destruction, was now engaged in a re-construction *(Wieder-Aufbau)* marking, in the similar exertion of hard work, the characteristics of what Freud called *Wiederholungszwang*. Repetition compulsion has been cited as the complex motivation behind the seemingly new, in fact resumed, immersion in work, this time with a liberating agenda and with reasonable assurance of a responsive political system.[32]

The compensatory nature of this process seems obvious. However, before it is buried under the verdict of the inability to mourn, the collective mental and behavioral patterns after earthshattering experiences such as war should be carefully examined and compared.[33] As Freud's individualistically patterned theory had neglected the working sphere that generates different dynamics of collectivity – a lacunae already criticized by Alfred Adler in his master's analysis – the Mitscherlichs fall short in similar terms in defining the social incentives for identity-building after 1945. To be sure, in their book, *Die Unfähigkeit zu trauern* (The Inability to Mourn), Alexander and Margarete Mitscherlich categorized convincingly the need for working through mourning and coming to terms with guilt. They confirmed the moral criteria for a psychological narrative on the failure of the Germans to accept their responsibility for the murder of the Jews. They went further than literary authors in establishing a language for working through loss and guilt. And yet, their most effective contribution to this crucial issue was less the analysis of the postwar developments than the setting of an agenda for acting out what had not yet been worked through.[34]

32. Frank Trommler, "'Deutschlands Sieg oder Untergang:' Perspektiven aus dem Dritten Reich auf die Nachkriegsentwicklung," in *Deutschland nach Hitler: Zukunftspläne im Exil und aus der Besatzungszeit 1939-1949*, Thomas Koebner, Gert Sautermeister, Sigrid Schneider, eds. (Opladen: Westdeutscher Verlag, 1987), 226 f.

33. Comparative histories of the reconstruction of Europe contain much material, for instance Walter Lacqueur, *The Rebirth of Europe: A History of the Years since the Fall of Hitler* (New York: Holt, Rinehart & Winston, 1970); Henry M. Pachter, *The Fall and Rise of Europe: A Political, Social, and Cultural History of the Twentieth Century* (New York: Praeger, 1975).

34. The terms are juxtaposed somewhat differently from Dominick LaCapra, *Representing the Holocaust: History, Theory, Trauma* (Ithaca: Cornell University Press, 1994), esp. 205-23. – Important contributions to this topic from both East and West German

In other words, representing psychoanalysis as a viable tool for analyzing the case of the Germans as a case was one thing, surpassing the writers' search for remembrance with a Freudian agenda was another, more questionable undertaking, as long as the exclusion of the working world, the crucial place of a first working through, failed to be addressed. It is my thesis, then, that the Mitscherlichs's book which appeared in 1967 when the conditions of the public debate about Germany's past had changed, had its unique value in shaping the psychoanalytic agenda of a later generation. Less an analysis of the postwar mind of the Germans on the subject of the persecution of Jews, it was on the mark in defining the de-realization of the Nazi past. By making a case for a new "realization" of the Nazi past, it became a guide to the psychological needs of the second and third generation of Germans after those events. These needs encompass the emotional re-creation of the predicament of crime and perpetration, as well as that of loss and victimization from which the members of these generations wish to be liberated. Mitscherlich's public success signifies the moment when the fictional and metaphorical projection, with which literature involved audiences in recasting memory, gave way to a more directly articulated engagement with the reality of the Nazi past.

Culminating in the explosive confrontations of the 1980s that included huge anti-nuclear demonstrations, Richard von Weizsäcker's Bundestag speech of 8 May 1985, President Ronald Reagan's visit to the Bitburg cemetery in 1985, and the so-called *Historikerstreit* in the following year, the public debates on this topic took on the dynamics of an acting out, a projective identification with, and obsessive repetition of, the victim-perpetrator constellation as a present reality. These dynamics need to be seen under the auspices of a different stage of psychological confliction, as remembrance itself had shifted from a first-hand experience to a second- or third-hand reworking of a trauma.[35] Also crucial is the will of a later generation to re-engage society in the acting out of the part of the victim that had been excluded in the earlier phase of documentary rationalization. Taking this will in its various modes of expression leads invariably into the emotionally charged public manifestations of victimization in the protest demonstrations against the nuclear confrontation policies of the early 1980s. Nowhere were these manifestations of nuclear-war *Angst*, inflamed by the NATO decision to install American Cruise and Pershing

---

perspectives can be found in *Erinnern, Wiederholen, Durcharbeiten: Zur Psycho-Analyse deutscher Wenden*, Brigitte Rauschenbach, ed. (Berlin: Aufbau Taschenbuch Verlag, 1992).

35. Rafael Moses and Friedrich-Wilhelm Eickhoff, eds., *Die Bedeutung des Holocaust für nicht direkt Betroffene* (Jahrbuch der Psychoanalyse 14) (Stuttgart: frommann-holzboog, 1992).

II missiles on German soil, and ecological disaster fantasies more intense than in Germany. They represent, on closer examination, a convoluted and little understood acting out of the experience of victimization, a collective antidote, so to speak, to what Robert Jay Lifton and Eric Markusen have portrayed as *The Genocidal Mentality* among the professionals of these practices.[36] There was no lack of reference to Auschwitz in public discourse. Whether the "doubling" of Nazi genocide through the projection of nuclear genocide can be understood as a mourning maneuver of a later generation might remain open, at least for now. What cannot be overlooked, however, is the fact that the political and, finally, the academic confrontations of the mid-1980s about the accountability for the Holocaust were a response to the unprecedented collective immersion in a catalytic notion of victimization that coincided with broad efforts to "emotionalize" the approach to war and the Holocaust.[37]

Instead of concluding the long answer about the contribution of literary writers, this leads into another discourse about the psychological stages of coming to terms with *Massentod* in Germany which, in the 1980s, tended to concentrate on Auschwitz,[38] but which remains bound by the experience of war. This discourse has left the purview of literature. It was symptomatic that writers such as Böll and Grass let it be known in the early 1980s that their contribution to working through *Angst* and apocalypse was by participating in a demonstration rather than by inventing another story. And yet, writers *did* try to use the new perspectives and overcome the earlier poetics of identity creation that was analogous to aesthetic trends in other countries.[39] Günter Grass made a case with his most violently attacked book, *Die Rättin* (The Rat, 1986) , in which he took the newly invigorated apocalyptic thinking as another attempt of Germans to avoid mourning. As self-righteously wrong as Grass might have been in his moral verdict, he was truly inventive and bold in the choice of his allegorical poetics. The critics of 1986 were

36. Robert Jay Lifton and Eric Markusen, *The Genocidal Mentality: Nazi Holocaust and Nuclear Threat* (New York: Basic Books, 1990).

37. For a typical statement on the teaching of Nazi history in schools see Gerhard Schneider, "Mehr Affektivität im Geschichtsunterricht? Die Darstellung des Zweiten Weltkriegs in der trivialen und populärwissenschaftlichen Literatur und ihre Verwendung im Unterricht," in *Aus Politik und Zeitgeschichte* B 45 (1980), 16-38.

38. See the ongoing debate in the journal *Psyche*, esp. Tilmann Moser, "Die Unfähigkeit zu trauern: Hält die Diagnose einer Überprüfung stand? Zur psychischen Verarbeitung des Holocaust in der Bundesrepublik," *Psyche* 46 (1992), 398-405; Margarete Mitscherlich-Nielsen, "Die (Un)Fähigkeit zu trauern in Ost- und Westdeutschland: Was Trauerarbeit leisten könnte," ibid., 406-18; and the replies in *Psyche* No 8 (1993), 727-94.

39. See Richard Dellamora, ed. *Postmodern Apocalypse: Theory and Cultural Practice at the End* (Philadelphia: University of Pennsylvania Press, 1995).

looking in vain for the exploration of existential empathy that they routinely demanded from German novels. A future generation of readers, overlooking the twentieth, together with previous centuries, might find his approach appropriate to the deathly wind of banality blowing through all of them. Painfully, postwar writers had debated the possibilities and limits of representing the persecution of the Jews. Later writers, after less than satisfying attempts to engage in such representation, ceded their place in the public sphere to historians. Historians painfully debated the possibilities and limits of historicizing National Socialism and the Holocaust. This left a void as much as it filled one.

Future scholars will be able to sort out the various undercurrents, psychological, generational, and institutional, that converged in these manifestations of acting out an uncompleted history in the 1980s. What they will also be able to trace is the reciprocal emergence of a public discourse of Jewish intellectuals living in Germany, among them Henryk M. Broder, Micha Brumlik, and Dan Diner. This discourse, which assumed a broadly recognized role in the public debates about German unification and its effect on minorities in the 1990s, reflects a new stage in dealing with the "negative symbiosis", as the relationship between Jews and Germans since the Shoah has been labeled. It has reversed the "overall sense of self-imposed invisibility among counterparts," that older participants of German cultural life such as Hans Mayer or Marcel Reich-Ranicki had maintained about their Jewishness in earlier decades.[40] In this respect, the 1980s should remain the threshold decade for a new public engagement of Jews, Germans, Jewish Germans, and German Jews united in a common purpose: living together in the same state, though with different identities.

Literature Is (Was) the Message

A final flashback to the issue of creating literature. In a typical headline, the weekly *Die Zeit*, the foremost public supporter of Group 47, told its readers in 1959: "Our literature cannot be entirely dead as long as these twenty-one writers are alive."[41] The paper presented these authors,

40. Sander L. Gilman, *Jews in Today's German Culture* (Bloomington: Indiana University Press, 1995), 35. See also *Reemerging Jewish Culture in Germany: Life and Literature Since 1989*, Sander L. Gilman and Karen Remmler, eds. (New York: New York University Press, 1994); *Speaking Out: Jewish Voices from United Germany*, Susan Stern, ed. (Berlin/ Chicago: Edition 9, 1995).

41. "Der deutsche Roman 1959: Unsere Literatur kann nicht ganz tot sein, solange diese einundzwanzig Schriftsteller leben," *Die Zeit* No 41 (9 October 1959), 9.

among them Böll, Lenz, Koeppen, Schmidt, Gaiser, Andersch, and Schnurre, in an attempt to ward off the strong and often prevailing criticism in the 1950s that the highest goal, literature, had escaped all endeavors by writers. The defense was geared toward the writers as guarantors of literature, clearly a reflection of the aesthetics practiced in the meetings of Group 47. In his rules and pronouncements, Hans Werner Richter always insisted on the literary character of the group, fearful of having this goal diluted by the politics that he himself practiced outside the Group. Only in this constellation were writers able to create themselves by creating literature, and by creating themselves they were able to champion the rescue of literature. This accounts for the tendency to close off their poetic worlds against non-literary intrusions, and also for a surprisingly strong success in elevating the status of literature as a social achievement.

Thus, when other groups tried to assume a higher profile in public, as in the case of working-class writers in the early 1960s, literature was still used for personal and collective self-promotion. The ascent of the worker-writer Max von der Grün, who became the co-founder of Group 61 and attained at times a Böll-like stature in his popular novels about the working world (which Böll had kept on the margins), is another example of the representational alliance of work and author. The advancement of feminism on the part of woman writers since the 1960s initially partook of this self-promotion through literature, with books and book series dedicated to their cause. As the goals changed toward a new social activism, however, the – mostly autobiographical – literature moved to the background. Essayistic writing, as preferred by prominent American and French feminists, reflected the changes. Christa Wolf, yet another example for the work-author "partnership," was able to maintain a literary approach, though one less esoteric than Ingeborg Bachmann, who had moved away from the constraints of Group 47.

In promoting literature as the aesthetic, symbolic, *and* commercial message, the enormous growth of literary sections in newspapers, journals, radio stations, and publishing houses has played, of course, a crucial role. Maintaining the allegiance of this industry, a communication industry, will become crucial to literature in the twenty-first century. This is a tough proposition, not least because the advocacy of literature as a whole that regained ground as a part of the poetics in the 1950s and 1960s, has lost its prestige. Some of it has been picked up by universities whose institutional setup provides continuous though narrow interest. Yet, as questionable as it is when painters produce directly for the museum, the outlook when writers publish mainly for a certain academic clientèle is just as questionable. What threatens to get lost is the presence of the literary word in the public sphere. What threatens to increase is the perception that literature is something for professional readers. Yet again, while writers nowadays earn their living by engaging in many forms of publishing and media work, status recognition is to some extent still connected with literary success. The academic museum is increasingly part of the survival strategies for texts.

In this essay I have taken the liberty and avoided the established pattern of projecting a literary history by placing texts in a sequential order. I have gone after the various forms in which the literary word after 1945 became a lived experience, be it through the alliance of work and author that helped shape new identities, be it through a theatrical presence that acquired an explosive dynamics in the 1960s and 1970s, or be it in a retreat *vis-à-vis* other forms of recollecting memory and emotion when a new generation reshaped the language of guilt, anxiety, and understanding. While literature became a medium in which a post-Nazi, post-World War II society shaped part of its identity, it should not be just reduced to this function. Likewise, it also should not be misjudged as a mere text, a web of intertextuality, an assemblage of scriptures to be used as a screen for the message: Literature is not dead as long as *we* read it.

Satisfying the public's demand for identification with the literary word is a challenging task at a time when the same public tends to prefer identification through the language of the mass media and visualized discourse. This preference is probably a stronger challenge than the effort on the part of academic literary critics to dismantle the strategies of poetic identity creation. Should the literary work be seen as a catalyst for identity, or rather for non-identity? In postwar Germany the most challenging answers came from Adorno but, aside from Andersch and Enzensberger, they hardly enjoyed a wide reception among writers. Other, less strident yet publicly more successful answers came from literary critics with whom the writers were engaged in a constant quarrel. The two most influential literary critics between the 1950s and the 1990s, Friedrich Sieburg and Marcel Reich-Ranicki, articulated an advocacy for the whole of literature that was predictably reassuring and old-fashioned. The fact that Reich-Ranicki has been able in the 1990s to draw a devoted TV audience to his critical reviews of literary works has obviously something to do with his old-fashioned trust in the power of story-telling to allow for identification. Answering the question, "What Should Remain?" on TV opens a great opportunity for literature. Or does it?

NOTES ON CONTRIBUTORS

Nora M. Alter is Assistant Professor of German at the University of Florida.

Stephen Brockmann is Assistant Professor of German at Carnegie Mellon University.

Keith Bullivant is Professor of German at the University of Florida.

Carol Anne Costabile-Heming is Assistant Professor of German at Pennsylvania State University.

Barbara Kosta is Associate Professor of German at the University of Arizona.

Helga Kraft is Professor of German at the University of Florida.

Siegfried Mews is Professor of German at the University of North Carolina, Chapel Hill.

Jennifer E. Michaels is Professor of German at Grinnell College and a former President of the German Studies Association.

Walter Pape is Professor of Modern German Literature at the University of Cologne.

Jay J. Rosellini is Professor of German at Purdue University.

Frank Trommler is Professor of German and Comparative Literature at the University of Pennsylvania and a former President of the German Studies Association.